BLOODLINE OF THE SCROLLS

"I became a 'fan' of Russell L. Martin after reading his first book, *Scars of My Guardian Angel.* I had the privilege of getting to meet Mr. Martin, and I must say that he simply radiates the love of God when he's talking to you.

Having been a teacher for more than 20 years, I offered my proof-reading skills (teacher's way of grading ;) whenever he needed me. While reading "Bloodline of the Scrolls", I found myself so caught up in the story that I actually forgot to "tear it apart", like Russell had asked me to do! I was caught completely off guard by one of the heaven scenes and the emotions it provoked so deep within, that I literally wept as I read. I am a true believer in the Spiritual Realm, and I think it's a true blessing that God doesn't allow us to see into that realm for our protection. This book gives you a bit of insight of what it might be like in that realm—the battles that are not of flesh and blood.

This book is more than just a "made-up" story. It reminds us that there is truly a Heaven and a Hell. There are angels to protect us, and demons to tempt us, but above any and all decisions, God is there to love us and to forgive us.

Mr. Martin has creatively integrated several stories at once, in order to hook a wide range of readers based on their interests. There's a little bit of everything for everyone wrapped up under this one title..."Bloodline of the Scrolls."

Melisa James
Retired Teacher from Louisiana
Pharmacy Technician (cPht)
Chadmelisa@bellsouth.net

"After reading *Scars of My Guardian Angel*, I could not imagine that Russell L, Martin could tell another amazing story about Heaven and the Spiritual Realm. His second book exceeds all expectations. He combines his astonishing imagination and knowledge of the Bible to tell the story of a young man's mission from God. *Bloodline of the Scrolls* takes you deep into the spiritual realm of good and evil, providing glimpses of what heaven and hell may be like. This fiction book is very thought provoking and makes you want to learn more about what is to come after death. *Scars of My Guardian Angel,* the first in the series, has impacted many lives, giving all a sense of peace and an insight into God's mercy and love for mankind. The second book, *Bloodline of the Scrolls*, continues Chado Cole's journey as he attempts to complete a mission from God. Though this book is a work of fiction, it is filled with scriptures that provide fundamental truths throughout. This book will keep your interested and wanting more at the end of each chapter. Mr. Martin has an exceptional gift of storytelling that God has used once again to tell others of His great love for mankind

Jackie Lewis
HSE
Grant Junior High

"I was extremely pleased to have the opportunity to read *Bloodline of the Scrolls* after falling in love with Russell L. Martin's first novel, *Scars of My Guardian Angel.* Once again, Mr. Martin delivered a fantastic and entertaining story with a positive message that flows with ease from start to finish. It is truly an honor to be a part of this ministry and help promote a message of hope and kindness to readers everywhere. Once you begin "The Portal Series", you will be hooked and have trouble setting it down, but when you do, you will find yourself reflecting on your impact on the world."

Blake Blevins
Customer Service Director
DELIVERYMAXX

BLOODLINE OF THE SCROLLS

THE PORTAL SERIES

ECHOES OF TRUTH;
CLOUDS OF DARKNESS

RUSSELL L. MARTIN

Lift Up Solutions, LLC
Dry Prong, Louisiana

Bloodline of the Scrolls
Echoes of Truth; Clouds of Darkness
The Portal Series
Book II

By Russell L Martin
www.russellmartinauthor.com

ISBN-13: 978-0-9998366-3-7

Library of Congress Control Number: 2018913101
Lift Up Solutions, LLC, Dry Prong, LA

Published by Lift Up Solutions, LLC
Printed in the United States of America

Cover design by 100Covers

Contents

From the Author:

Throughout my life, inspiration to be a better person has presented itself in many different forms. To be the first, I would have to say, is my mother and father. From their being brought up inside a Christian home and community, God definitely plays the main role. He has inspired me to do my best and always acknowledge Him. Feeling His presence helps me strive to be a better man.

Other ways of inspiration have come from my childhood heroes on television. Thinking back, I would have to say some were Daniel Boone, Davy Crockett and maybe even Underdog or Superman.

I know this may all sound strange, but after writing my first novel, I felt like I was cast down inside a bottomless pit of authors with no hope of ever reaching the surface.

Then one day, through our social media company, I heard a testimony from a very kind and wonderful man that had read "Scars of My Guardian Angel". Through his heart-felt testimony, he unknowingly has given me an abundance of confidence. He has truly inspired me to continue on with "The Portal Series". Through my writings, it is my prayer that we continue to give comfort and hope to others, as so it did with this gentleman. Mr. Wayne you are truly a Godsend hero to me.

"Thank you for writing the wonderful story of *Scars of My Guardian Angel*. I am very much looking forward to continuing to read the series with *Bloodline of the Scrolls*, and truly hope that I live long enough to see your third book of the series come to print. Although based on the Bible and I know the books are fictional in nature, however I love the imagery you have depicted in your writing. Recently, I was diagnosed with cancer and I know that my time on Earth is limited. Soon I will enter into God's Kingdom. I take great comfort imagining that Heaven will be something so special that words cannot truly describe it. This book has meant so much to me and brings me the Lord's Peace, as I'm sure it touches everyone who reads it. Friends and family who also read your work feel the same way. These stories have a special place in our hearts and hope they touch others as much as they have touched me and my family."

Wayne Bates
Terrell, Texas

FOREWORD

I purchased Mr. Russell L. Martin's first book, *Scars of My Guardian Angel*, at a book signing and was fortunate enough to meet him and his wife Laura at that time. I became enthralled with Mr. Martin's storytelling style, how The Word of God was woven into his storylines.

I can honestly say I have read thousands of books, but absolutely none of them were anything like these unique stories. I was inspired and uplifted, and found a new hunger for God in myself, being so deeply exhilarated and filled with hope. I met up with Mr. Martin again and was so touched by his kind spirit and pure enthusiasm, I asked to assist in his ministry.

I have written and proofread many manuals and evaluations during my working life, and was thrilled to be asked to edit and proofread for Martin's second effort, *Bloodline of the Scrolls*. Admittedly, I began by proofreading the chapters I received, but soon began to selfishly read for my own edification, before proofreading and making any edits. On more than one occasion, I texted Mr. Martin after reading a section, to tell him how I was touched by something I had read. This book includes mystery, intrigue, emotion, love, laughter, and of course hope and inspiration. It should be well received by both men and women. Mr. Martin's clever use of the appropriate vernacular and jargon for the different characters is skillfully woven through the storylines.

Bloodline of the Scrolls is uniquely written and is a continuation of Chado Cole's journey from *Scars of My Guardian Angel*, and how his story, and those of two chosen people at the brink of death converge for God's mission. You will be taken from the 11th gate of Heaven to the gates of hell in this journey as *Bloodline of the Scrolls* ties together seamlessly with *Scars of My Guardian Angel*. I believe you will be blessed, as I was, as you read Martin's books. They are more than words, so let yourself receive the messages and visualize where he takes you.

I call myself blessed to have worked on this project and spent many hours with this author. He is a gentleman and a true man of God with vision; mostly I feel blessed to call him a friend. I will be waiting eagerly for the next book as I know he has more stories to tell!

Diana Rhodes
Administrative Programs Manager
Retired, State of Louisiana

1

A Toddler's Heart

Summer Allyce Cole sits peacefully at the crest of a hill in front of her home overlooking the Valley of the Children. On her arrival in Heaven, God had placed in her heart an overwhelming desire to come to this valley and have a part in receiving the souls of babes. This giant valley is filled with magnificent structures designed by the One True Architect, God Himself. It is well known throughout Heaven to be a very special place; and is very close to God's own heart.

Thousands upon thousands of unborn children, some of whom have been judged and sentenced back on Earth, arrive here in the valley. They are passed through portals from the hands of angels, into the hands of their ancestors.

This constant flowing river of children arriving in Heaven, are embraced and met with rejoicing hearts and a deep love like no other.

* * *

Summer Allyce feels a cool breeze on her face as she hears and watches the movement of this invisible force. It gently sways the tall plush grass growing along the hillside. Her mind runs away with memories of family and friends she had left behind on Earth several years ago.

Staring at the grass dancing across the hillside almost in a daze, Summer whispers a prayer, "Lord, you know I've never really thought much about why you took me at such a young age. I was only 22, and I thought I had big plans for the future. Not understanding why is okay. I guess it really doesn't matter. I'm just grateful You allowed me the honor of serving You. As I look down on this valley, I feel in my heart that this is my final destination. For that, I thank you Lord."

Summer breaks out in a huge smile as she hears the pitter pat of little feet running up behind her. It's the green-eyed toddler, Rosie.

God had placed Rosie on Summer's heart, giving her a desire to take Rosie in, and be a mother to her. Rosie was another casualty of abortion, with hardly any relatives who made it to Heaven. The few ancestors she had were already so overwhelmed with the many children they received to care for; God made this choice of where Rosie belongs.

Summer braces herself as she hears Rosie getting closer. Then suddenly the toddler goes airborne as she jumps on Summer's back. They both break out giggling as they roll around on the ground. "Hey, my Summer, what ya doing?"

"Oh… I'm just sitting here in the soft grass watching the wind dance. What you doing?"

"I have a question."

"You always have questions, Silly Willie."

The toddler laughs, "I'm not Silly Willie. I'm Rosie!"

"Yes you are. So what's your question, sweetie?"

"So if Chado Cole is your daddy and you're my mommy, does that mean he's my grandfather?"

"Yes, I guess so. You could say he's your heavenly grandfather. He would probably like it if you continue to call him Pawpaw."

"Why did Pawpaw and his angel have to leave? I want him to come back. I really love my new Pawpaw, and I miss him."

"He'll be back soon. Don't you worry; I believe he really loves you also."

"But why did he have to leave?"

"Well, Rosie, from what Daddy told me, and what I also overheard Jesus telling him and his angel Uriel, they are on a fantastic mission! This mission is really top secret, not even the angels know. So, Rosie, can you keep a secret?" The toddler grins from ear to ear as her green eyes glisten with excitement. "Yes, my Summer, I can keep a secret forever!"

"Okay, sweetie, listen closely. Your Pawpaw Chado has been chosen. He had to travel back down to God's Mountain on Earth. There he will write down all the things he witnessed while he traveled through the spiritual realm and here in Heaven. He documents everything inside two scrolls. He is to give one to a lost soul who doesn't believe in God, and the other to a believer of Christ. They both are caught between life and death as your Pawpaw hands the scrolls over to them. He has to meet the unbeliever at the Gate of Hell and the other at the Eleventh Gate of Heaven.

"As these two spiritual souls return to the living, the scrolls, along with their testimonies, will make the unbelievers believe. You see, God is going to use this in a special way to open the eyes of millions of lost people. When the people of Earth realize they've been fed lies all along, hopefully they will run to the Lord and seek His saving grace."

"So does that mean we will have more friends here in Heaven?"

Summer chuckles, "Yes, sweetie, we will."

"How did Pawpaw Chado lose his life back on Earth?"

"You are full of questions, little one, but I guess we have time to answer one more before we head down into the valley.

"You see, back on Earth people have jobs, kind of like we do here in Heaven. Your Pawpaw was a deep-sea diver working for the oil and gas companies, and his job, was to help build pipelines on the bottom of the ocean. Your Pawpaw and his friends lived and worked on a vessel that floats on the water. He called it Barge 101. He had lots of friends out there, from Captain Lee to the rest of the dive team. Some had silly names like Bones and TC. Others were normal names like Joey and Matt. He even had a friend who lived in the swamps of Louisiana he called Cheese Hound."

Rosie laughs, "Cheese Hound is a funny name!"

"Yes, he's one of your Pawpaw Chado's childhood friends. Well anyway, while they're under the water they need air to breathe. The air is supplied through long hoses hooked to big machines that make and pump the air. This keeps them alive while they work.

"One cold winter night it was your Pawpaw's turn to go down to the bottom of the ocean, and the air machines quit working!"

Rosie's face lights up with expression, "What happened then?"

"Well, Rosie, Pawpaw ran out of air while he was on the bottom under water, and right before he died he spoke to God."

"What did he say?"

"He said, 'God, I guess you've got me.' That's when God sent three angels to carry him over into the Spiritual Realm… and that's where his mission began."

2

BARGE 101

At 2:00 am, January 9th, 2020, Captain Lee rolls out of his bunk as he hears the loudspeaker echoing through the living quarters. His bare feet touch down on the cold tile floor of the pipeline lay barge and with a huge yawn he reaches over for a chew of tobacco. Divers a few bunks down are mumbling, "I wish they would shut the heck up, it's too early to hear them yapping."

Intercom repeats, "Captain Lee, report to the mess hall, Captain Lee, report to the mess hall."

"Ok, boys, drop your rocks, and grab your socks; we've got work to do! Hey, Joey, wake Matt up. Let's go! I'm not your sweet dear old momma. Get up!"

Joey walks over grinning from ear-to-ear, as he reaches up grabbing Matt's blanket, and with a swift motion jerks the cover off.

"Hey, Joey, you know what your name means in Australian?"

"No, what does it mean?"

"It means baby kangaroo. Now give me back my cover, I'm calling in sick."

"You can't call in sick, you're already here. You better get up' we've got a long day ahead of us."

Captain Lee walks in the mess hall facing a table filled with company men and supervisors.

One of the men hollers across the room, "Good morning, Lee. Grab some breakfast and let's go over today's work schedule."

Reggie, the barge supervisor, glances over at Lee. "Hey, bud, looks like we've been ordered to bring the lay barge in to dry dock."

"What the heck is going on?"

The company man, Mr. Brunson, reaches over and fills Lee's coffee cup. "Lee, it looks like the Gulf of Mexico is being shut down. Oil prices have bottomed out and our oil and gas reserves are full. It's some kind of a deal the government made with the Saudis, not to mention they're bringing in oil from Canada. I hate to be the one breaking bad news, but it is what it is."

The dive team is walking into the mess hall laughing and cutting up, as usual.

Cookie, the cook, looks up at the team, "Good morning, guys!"

Matt lets out a big yawn, "Morning? It's not morning until at least 6:00 o'clock."

Captain Lee shouts out above the rumbling conversation at the table. "You guys, get quiet! We have a bit of bad news. Mr. Brunson, you want to give everyone the low-down?"

The room goes silent as Brunson looks up. "Sure, Lee. Guys, I won't beat around the bush. I hope you divers have saved your money, or know some other trades. Boys, the oilfield is being shut down, at least for the next few years."

Reggie, the barge supervisor, pops off from the kitchen. "I hear they're hiring divers down in Florida to scrape barnacles off pleasure boats."

Matt smirks, "Thanks, but no thanks! If it isn't oilfield, we don't want it."

Bones taps a butter knife against his plate. "I'm with you, Matt; the heck with scraping boat hulls!"

Matt looks over at Lee, "Captain, what are you going to do for income?"

"Well, I've saved a few bucks along the way. My wife makes a decent little check, and that covers our health insurance. I guess I could pull out my old tool bag and do a little carpentry. Heck, I might even mow a few yards; I'm not too proud."

Reggie shakes his head. "Hey, fellows, I didn't mean anything by what I said about scrapping hulls. This oilfield crash will hurt a lot of families."

Mr. Brunson stands up after his last sip of coffee, "Don't throw in the towel yet, boys. We have at least one more full day of diving before wrapping this project up. I'll call a connection of mine back at the home office and see if I can get you fellows paid an extra couple days. So, y'all be careful down there; God's speed."

Mr. Brunson dumps his dishes over in the galley sink as he walks past the crew. Lee whispers as they watch him exit the galley, "You know he turned out to be a pretty decent company man."

Reggie smiles, "Yep, he is one of my favorites, pretty good ole boy."

Matt shakes his head in disgust. "I can't believe we are about to get laid off. This really stinks!"

Lee cools his coffee as he lightly blows across the rim of his favorite mug. Slowly leaning back in the chair he smiles, "Well, fellows, on a positive note, y'all do know you can draw unemployment for a few weeks."

Joey says with frustration, "A few weeks? With the bills I've got, I need to be knocking down some serious cash. Louisiana unemployment only pays around 200 bucks a week. Man, I'm in trouble. I knew I shouldn't have bought all those toys. My whole shop is covered with hot rods, ATV's, and motorcycles. Heck, I even have a small plane I picked up the last time I was home."

Bones begins his irritating butter knife tap on his plate, "Yeah this blows. We didn't get any kind of warning."

Matt reaches over snatching away the butter knife, and moans, "I know. We went from hero to zero, with a three minute warning."

"Hey, I've got an idea."

Matt hands his butter knife back, "What you got, Bones?"

"Ok, y'all stay with me on this... I heard you can dive for diamonds down in Africa; maybe we could all go there. What do you think, Matt?"

"Bones, I think you've smoked way too much hooch, Africa is a bad idea, and here's why. I shared an apartment back in dive school with a guy named Andre from South Africa. He told me stories that would make your skin crawl. Hey, check this out: this guy was a very neat, short haired, well-dressed dude; but he showed me a picture of when he was in some kind of African Special Forces. In this photo, he had super long hair with a beard almost covering his whole chest. He had guns and ammo strapped all over him. Trust me. The photo he showed me made him out to be one bad-to-the-bone dude. Andre described how their strike team would go deep into the bush, slip around for weeks, make one kill, and then slip back out. I guess kind of like our sniper teams."

Joey widens his eyes, "What's that got to do with diving for diamonds?"

"He told me if the gulf jobs didn't work out, he would head back to Africa, and that's what he planned on doing; you know, diving for diamonds."

Joey slaps the table, "Man, that sounds exciting, let's do that!"

The other four divers all have a sparkle in their eyes, "Yeah, call him up and get us hooked up. I have a passport."

"Yeah, me too, let's do it!"

Matt shakes his head, "Hang on, guys. Don't buy your plane tickets just yet."

TC wipes milk from his mustache, "What do you mean, don't you want to go? The gulf work is belly up!"

"Andre told me that if you dive off that coast anywhere, the sharks will eat you alive!"

TC continues, "Sharks...? We've got sharks here and they don't bother us."

Matt holds his hand up. "Hang on, guys; it's a bit different down there. They have great whites that feed along their coast, and divers are on the menu."

Everyone chuckles as Matt continues. "He said they have surveillance helicopters constantly circling, watching out for the sharks."

Bones laughs, "Well there you go. They have protection to warn the divers. I've also heard you can search the inland rivers, if you didn't want to deal with the sharks."

Matt grins, "Ok genius, what are you going to do if the water is murky and the choppers can't see the sharks? He said even with the choppers circling, they still lose quite a few divers each year."

Joey butts in, "Well, what about inland diving?"

Matt continues, "Oh yeah, that's so much safer! He said that terrorist groups have their people watch and follow diamond miners. They let you work your tail off finding the treasures only to strike, taking everything and leaving you with nothing. If you're lucky they might let you live. Sometimes they have kidnap orders and will take your skinny buttocks deep into the jungle, maybe never to be seen again. Nope, I think I'll stay right here in the good ole USA!"

Captain Lee slides his chair back under the table. "You guys, quit worrying about your future. Hurry up with breakfast, and I'll meet y'all at the dive shack. Bones, TC, you two are in the lineup to jump first. Matt, you give me a hand in the shack."

Matt answered, "Ok, Captain, we'll be there in a minute."

The old cook fills two gallon jugs with hot water and sets them on a table near the door. TC and Bones smile, "Thanks, Cookie. It's going to be a cold one down there, and there's nothing like pouring hot water in your wetsuit on a cold winter morning!"

Grabbing their jugs of hot water on their way out, Joey lets out a nasty long burp. With the pungent smell of onions hanging in the air, Bones says, "Thanks a lot, Dooger! That was just plain gross."

TC holds his nose, "Yeah, knot-head, that wasn't how I wanted to remember the galley on Barge 101."

With everyone knowing what to do, they all separate, with Matt heading for the dive shack.

"Hey, Matt, you want to get Joey to make sure the decompression chamber is ready? I see he's down there helping the tenders hook up helmets."

"Sure, Captain." Matt reaches over and slides the intercom mike across the small table. "Hey, Joey, prep the chamber. The tenders can handle the helmets." Joey waves back in response as the barge two-way radio starts crackling with someone keying a mike.

"Come in, Lee. You got a copy?"

"Yeah, go ahead TC."

"Hey, Boss, this 5120 air compressor doesn't want to crank. I guess it's this cold weather."

"10-4, TC. Look here, bud, there's a can of starting fluid in a tool box right behind number two compressor."

"Ok, Captain."

"TC, don't spray too much; that ether might burn it up."

"Roger that, Captain."

Only a couple minutes pass when they hear the sounds of two 5120's, as they blast off. All the air gauges start showing signs of life.

"Hey, Captain."

"Yeah, Matt, what's on your mind?"

"You know what the day after tomorrow is?"

"No, am I supposed to?"

"It's January 11th, the day Chado Cole got killed out here."

"I'm sorry, Matt, I had forgotten. How long has it been, four years?"

"It's already been five years, and seems like it just happened yesterday."

"Yeah, I sure miss Chado. He was a good guy. That man really had a funny way of rubbing off on you… couldn't help but love him."

"Well, Captain, all the guys are going to meet up for his fifth year anniversary at the Bayou Rose for a few drinks, after we get back to shore."

"Come in, Lee, this is Reggie."

"I read you, sir."

"You guys ready on your end?"

"10-4 Reggie, we are ready to jump divers."

"Roger that, Lee. We have all-stop, I repeat barge is all-stop; jump divers."

"10-4 we read you, barge has stopped and we are jumping divers. I repeat; we are jumping divers."

Lee grabs the barge intercom, "Ok, TC, let's do this, jump divers. I say again, jump divers."

Lee leans back as he releases the button on the intercom. "Matt, that bar you're talking about, isn't that a biker bar located way out near Belle River?"

"Yes, sir, that's the one."

"Matt, I believe I'll pass on that invite. I have a cop friend that worked around Pierre Part, and he told me they wished someone would torch that hellhole. It's a drug den, run by a Russian that moved in down there a few years ago. Matt, if I was you, I wouldn't fool around anywhere near that place. You might end up floating in the swamp with critters feasting on your corpse. Why don't you all meet up in Lafayette? At least you would have a few street lights."

"Well, Captain, if you saw how fine the strippers are there, you would probably throw your Bible down and join us."

"Matt, I believe you have completely lost your mind. I wouldn't give up God or my sweet family for all the strippers in Louisiana! Anyways, ole buddy, you really should be trying to find you a good, solid church-going girl like I did, and settle down."

"Hold up, Captain. You know my feelings about the whole God thing, and I don't need some Christian woman nagging at me, trying to get me to go to church."

"Matt, I have never really asked you, but are you a full blown atheist, or is it you just don't know what you believe?"

"I guess I am an atheist. I believe when you die you just rot away, and there's nothingness. I mean you're just done and over."

"My goodness, Matt! I had no idea that's what you thought! What a hopeless outlook you have about death. We believers have a sort of peace, knowing in our hearts there is an afterlife. I believe it gives a person a happier life as we live out our days on this Earth. Well anyway, it's something you might want to look into. Face it, we live dangerous lives; diving, riding motorcycles, not to mention you going into a bar like the Belle Rose. My goodness, Matt, you really need to make an appointment with Jesus, and I wouldn't wait too long, because one day he might stop taking patients!"

Matt laughs, "So Jesus is a physician, I mean… like a doctor? What are you trying to say, I'm sick?"

"Yes and yes. He is the Mighty Physician, and you have a sick and empty heart. Matt, we've been friends for over six years and I care about you. I just feel that since we are shutting down in the gulf we might not see each other for a long time, and I needed to tell you this. As a Christian, if I fail to share the Gospel, I might have your blood on my hands. So there, I said it!"

"Hey, Lee, I appreciate what you're trying to say. Chado used to play the same ole song you're singing. As I told you the day he got killed, I don't need God. All I need is a few bucks in my pocket, a motorcycle, a few brews, and a good-looking, hot momma to ride on the back. If I can hit those goals, my world will be fine."

"Boy… you are stubborn!"

Bones breaks in on the com, "Hey, Captain, I lost communication with the crane operator. Can you relay for me? I believe we can wrap this up faster than we thought. Another couple hours and we can get the heck out of here."

"Roger that, Bones, we read you."

After a few more hours, the dive crew finishes their task on bottom and starts heading for the surface. Their last project is complete.

Mr. Brunson is notified the dive crew is finishing ahead of schedule. He calls in for a chopper to pick up a crew of six divers plus one galley hand. The remainder of the crew on the barge will ride it all the way back to Morgan City, Louisiana. Old Barge 101 will join others just like it, which will be put to rest in a coastal rig graveyard.

After showers and packing bags, the disgruntled divers make one last pass by their bunks and lockers, making sure they collected all their personal belongings.

TC, with a sad look, places his hand on Lee's shoulder, "Hey, Captain, you think we might ever see the inside of Barge 101 again?"

"Boys, who knows; our company man didn't seem to be bluffing. He told me a while ago that he hopes he might get a position on a production rig. Heck, if the gulf is shut down for four or five years, I know I won't be back, I just turned 53. Some of you younger divers might get to see it again, but I'll be too old for this cold hard life. Besides that, my family has been ready for me to lay it down for a long time now."

Joey holds his hand up, "Listen, I think I hear the chopper."

TC grins, "Yep, I hear it. Let's get the heck out of here."

The divers hang their heads in despair as they all move toward the helipad located on top of the galley. Each one, except for Captain Lee, reach up and tap a playboy photo hanging over the doorway of the sleeping quarters as they pass. Bones jumps up on Matt's back, reaching up and kissing this skimpy dressed bombshell, "Goodbye, Bugles, I'll miss you."

The despairing divers break out in laughter. "Get off me, Bones, you crazy rascal!"

* * *

They all hunker down as they walk across the helipad, underneath the rotating blades of the chopper, with each tossing their duffle bags on the floorboard... Bones and Matt stop on the helipad grinning from ear to ear as they start playing Rock-Paper-Scissors, to see who gets the outer seat. Captain Lee turns and starts shouting, "Hey, you two lug heads, get your butts in a seat! Let's go!"

Captain Lee grabs the vacant seat up front with the pilot. "Lee, they didn't tell us where to let you guys out. Where will it be, Lafayette?"

"No sir, we caught out in Port Fourchon. That's where all our vehicles are parked."

"Ok, Captain, Port Fourchon here we come."

Upon liftoff, the crew stares from windows of the chopper as the morning sun peeks over the edge of the horizon like an awakening giant; shooting its first rays across the gulf causing the invisible fog to be revealed as it slowly rises. With saddened hearts, they all look back at Barge 101 as the pilot respectfully makes a slow circle around the old pipe-laying rig. Since it was built in the early sixties, this floating piece of iron has provided many paychecks over the last three generations. It disappears into a hazy, winter fog hovering over the gulf water as they head for the Louisiana coastline.

3

God's Mountain

Chado has spent the last four years and eleven months in Heaven. To Chado, it only seems like he's been away from Earth a few days. He has been directed by God to follow Uriel, his guardian angel, along with his dog Buck, through a portal that takes them back to the hidden Mountain of God, located on Earth. On top of this holy piece of ground at the Plateau of Portals, Chado is to document everything he experienced and saw from the time of his death and during his heavenly journey on two scrolls. After 21 days, upon completion of the scrolls, Chado, Uriel, and Buck are to travel and witness many profound events which will unfold on Earth.

* * *

It is December 18th, 2019, earth time, and Chado Cole steps out of a portal located on top of God's Mountain, followed by his guardian angel, Uriel, and Buck. Without saying anything, Chado walks over to the cliff wall overlooking the lake.

"Hey, how far would you say it is to the village?"

"Oh, I would say around 70 miles or so. Why do you ask?"

Chado chuckles, "Well, if I can't pull off writing everything God wanted me to write in these two scrolls, I might just go hide in that ancient village until it's all over."

Uriel smiles, "You cannot hide from God, especially after he chose you for this assignment."

"Yeah, I reckon so. Well, what do you think? Or should I say, what do we do first?"

"Chado, this is as good a spot as any. Well, actually this is a perfect spot."

"It's a perfect spot for what?"

"Before I answer, we need to take off our sandals."

"Hey that's right. We are standing on holy ground!"

"Chado, when Allayer and Nipper were transporting you, did they show you the face of this cliff?"

"Oh yeah, they made me guess what the writing meant and who the author was. It took me a while to figure out that it was the Ten Commandments, and it was written in an ancient Hebrew language. To top off their guessing game, I couldn't figure out how the words were so deeply chiseled into the cliff, until they finally told me I was witnessing the fingerprints of God. So, Uriel, you were talking about a perfect spot?"

"Yes, we need to go to the Lord in prayer before we get started."

"Ok, bud."

Uriel draws his sword and jams it into the soft ground only a few inches from the edge of the cliff. He slowly drops down to his knees with his hands draped across the handle of his mighty blade. Chado follows the guardian angel's lead as he kneels beside him and places both scrolls on the ground, one on each side, while lowering his face to the ground. Wanting to join in, the huge mixed breed canine does his crawling trick as he wedges in between Chado and Uriel, as if to be praying also.

After a short hour of prayer a soft warm breeze comes across the lake hitting the trio in the face. Feeling the presence of the Holy Spirit, they open their eyes to find heavy clouds now hovering just above the mountain plateau.

"Chado, follow me."

They all walk over to a stone bench just past the three portals.

"Let us take a seat and wait."

"Uriel, I feel the urge to start writing but I only have the two scrolls, nothing to write with!"

"Have patience, Little Soul, have patience."

After sitting on the stone bench for a short while, Uriel points up at the low hanging clouds. "Does that look familiar, Chado?"

Suddenly the legs of a stone table appear out of the clouds. "I can't believe what I'm seeing. It's just like the dream I had several years back before I died! The table in my dream had gold coins and ink pens lying on top, and I was to choose between the two."

"Yes, Chado, just like your dream."

The table slowly comes into full view as it lowers out of the clouds. The legs look to be made of brass, and the feet of the table from iron. Finally resting directly in front of the stone bench, they stand and admire the tabletop. Chado rubs his hands across the cool slick surface, and realizes it looks like pure white marble, polished to a brilliant gloss finish. Uriel reaches over and slides two square jars filled with ink from the center of the table over in front of Chado. One of the glass containers is filled with dark, red ink and the other one filled with black.

"Ok, bud, looks like we won't run short of ink, but what are the small skinny sticks for?"

"That, my modern friend, is a bundle of Egyptian reed pens. This type of writing tool comes from a time around 400 BC, along with the ancient scrolls made from an aquatic plant called papyrus. You should not have any trouble getting everything written down."

"Uriel, I need a little direction on how to use these reed pens."

"Dip, write, dip a little more."

"Boy howdy, I just knew I would get a good ole 21st century ink pen, and boom, knock this thing out right quick and snappy."

Uriel said, "You might as well face facts—dip it, write it, dip it, write it."

"Okay, okay, I get the picture. We're going to be here for the full 21 days."

"Yes, sir, just like Jesus told you, 21 days."

"One more thing, what's the different colored ink for?"

"Come on, Chado… you should know that. It is just like in the Bible—red ink when you are writing down what God has spoken, and black ink for everything else. Also, Chado, remember God spoke to you quite a bit in your dreams, so take heed of His words."

Reaching over, Chado removes the glass lids from the jars, takes the first scroll and slowly rolls it out over the marble table. Staring at the blank sheet of papyrus, he feels overwhelmed with this task set before him. As he lets out a long deep sigh, he closes his eyes; *"Father God of all who breathe in Heaven and Earth, help me fulfill this mission as we continue our journey. I humbly ask for knowledge dear Lord and that I may never fail you. Fill my mind with the words so that I may fill the pages of these two scrolls with your truth, wisdom, and message to the saved and the unsaved. I am nothing without you dear Lord. Help me in this time of need. I love you this day, tomorrow and forever. Amen"*

He opened his eyes to see Uriel with his hands and sword raised toward Heaven, praising God, shouting to Heaven. "We praise you, oh Holy One, we praise you!"

Suddenly, Uriel's sword and arms disappear as the mist of the cloud lowers itself to only a few feet above their heads. Chado quickly stands with the overwhelming need to reach up into the dense canopy. He slowly pushes his hands through the haze of the cloud, when suddenly the Holy Spirit floods over him consuming all his thoughts and igniting his senses.

Buck leaps up on the table. He turns facing Uriel, sits down and begins staring up into the clouds.

"Hey, Buck, you ok? What are you looking at?"

Suddenly, a deep rolling thunder starts. The continuous rumbling creates vibrations and the small pebbles on the ground begin to move. After several minutes of thunder, an eerie silence falls over the mountaintop. Chado reaches over and places his hand on Buck's head as the huge mixed breed gives off a small whimper.

"Hey, buddy, it's going to be ok. We've got Uriel with us. There is nothing to worry about."

The low tone of a soft still voice echoes across the plateau. "Little Soul, where art thou?"

Chado looking around while cupping his hand against his mouth, quietly whispers, "Hey, Uriel, was that you? Are you, jacking with me?"

Uriel shakes his head no and points up into the clouds.

"Little Soul, where art thou?"

With his voice quivering, "I'm here. Is it you, Lord? Is that really you?"

"Little Soul, I Am."

Chado turns and looks over at Uriel, who is now already bowing and on his knees.

Turning back and looking into the midst of the clouds, Chado falls to the ground, humbling himself, as to be a dead man.

"Little Soul, arise; stand up my child, I am with you. Have joy in your heart."

"Will you help me, God?"

"Help you? Chado, you have everything you need. Oh, I see, you need confidence. I have gifted you with an abundance of confidence. You just need to find it. Is it imbedded in the rock bench beside which you stand? Has it flown away in an eagle or swum away in a fish? Where could it be? It is right here, deep down in your heart. Just close your eyes and let the Holy Spirit help you search for it. Soon you will recognize the hidden places of your soul, and that all your strength comes from me. Chado, you have to understand, it is I who dwell in your mind, soul and spirit. Once you truly understand the mysteries of Heaven and my ways, you will accomplish all things set before you. I hear your prayers and I Am with you."

"Father God, I am in fear of failing you as I attempt to write in the scrolls… The last thing in Heaven or on Earth I would ever want is to fail you."

"Fear not, Chado, I Am with you. My Holy Spirit takes away all fear, not only for the writing, but for the dangers that lie ahead. On this journey, you will be attacked by the enemy. Know this; I have set before you mysteries which will unfold.. I have assigned angels that have waited on this season for ten thousand lifetimes. So now, be about my good work and rejoice in it. Little Soul, it is time; this day you will begin the writings!"

"Yes, Lord, I will begin."

4

Family of Soldiers and Lily of the Valley

Christy Moody proudly stands in front of an audience of several hundred people. Her family and friends are looking on from two rows deep in the outdoor auditorium. All are attending the graduation class of a military unit scheduled for deployment in three weeks.

Christy was raised in the foothills of Arkansas, near the small town of Mountain View. She is the only girl of five children, having four brothers, with her being the youngest. She enlisted in ROTC during her high school years and shortly after high school, she joined the Air Force. Today she is graduating as an officer with the rank of Second Lieutenant.

As the National Anthem is played, Christy stares over the crowd focusing on her family. At the point of tearing up, she feels a sense of sadness, mixed with a proud heart, as she can see clearly four vacant seats that were left open in honor of her father and three brothers. Her father served in an army Special Forces unit, when he lost his life on a mission in South Africa. She was only twelve years old at the time. The other three vacant seats were for her brothers, who are alive and well. They couldn't attend the ceremony because they have proudly followed in their dad's military footsteps. Two are assigned to separate forward operation bases located in Afghanistan, and the third on detail at the U.S. Embassy in South Korea.

Christy looks past the vacant seats at the oldest of the four brothers. She is just as proud of Jed as the other siblings... She feels that he has made the right and good choice in becoming a pastor. Jed has served at their church in the small town of Mountain View for the last six years.

She sees her mom, Sarah, give a small passionate wave... The tissue she is holding blends with her white glove. She has worn those same white gloves at every event having to do with any of her five children. After the small wave, she reaches up and wipes away tears of sadness. Jed, having a heart of gold, reaches over and places his arm around their mom. Christy notices something a bit strange as the morning sunlight peeks through the trees behind the audience. The rising sun forms a beautiful glow around her mom and Jed. It is as though the sunlight creates a halo around Sarah's long, blond hair, mixed with silver-grey highlights. At the age of 57, her mother's beauty is even more evident as the sun continues to rise.

Christy is overwhelmed with this beautiful sight, as she whispers a prayer: "Heavenly Father, thank you for my sweet family, and thank you for this sunrise. I pray I will never forget this wonderful picture you paint in my mind this day."

Suddenly without realizing it, all of her classmates had tossed their graduation hats into the air, and were shouting with joy. Being caught off guard while focusing on her moment of prayer, she is a few seconds behind with her throw. Christy rears back and throws hers as high as a girl of 5'9" and 145 pounds could throw. With her hat being the last one tossed, everyone in the audience, as well as her class, focused on the last and only cap flying through the air. A strange gust of wind takes her headpiece higher and higher.

Christy looks back down at her mom and completely loses sight and thought, of her headpiece… still flying through the air. Out of nowhere, a sudden burst of cheer and laughter breaks out! Not realizing what had just occurred, she notices her classmates pointing up. As she looks up in the direction they're pointing, to see what all the excitement is about; "O Lord, My God!"

The dark blue headpiece had landed perfectly on top of one of the nearby flagpoles with old glory waving right underneath. The entire audience goes ballistic! She had unintentionally pulled off something that had never happened in all the history of the Air Force Academy at Colorado Springs, Colorado.

With a blank expression, Christy turns and looks at her commanding officer as he begins shaking his head. Within seconds, he finally breaks out into laughter, joining in as he witnesses this odd sight.

* * *

The short three weeks before Christy's deployment seemed like only a few hours, as the days quickly clicked by. Sarah was having a hard time knowing her little girl would be stationed overseas some 6,000 miles away, at Akinci Air Force Base.

"Hey Mom, are you going to be ok?"

"Oh, sweetheart, you know I'll be fine. It's just that you're my baby girl, and baby girls shouldn't be zooming around in A-10 Thunderbolt jets, shooting at bad guys."

"I'll be fine, Mom. You know God is watching over us. Just have a little faith."

"Have a little faith? I have plenty of faith! I had faith your dad would make it home, but God had other plans. Sweetie, sometimes I truly wish I would have had all girls and your dad would have been a shoe salesman. Maybe then, you wouldn't have turned out to be such a tomboy. I don't understand why in the world you were so set on going into the military. Even in joining the armed forces, you could have easily picked something safer, like a recruiting officer, or a desk clerk for some General. You are just as hard-headed as your dad and brothers!"

Christy steps a bit closer and wraps her arms around her mother, who is now in tears. "Mom, please try to calm down, it's going to be ok. You know I hate making you feel this way."

The screen door on the carport entrance screeches open and bangs shut.

"Hey, Momma, where are y'all at?"

"We're back here, Jed, be out in a second."

"I've got the truck warmed up. We need to get going. We're having the Lord's Supper today and I need to get there a little early, so let's hurry along."

"I tell you what, that boy is a fine preacher but he is short on patience. Hand me that dishtowel. I don't want him to see me like this.

* * *

As they pull in the parking lot of the Mountain View Open Door Church, Sarah starts humming a familiar praise song. Jed and Christy break out in a big grin looking over at each other, without saying anything, remembering their mom has done this for years. Each and every time they have rolled up to their church it was mom's way of getting ready to go into worship.

While Sarah begins visiting with a few elderly early birds, Jed and Christy hurry in to prepare for the Lord's Supper. They carefully fill each cup with grape juice and place the unleavened bread wafers on the silver dish. Just as they finish setting it all up on a table in front of the pulpit, a hometown favorite, everyone calls the Lily of the Valley, walks through the door. She has with her a giant bouquet of roses.

This humble 99-year old servant of the Lord has provided flowers for their church for the last 75 years. She smiles from ear to ear as she proudly walks up the aisle setting her masterpiece on the table. Lily turns and wraps her arms around Christy and whispers, "Sweetie, the Lord has had you on my mind for several days. Last night I had an odd dream about you."

Still in this long embrace with Ms. Lily in front of the pulpit, while members are filling the pews, Christy whispers, "Ms. Lily, what kind of a dream did you have?"

"Well, I know you're going on a distant task with the military, and child, I don't want to scare you with this, but I felt the Lord prompting me to share this dream with you before you leave tonight."

"Ms. Lily, you have my full attention."

"I saw in my dream where there is a great battle with a number of soldiers who lose their lives and you are caught right in the middle of it. You, with all your training and firepower try to defend these men and women on the ground, but can't save them. As you're in the midst of the battle, I saw black smoke coming from the engines of your plane. Now child you have to understand, I'm an old lady and I forget things. Now if memory serves me… I saw you hiding and injured in a mountain range with mountains much larger than we have here in Arkansas."

"O my goodness, Ms. Lily. That was probably just a silly ole dream."

"No, sweetie, God has given me dreams before, just please listen! God wants me to let you know, He is going to send angels dressed as shepherds who will rescue you from the hands of the enemy, and will deliver you to a safe place. One more thing, He wants to let you know that He has chosen you for a journey into the light and wants you not to have a spirit of fear, but to rejoice in obedience to Him. I know all this must seem very strange."

"A journey into the light, what light?"

"I'm not sure, but I saw you in the presence of three angels. Two were small and looked a lot like children. The third was huge and he was adorned with armor, but he stood off in the distance and seemed to be just watching. Sweetie, that's all I can remember, but before we are dismissed from church, I would like to pray over you—if you don't mind."

"I would like that, and thank you for sharing your dream." Christy watches as Ms. Lily heads for her favorite spot on the front row, a spot she has occupied for the better part of a century.

While the last of the folks visiting in the back of the sanctuary find a seat, Jed walks past Christy and whispers, "What was that all about?"

"I'll tell you later. It was a bit spooky."

The small choir finished singing the last hymn, then Jed steps up to the pulpit.

"Good morning, everyone, doesn't it feel good to be in the house of the Lord on such a beautiful Sunday morning?" The church members let out several amens.

"Yes indeed, wonderful morning. Would you all show your appreciation and give Ms. Lily a hand for those beautiful flowers she grew herself, trimmed up, and delivered right here in front?" Everyone claps with a couple mild whistles as the congregation cheers for Ms. Lily.

"You know I'm not much to look at, so I think she does that with those gorgeous flowers so when y'all look in this direction it makes it a lot easier on your eyes." Laughter and chatter ignite across the church.

"Ok now, calm down, it wasn't that funny. Folks on a serious note, I have a lot I want to throw at you this morning and a short time to do it. We plan on leaving here right after church and heading straight to the airport in Little Rock. We have to put little sister on a plane. She's heading almost to the other side of the planet. As you know, it's going to be a bit rough on Momma. I also want to remind everyone about our family losing Dad several years back; and we can't forget our three brothers who are currently serving in the military overseas. Saying this, please keep Mother and our family, in your prayers.

"Now, I have a couple of different things I feel the Lord wants me to go over with you. After we finish, I would like anyone who feels the spirit of the Lord to come forward and lay hands on my sister and pray for her. I don't care if you're a 70-year-old elder or a 2-year-old toddler. God hears the prayers of all who love Him. It's not about status; it's about the love of our Savior!

"If you would, I want you all to open your Bibles and turn to Matthew 7:1-6. Folks, these few small verses of the Bible have always given me a bit of fear, because I stand before you, guilty of this very thing God's word speaks of here today. If you will, stand in honor of God's word. You folks with bad backs or knees, you stay seated if you would rather. God knows your heart.

"Chapter 7, verses 1-6 says, '*Judge not, that you be not judged. For with what judgment you judge; you will be judged; and with the measure you use, it will be measured back to you. And why do you look at the speck in your brother's eye, but do not consider the plank in your own eye? Or how can you say to your brother, Let me remove the speck from your eye; and look, a plank is in your own eye? Hypocrite! First remove the plank from your own eye, and then you will see clearly to remove the speck from your brother's eye. Do not give what is holy to the dogs; nor cast your pearls before swine, lest they trample them under their feet and turn and tear you in pieces.*'

"You can take a seat, and I'll try and explain why fear comes over me sometimes when I think about this scripture.

"Throughout our lives Satan has laid traps which we continually fall into. Even with this knowledge handed over from our Maker, we find ourselves guilty. I'll give you an example: I was over in Little Rock on business in the downtown area. These young adults walking right in front of me were wearing their pants all the way down, below the crack of their butts." Chuckling comes from the congregation.

"Hold on, it gets better. They passed right by a big trash can, and just a few feet past it, one guy tosses a half-eaten sandwich with the wrapper still on it over on the sidewalk. He then finishes his pop, tosses his empty can on the edge of the street. At this point, I was steaming and had to get away from these guys. So, I plopped down on a bench facing a little park and allowed some distance between me and the street urchins. While I was sitting on that bench this very scripture came to mind. I started thinking; well I guess I had judged them in three or four different ways. *'Ok, Lord, how can I not judge someone like this?'* God, at that point, put me under conviction to lose the anger, along with the judgmental spirit, and to pray for this unsightly crew. Being obedient, I began to say a little prayer still hiding my prejudice deep down inside.

"Suddenly, I started to have thoughts of how some of these kids are raised. Some without Godly parents, some without any parents at all. Some are born and raised on the street with no recollection of God. Then I began to wonder: If I wasn't raised with parents and grandparents praying for me, taking me to church, and teaching me something as simple as respect, where would I be?

"Giving it more thought; what if I had a mom on drugs, or a dad that came by once a month to share a few food stamps, or slap me around because he was raised without God in his life? Where would

I be? I would probably be walking with those guys with my pants sagging, and tossing trash.

"At that point, I asked for forgiveness for being so shallow-minded and judgmental. So I sat there for a while and continued to pray for all the people living in Little Rock and that they would all come to know the Lord.

"So now are you seeing how easy it is to fall into the snare Satan sets in front of us?

"I said I was going to cover a couple things so here's number two: I have been watching the news and I've never seen so much division between the races of mankind. The crooked media and politicians are trying to get us to believe their lies.

"Here's my thought; we have blacks, whites, Spanish, even Mr. Lee over there who's from the Philippines, all who attend our church and serve as Christian believers, working in our community side by side. We love everyone as brothers and sisters.

"I'm going to do a little test. Is there anyone here who feels, or has ever felt like someone in our church body is prejudice against them? Go ahead, lift your hands, and speak out. Come on help me with my test, lift those hands!"

One old man slowly lifts his hand as he stands. "Ok, Mr. Simmons, talk to us. How has anyone in our community or our church ever shown prejudice toward you?"

"Well, Pastor Jed, the last three times I went fishing with my black friend Jimmy Johnson, he caught more fish than I did. Two times, he caught the biggest. Does that count for prejudice?" The whole church bursts out laughing.

"No, that doesn't count, Mr. Simmons."

"Oh I know, I was just funning, I couldn't do without my fishing buddy Jimmy. We've been fishing partners for over 30 years."

Jed begins shaking his head as he breaks out into a big smile.

"Now we are getting somewhere. If the world could see the true hearts of men, women, and children who first love the Lord God with all their heart, there would be no prejudice toward one another. I say this is another trap set by Satan himself. His key element is using the media and lost politicians like puppets. They try to sway votes in their favor by dividing the races and promising the moon and stars, only leaving empty pockets and angry hearts.

"Tell me, who does that sound like? Remember, Satan's number one tool is lies, and then comes division."

Everybody in the congregation stands in agreement clapping and cheering. "Amen, brother, Amen"

Jed steps down in front of the communion table, while the ushers come forward. After the prayer, they slowly make the rounds with the bread and juice.

After the Lord's Supper, Jed asks anyone and everyone to come forward and pray over Christy. They anoint her with oil, and as many prayer warriors that could reach, lay hands on her shoulders and head.

Christy, on her knees feeling the spirit of the Lord, begins to weep. She is humbled by the presence of God and the love from her friends and relatives as they pray.

After the prayers were over, Ms. Lily begins singing, "*Onward Christian Soldiers, marching as to war, with the cross of Jesus going on before.*" The entire congregation joins Ms. Lily in song as they walk out of the sanctuary. *"Christ, the royal Master, leads against the foe; Forward into battle see His banners go!"*

Jed stands just outside the front door, with Christy and Sarah at his side. Each and every one passing gives Christy and her mom warm loving hugs.

Ms. Lily doubles back, leans in, and whispers, "Remember, the

Lord will be with you and lead you in your time of trouble. I will also be with you in prayer and spirit."

Christy smiles, "Okay, Ms. Lily, thank you. I'll pray for you too."

* * *

During the short 103-mile drive from Mountain View to Little Rock, Jed could sense a sadness looming over their mom. All sitting side by side, with Christy in the middle, she starts giggling as they drive over a rough stretch of highway. The worn out spring seat in this old antique 1960 model Apache 10 pickup would almost launch all three in the air as they hit the swells in the rough blacktop. Being overtaken by the bouncing and Christy's adorable giggle, Sarah and Jed begin to laugh.

Not saying anything, Jed reaches up and clicks on the AM radio. Christy immediately takes over the controls, trying to find a decent channel. After twisting the knob back and forth, they only hear static along with some silly talk show. Showing a touch of aggravation, she gives up and turns it off. "Jed, why haven't you ever installed a CD player or maybe even splurged, and gotten XM in this old heap of nuts and bolts?"

"It's a classic; I want to keep it original."

"Oh, I understand, so leaving the unpainted primer and the rusted out fenders help keep it original?"

"Well no, it's a work in progress!"

"You haven't done anything to this truck ever since Dad died."

Sarah jumps in the conversation. "Okay, that's enough. The truck's fine. It's getting us down the road and I'm not in the mood to listen to the radio!"

"Sorry, Mom, we were just jacking with each other."

"I don't like bringing your dad into a conversation on a day when Christy is going off to war, if you two don't mind."

Both at the same time with soft voices, "Sorry, Mom…"

"Christy, I want to ask you something."

"Okay, what you got, Mom?"

"Well, I would like to know what Ms. Lily was telling you before church started, and I noticed she was whispering something as we were leaving. What was it?"

Jed jumps in, "Yeah, Christy, I want to know too. You told me you would share later. So, here's later!"

"Oh, it was nothing. She was just saying she would be praying for my safety, you know stuff like that."

Mom raises her voice, "Girl! I saw the look on your face when she told you whatever she told you, and I can read your face like a roadmap. Ms. Lily is a bit different from most folks. She walks a little closer to God than most, and she has said and done things that can't be explained. So come clean."

Jed chimes in with excitement, "Yeah, I have to agree with Mom, she is a little more in touch with God than most. I would even go as far as saying she might be a sort of 21st century prophetess."

"Okay I give. Lily was telling me about a silly dream, she had and that I had been on her mind for some time now. So there, I told you it was nothing."

"Christy Lee Moody! What was her dream about?"

"Well, she saw me in a great battle where I was trying to save some of my soldiers, but couldn't. She also saw black smoke coming from my engines, and said I would be saved by angels dressed as shepherds, and something about taking a journey into the light. That was about it, just a dream."

Sarah slams both hands against the dash. "Stop the truck, turn this piece of junk around, we are going home right now! Young lady, I forbid you to get another step closer to that plane!"

"Whoa, Mom, I can't just go AWOL because an old lady from the mountains had a dream. They would lock me up in a military loony bin. Drive on, big brother!"

The conversation came to an uncomfortable silence. The only sounds were coming from the old six cylinder engine chugging along with the howling of a worn out rear drive train. The mesmerizing sounds cause Jed to let out a big yawn. "Well, we are almost there. Don't y'all think we need to get over our little misunderstanding?"

"Yeah, Mom, don't let that silly ole dream scare you. God has a plan for all of us and we need to accept it."

* * *

Walking through the Little Rock National Airport, Christy spots two of her classmates heading in the same direction. Just before entering her gate, she hears the airport intercom announcing, "Boarding flight 332."

Christy stops in front of her gate, "Well, I guess this is where we part." Sarah, with tears in her eyes, wraps her arms around Christy and whispers, "Just don't take any unnecessary chances out there. I will be praying for you constantly. I love you, my sweet baby girl."

Jed steps up as he reaches around both, "Okay enough of this sobbing, you'll ruin your uniform. Know this, kiddo, the whole community will be praying for you, including big brother."

After a few short waves, Christy disappears through the plane access door, heading for the country of Turkey where she will join up with her flight team for two weeks of training and military drills before her final destination, Syria.

5

Hot Rods and Hogs

Back down in Louisiana the dive team steps off the helicopter throwing their gunnysacks over their shoulders. They all head for the row of vehicles on the backside of the lot. From being out on a six-week diving project, their cars are completely covered and caked with grey dust and salt from the moist gulf air. Matt shakes his head, "Look at my car. That makes me sick. I paid 70,000 bucks for this Dodge Demon, and just look at it." Laughter breaks out across the parking lot as Captain Lee pulls the cover off of his old 1979 Chevy S-10.

"What are you laughing at, Lee?"

"Oh nothing, I was just admiring those fancy hotrods y'all are driving." Lee rolls up his cover and tosses it over in the toolbox. "You boys get a few more years on you and maybe, just maybe, there's something to be said about wisdom. Well fellows, you have my number and my address, so don't be strangers. Check in with me, because I am checking out! See y'all in the funny pages."

"Later, Cap."

"Yeah, see ya, Cap."

"We enjoyed it, and we'll look you up one of these days."

They all wave as Captain Lee drives out of the heliport parking lot. Before his dust settles, TC grins from ear to ear, "Roll one, Bones."

"What…? You got it, TC!"

Matt pops the trunk of his car, "Does anyone want a hot beer?"

Laughter begins as Joey proudly sticks his chest out, "I'll do one better than that. I've got some homemade moonshine."

Joey opens the trunk of his Shelby Mustang, when Matt suddenly becomes alarmed and whispers, "Bones, ditch the joint. The security guard is heading straight for us."

Bones starts laughing, "Who do you think I got this weed from, Matt?"

"You have got to be kidding."

"Nope, he gets it off a shrimp trawler that meets up with a sea going speedboat off the coast about 30 miles out. Yeah, he's been getting me fresh weed for several years."

Matt chuckles, "Where does it come from?"

"I believe it comes straight out of Columbia."

The security guard gets close enough to hear everyone talking and with a strong Spanish voice, "Hey, my amigo, El Bones, I smell something a little funny coming from this way… you know Chico has to investigate…"

The whole crew bursts out laughing with Bones waving him over. "My good friend, Chico, I missed seeing you last hitch."

"El Bones, I was out of town. I had business with the Russian down in Belle River."

"The Russian they call Nikolai, at the Bayou Rose?"

"Si Señor, that's the one… He's no good… His bouncer Shafer gave me this."

Chico pulls his shirt up and you could see stitches across his ribcage.

Bones reaches over lifting Chico's shirt a bit higher, "Dang, son, what happened and who sewed you up? It looks like a horse doctor got a hold of you."

"My sister... sewed me up. Bones, you make Chico feel bad... I thought it look good..."

Matt takes a pull off the joint handing it over to Chico. He coughs, while asking, "So why did the Russian do this to you?"

"Well, Señor Matt, you have to understand, Chico only deals with a little weed. I don't touch the hard drugs and the Russian say if I don't start moving his product, he will kill me and my family. This knife wound is just a warning. He says, not only will they kill my family, they will kill them one by one in front of me. Si you know, Señor Matt, Chico has big family."

Joey with an angry look, raises his voice, "We should go down there and smoke his butt!"

"Señor, don't mess with them. They are evil, and the Russian is El Diablo, the devil."

Bones takes a big swig of homemade moonshine, wiping off his chin as he slowly hands the jug over to Chico. "My friend, where are they cooking that poison?"

"In the basement off the back of the bar they have four cargo containers buried underground."

"Containers like the ones that come in on the big ships?"

"Si, Señor Bones, just like on the cargo ships, muy grande my friend, really big. They have them side by side, two on one end, and then two more. They have lights; propane burners and they have air-conditionin'. Ah no es bueno, I mean no good, it's hot like hell. They have women working down there naked, no clothes man! The Russian checks them in their mouths and even look at their butt crack so no one can steal. One girl he catches stealing. No work no more. They find piece of her in swamp, alligators take the rest. I tell you, Bones, he is the devil!"

"Okay, Chico, thanks for the info, my Spanish friend. Tell your sister Louisa, 'Bones says hello...'"

"You got it, my friend. Here's a little something special. It's pretty strong, so don't smoke too much… It will make you laugh all day and people see you and think you loco… Bones, I think my sister Louisa, she like you too much… She had a baby that looks like you, ahhhh my friend, maybe become my brother-in-law someday."

They all burst out laughing at Bones, with Matt shouting, "Bones, you done knocked up a Spanish chick! Go ahead, big daddy Bones, now you're a dad."

TC joins in, "Yeah, a laid off dad."

Bones holds his index finger in the air, "Gentlemen, the laid off with no money gives me an idea! Y'all know where Cheese Hound's place is down on the Belle River? We need to give the Hound a visit."

Everyone is shaking their heads, with Matt mumbling, "Why you want to meet at Cheese Hound's? I think he's still mad at me for scooping up that stripper at the Bayou Rose."

Bones grins, "I'll tell you my idea when we get there, and by the way, he's not mad at you. Matt, ole buddy, Cheese Hound was actually jacking with you. The stripper you're talking about is his first cousin, and they were both in on the joke."

Matt shakes his head, "You mean to tell me Lela is his cousin? Dang, they got me for sure." Everyone laughing… "Okay, okay, laugh it up guys, payback will come out of nowhere!"

TC pops off, "Hey, my Bro Bro, I wasn't in on that one, so leave me out of the payback!"

Joey says, while displaying his little gangster smile, "First, let's hit a car wash in Morgan City and catch dinner in Lafayette before we head out to Cheese Hound's. I don't want to go all the way out there and find the Hound's fridge is empty."

TC chuckles, "Yeah, the last time we were over there I saw three freezers, each one having all kinds of animal heads waiting for the taxidermy."

Bones mumbles, "Yeah, Cheese Hound dropped out of the social life and become a bit of a loner after he got back from his last tour of duty. He hasn't opened up to me on what went on over there, but I could tell it changed him. He told me other than this small crew he just wants to be left alone. All he does anymore is hunt and fish on those bayous. One thing about it, he grows some killer weed, and his fridge is always full of cold beer. He even cranks out a little moonshine certain times of the year, down there in the swamp."

Matt chimes in, "That whole swamp thing kind of scares me."

Bones shakes his head, "You big wuss, you're a deep-sea diver and you're scared of the swamp?"

"Give me a break, Bones; I watched a movie when I was a kid that scared the tar out of me. The movie was called Bigfoot and they claimed it was a true story!"

Bones, knowing Matt was from Minnesota and raised in the city, sees a perfect opportunity for another prank. He slowly turns away from Matt looking at the dive team and gives everyone a big wink. This was a signal to let everyone know to get on board with the leg pulling, or in land lovers terms, a prank.

Bones quickly turns back to Matt, "Well, brother, the rumors around Louisiana about Bigfoot are true. Chado Cole told me a story about a time when he was just a teenager. They had several events around a place called Iatt Lake that led the whole community to believe there was a monster that lived in the swamp."

TC joins in, "Where is that lake at, Bones?"

"It's up in central Louisiana. He said there are areas up there that if you were to ever get lost, you might never find a way out." Matt's eyes widen as Bones continues, "Chado said they heard one while they were shooting wood ducks coming into roost just before dark. They were standing in waist deep water out in the middle of Iatt Swamp when they heard it."

Matt chimed in with excitement, "What did they hear? I mean, what did they do when they heard it?"

"Well, he said he and two of his buddies got the heck out of there. He also mentioned several days later that they found tracks about two miles from where they were hunting. This thing had a huge foot. It was at least twice the size of a human's. His stride between steps was double that of a man. Kind of like if you were stepping off a yard at a time. Hey check this out, the local college, LSU, sent people out there and they poured plaster compound in the tracks, and brought their findings back to their lab." Silence falls over the dive team.

Matt, with a lost look, asks, "Well?"

The silence continues as everyone watches Bones take a long slow sip of moonshine. He wipes his chin off, looks over at Matt, and with a smirk, said, "Well what?"

"Come on, Bones, don't leave me hanging! What did the college gurus find out about Bigfoot's tracks? Were they real?"

"I think so, from what Chado told me. It was if the story went hush, hush. He believed they wanted the story to go away. The reason being they were trying to protect the animal. They didn't want thousands of people running around in Iatt Field Swamp hunting a Sasquatch."

Matt's eyes widen again, "Wow, so it could be true; I mean the whole Bigfoot thing. I wonder if there are any in the swamp where Cheese Hound lives."

Everyone was still playing along with the look of fear in their eyes as Bones continues, "Oh yeah, there are sightings all over the US. Yep, Chado told me other stories that would make your hair stand up on your neck. Let's change the subject, because I'm ready to go. This hot beer is nasty."

TC jumps in, "Hey, guys, I checked the weather and it's going to be warm and clear for several days. Let's pick up our bikes."

Matt shakes off the spooked look, "Yeah, I'm ready to hear the rumble of the new drag pipes I installed on my Street Glide, let's rock!"

6

SWAMP BEAST AND THE CAJUN BAT CAVE

After a few ice cold beers and a belly full of crawfish, the dive team all walk out of Little Cajun Restaurant in Lafayette, Louisiana.

Bones leans against his bike, "Matt, you still feel like riding all the way to Belle River?"

"Bones, you wimping out on us?"

"No, it's just when I eat a belly full of crawfish, I want to go lie down and snooze."

The guys all chuckle, with TC popping off, "We can sleep when we die, let's head to Cheese Hound's. He has plenty of dusty old beds in that big camp house of his. If we leave now we can probably make it before dark."

Bones steps away from his bike, "Hey, guys, let me make a quick call before we go." Not wanting Matt to hear his conversation, he walks across the parking lot. "Hello, Cheese?"

"What's up, Bones a Rou?"

"Hey, bud, we're in Lafayette and about to head your way and I want you to help us do a prank on Matt."

"I'm in; what do you need?"

"Well, we have him all worked up and he's scared of the swamp, and we've been telling him stories about Bigfoot."

Cheese Hound laughing on the other end; "Say no more. I've got just what we need. Oh, yeah. One more thing, Bones…"

"What you got, Cheese?"

"Check him for guns. I don't want to get shot!"

"Ok, I don't think he's packing, but I will check."

"Hey, when y'all get here, just go on in. Make yourself at home, and if anybody asks, just say he's probably out hunting."

"Cheese, what about all your guns?"

"Don't worry, they're all locked up."

"Cool deal, my brother. See you in a couple of hours."

Matt straddles his Street Glide, "Hey, Bones, who was that?"

"Oh… that was just an old girlfriend down on the bayou." Bones turns and winks at TC and Joey, smiling as they all fire up their customized Harleys.

Three teenagers standing on the sidewalk admiring the bikes quickly place hands over their ears, as the deafening sounds of the four bikes slowly drive away.

This crew of vagabonds head south in a staggered formation down I-49, having absolutely no cares in the world... Matt, dragging up the rear lags back a few car lengths behind his buddies... His joy and smile slowly slip away as he has thoughts of that dreadful night on January 11, 2015. This night has haunted him for the last five years. He has self-judged and self-convicted himself, feeling like he was responsible for killing his best friend.

The sun is slowly setting behind the tall cypress trees growing along the interstate. The rays shoot through the trees as the bikes move along, as the sunlight plays a silent song. This harmony, joined with the strobe of flashing rays along with the roaring engines, seem to almost be in time. Each one of the riders notices this strange phenomenon as they ride along. Bones, the lead rider, holds his hand in the air pointing at the setting sun. TC and Joey give each other thumbs up in agreement.

Just north of the Morgan City Bridge, Matt breaks formation and blasts up beside Bones. "Hey, bud, it's getting a little cool."

Bones shakes his head in agreement. With unison like a jet fighter team, they all gear down swaying their bikes to the side of the road. Parking in single file, with no one saying anything, they break out the leather. Each rider feels the evening chill in the air and he knows there is no time for chitchat. As the sun is disappearing, it won't be long before an enjoyable ride turns into a cold uncomfortable run.

Bones looks back to see his buddies all clothed in thick black leather and ready to face the cool evening air. He holds his hand in the air motioning with a half circle then pointing south. Joey suddenly throws up a fist signaling the crew to wait. Bones mumbles to himself, "What's wrong, Dooger? What are you waiting on? Oh, I see, you want to wait on those three crotch rockets coming up I-49."

They all watch as the three sport bikes zip by and suddenly with the sound of thunder, the four hogs rumble up the Morgan City Bridge. As they top the crest of the tall bridge, they all look to the west just in time to catch the last glimpse of the sun as it disappears behind the horizon of the swamp.

Riding in double formation down the steep decline of the bridge, they throttle down and quickly pull up behind the sport bikes. Each rider knows their hogs are no match, in speed, with the 200 mph crotch rockets. So intimidation is their message, as they have a bit of pride in their fancy customized Harley bikes.

Out of curiosity, Matt breaks out of formation and pulls up past the first two bikes, settling in beside the lead rider. As he rolls up, he gives a friendly wave looking over at the largest of the three super sports.

Matt is suddenly surprised to see the lead rider on a GSX R-1300, a bike identical to the one his best friend Chado Cole used to ride. Sadness comes over Matt as he remembers how he used to pick on Chado for riding a crotch rocket, and without warning Chado would always do something crazy. He would gear down and launch his bike, riding a wheelie for a half mile down a busy street. Or sometimes he would slide up on edge of the gas tank and light the back tire up, burning rubber while blowing his hog away. Matt also remembers Chado never trying to defend his choice of bikes verbally. He would get his message across without saying anything; his answer was just plain ole horsepower.

Matt, holding back the tears from his cherished memories of Chado, collects his thoughts while giving each rider another friendly wave as he slows down rejoining his crew.

After another hour in the saddle, they finally roll up to a locked gate. Bones steps off his bike, immediately stretching and letting out a huge growling noise. "Hey does anyone remember the combination to this lock?"

Joey laughs, "How could you forget that? It's your birthday, 6661."

"Very funny, Joey, now that was a good one."

TC joins in, "For real? That's kind of freaky if you ask me! Why would Cheese Hound use the Devil's number?"

Being the unbeliever of the crowd, Matt mumbles, "There's no such thing as the devil or a god!"

Bones laughs, "And there is no such thing as Bigfoot, right…?"

Matt suddenly takes his cell phone light and begins looking all around behind him. "Hey, can you hurry up with the gate? I'm tired and ready to chill out."

They all start laughing at Matt as they fire their bikes off and head down the narrow one lane dirt road leading in.

As they pull up to an old wooden bridge, there are homemade

signs on each side of the road with skull and crossbones painted in red. The paint resembles blood dripping down each sign.

They slowly begin rolling across the bridge, as they notice strips of boards are missing.

Bone yells out, "Watch the holes, and don't fall through, it's about a 30 foot drop!"

Matt mumbles, "You've got to be kidding me! Cheese Hound needs to fix this rotten mess."

After everyone slowly idles across the rickety old bridge, they all pull up side by side. Being relieved from not falling into the bayou, everybody is laughing and making small talk.

Suddenly Joey points down the road, "What the heck is that?" They all at the same time hit the high beams on their bikes. It was something standing in the edge of the road about 200 feet away. It looked like it was around seven feet tall and had moss hanging all over it.

Matt mutters with a tone of fear, "Bones is that Cheese Hound playing a joke and trying to spook us?"

"I don't think so, he lives another couple miles in. I don't know what that is."

The shadowy monster continues to stand still, and not move in any direction. Sudden anger grips Joey, "Okay, I've had enough of this bull crap." He begins hollering and throttling his bike up. "Yeah, get out of here, you mossy freak!" With everyone joining in, the two legged beast moves on across the road disappearing into the brush.

After a short ride down the dirt road, they roll up to Cheese Hound's swamp castle. The house is all lit up, and even has some soft shell crabs boiling on the stove.

Bones yells out across the house, "Hey, Cheese Hound! Where are you at, my ole buddy?"

Joey, looking over at the boiling crabs, blares out, "Whoa, Cheese is about to overcook our dinner! I wonder where that rascal could have gotten off to." He reaches over and turns the fire off. "Well he has to be close; you just don't leave a stove on and go off fishing. You might burn this sucker down!"

Bones heads for the back porch and suddenly stops. "Hey guys, come look at this." They all walk up behind Bones as he points at the floor and whispers, "A blood trail, fellows, this don't look good. Hey, Matt, grab that flashlight."

Matt clicks the light on and they all four bundle together, like frightened schoolgirls. They walk out on the back porch, continuing to follow the blood trail. Bones reaches up for the string to a single light bulb that hangs from the center of the porch. Like safari hunters, they follow the trail of blood down a long set of wooden steps leading to the bayou directly behind the camp. Just at the edge of the water, they see something glistening with bright red blood.

Bones cries out, "No, no… that can't be Cheese Hound!"

Bones drops to his knees, violently hitting the ground with his fist. "No, this just can't be!"

Joey and Matt walk up to the body with the dimly lit flashlight. "Hey, Bones, I don't know if this is Cheese or not, it's torn up so bad we can't make it out."

Without warning, a loud roaring sound comes from the front of the camp, near where they had parked their bikes. Bones jumps up from the ground with a frightened look on his face. "Get back inside, now!"

Matt starts freaking out, "What was that? Hey guys, what was that?"

Bones and Joey halfway up the stairs yell, "Go, go, go, it's Bigfoot, and he's mad!"

The roaring is getting louder and still seems to be coming from where the bikes are parked.

As soon as everyone is inside, Matt dives behind a sofa, and like the old Kilroy signs, he slowly peaks up over the back of the couch. "Someone, find a gun!"

TC rattles the door of a locked gun cabinet, "It's locked, and there's no way to break into it!"

Suddenly the lights go out. Matt whispers, "What's happening? Are we going to be eaten like Cheese Hound? Oh, my God, this must be it. We are about to die a horrible death!"

The screen door bursts open, with Bones being the first to be drug away. Bones screams, "Someone, save me! I can't take the pain, help me…!"

Then all at once, Joey and TC are taken. Voices screaming "Help us… Matt, help us…!"

Total silence falls over the musky camp as Matt hunkers down behind the couch gripping the small dimly lit flashlight. The loud roar of this massive beast shakes the windowpanes of the camp now only a few feet from Matt's hiding place.

Again, an eerie silence falls over the room for what seems like minutes, but is only seconds. Matt can now smell a strong pungent odor. It smells as like blood mixed with sour clothing or body odor. He begins whispering to himself, "This thing is going to leave; it doesn't know I'm even here. I've got to make it out of this."

With no warning, chills pass through his entire body as he feels the warm breath of this beast on his neck. Matt squeezes his eyes shut for a second and finally accepts his fate. He slowly turns around shining his light into the eyes of this giant man killer. He sees a blacked out face with long hair and moss hanging from the head and face of the killer. Matt's hands are now shaking out of control. He sees the long jagged blood stained teeth appear from the mouth of this beast. Matt, now facing sure death, decides not to fight it. He closes his eyes, takes a deep breath, and waits.

To his surprise, he feels the hand of someone rubbing his head, "Hey there, Matt, how the heck are you, mate? You have officially been punked, my brother from another mother."

Matt opens his eyes about the same time the lights come on and the laughter begins. It's Cheese Hound, dressed in his sniper ghillie suit, with a bloody towel draped across his shoulder.

The laughter continues as Matt leans down on the floor rolling over on his back, "Man, I can't believe I fell for this whole back-woods, hillbilly, Cajun, malarkey! I am going to get a gun and put everyone one of you nitwits in the ground."

With all four of the guys leaning over the back of the couch, their knees are sunk down in the cushions. Cheese Hound takes the fake vampire teeth out of his mouth. Then, he reaches over handing Matt a clear mason jar filled with Mayhaw White Lightning. "Here, Matt, take a swig of this. It will cure what ails you and make you forget about all that silly talk of revenge."

TC starts laughing out of control pointing at Matt's pants. "Man, you peed in your pants! I can't believe you peed in your pants!"

Matt immediately defending himself, "No, I didn't. I spilled my beer when I dove behind the couch!"

Bones grins from ear to ear. "You didn't have a beer. All you had was that flashlight."

"Well, it must have been some water or something spilled on the floor that got on me."

"Yeah right…"

After several minutes of laughter and kidding around Matt has to ask, "How were you making the loud growling sound that totally freaked me out?"

"That is called a Dumb Bull. Actually Chado Cole showed me how to make one when we were just kids."

"A Dumb Bull, what the heck is that?"

"Well, let me show you." Cheese Hound gets up, walks over behind the door, grabs the Dumb Bull, and sets it down on the table. "You see, Matt, when your buddy Chado and I were kids you didn't have too many toys to play with, so you had to improvise a bit. I guess you could call this your typical hillbilly kid's toy."

"Well, show me how it works! It actually sounded pretty convincing as a monster prop."

"Ok, it's just a 12-14-inch round, hollowed out log around 16 inches long, with a cowhide stretched across one end."

"So what's the string for?"

"Oh yeah, forgive me, the white lightning is working on me pretty good. So, after you stretch a wet cowhide across one end, you let it dry completely out. Then you poke a small hole in the center of the cowhide, running a string through it. You then tie a knot in one end so the string won't pull out. The secret is you have to use a certain type of string that you coat with pine resin. I've heard the old timers use beeswax. Anyhow, after the string gets dry and stiff, you'll then need a dried-out, hard piece of pine resin. Now, here comes the fun part… You take hold of your string, pull it real tight, and then reach up inside the Dumb Bull, scraping the chunk of resin down the string. That's how it makes the monstrous noise. Chado's dad told us you could make a horse break clean out of a pasture with one of these things."

"Wow! That is for sure one crazy contraption. So, Cheese, what did you use for a body? I mean, what was that bloody thing lying down at the water's edge?"

Cheese Hound chuckles, "That was a gator that's been killing my pet ducks. I figured this was the perfect time to smoke him. I shot him right after I got off the phone with Bones. I have to say, it took some work to set all this up, but it was worth it!"

While everyone was laughing, Bones pulls up a chair at the table.

"Hey, Joey, get rid of the Dumb Bull, I need to show y'all something." Bones pulls out several photos of the Bayou Rose Night Club, and shuffles them all out on the table.

Cheese Hound takes a big swig of shine and passes it over to TC. "Bones, what's on your mind?"

"Well, guys, ever since we talked to Chico back at the heliport, I've been thinking about taking that drug den out."

Matt childishly expresses, "Take the drug den out? What the heck, Bones! We're divers, not outlaws!"

Bones leans back in his chair, "Calm down, Yank. If we plan this thing just right, it will be a walk in the park."

Joey and TC agreeing with Bones, "Heck yeah, let's do it..." "Yeah, I'm in for sure!"

Matt stands up, "Guys, listen to yourselves! You crazy suckers actually sound like outlaws. Tell 'em, Cheese!"

Cheese reaches up grabbing Matt by the shoulder, and with a calm voice, "Sit back down, Matt. You need to hear what's been going on down there."

"Cheese... you're in on this crazy idea? If it's that bad, call the cops and let them sort it all out."

"I would but there are a handful of cops on the Russian's payroll. Heck, even the district attorney is on the take!"

Matt slides his chair back. "Well, I don't want anything to do with it. Actually, I wish you hadn't even told me about any of this."

Cheese Hound gets up and walks over to an old roll-top desk. He takes out five old-timey tobacco pipes and a sack of weed. He scatters the pipes across the table and sets the bag of weed in the center.

"Okay, boys, let's smoke the peace pipes. I am about to tell you fellows what's been going on over at the Bayou Rose."

Matt, with his hands shaking for a second time this evening, reaches for the weed. "Guys, there's absolutely nothing you can tell me that will change my mind."

Cheese, holding his breath lets out a huge cloud of smoke and coughs a couple times, "Matt, you loved our buddy Chado, did you not?"

"Sure, everyone knows I thought the world of him. What's Chado got to do with this?"

"Everything, my brother, everything… Did you know Chado had another daughter and she's been working for the Russians? They've got her strung out on crack and some new drug called Flakka. Heck… they've got all those young girls strung out on that poison. Beautiful young girls are being turned into helpless slaves."

Matt hangs his head, "Why don't we just go in and snag the girls, then bring them all back over here?"

Joey butts in, "That won't work. They're probably all so strung out on that crap; they would walk a mile through glass barefoot to get another fix."

Bones jumps in, "He's right. The only way to stop this is to kill the Russian and his whole crew. Then I say we burn that hellhole to the ground!"

Matt shakes his head, "I don't know, guys, what about the dirty cops and the DA?"

TC slams his fist against the table. "I say we kill every stinking one that ever took a penny from Nikolai or had anything to do with destroying those girls' lives."

Matt stands back up stuttering, "I… I… can't, guys. I just can't."

Cheese Hound looks up at Matt, "Hey, Yank, I didn't want to tell you this, but you know your new girlfriend, Lela?

"Yeah, what about her…? She's not mixed up in this, is she?"

"Yes, neck deep, Matt. She's hooked on that new Flakka drug they're manufacturing. It actually makes them go plumb crazy. Some people are calling it the demon drug."

Matt sighs, "I know what it is. I saw videos on the net. They had a doctor on there saying the drug causes a huge spike in body temperature. It makes them tear their clothes off and run around naked. They are totally out of control. They even said they speak in a foreign tongue. I believed it was just gibberish, because I don't believe in the whole demon, angel, God, and Devil thing, and surely not speaking in tongues!"

Cheese Hound slides the shine bottle over to Bones. "Hey, bud, you got mighty quiet. What's going through your head right now?"

"I guess I have to say anger, if you want me to narrow it down."

Matt grabs the bottle from the table and takes a big swig. "I'm in, but don't we need weapons and a dive plan? Well, I mean a plan of attack?"

Everyone quickly stands, cheering and laughing.

Cheese Hound motions, "Follow me, guys. I've got something I've wanted to break out for a long time."

The half-stoned dive crew follows Cheese over to his gun cabinet. "This old camp might look like a heap of sticks from the outside, but I've put everything I saved over the past several years back into it."

He unlocks the cabinet and slowly opens the door. Everyone waiting on this grand view of something special is now staring at an almost empty gun cabinet. Now with the room dead silent, everyone, including Cheese bursts out laughing.

Matt slaps Cheese Hound on the shoulder, "Man, you had us going, Cheese. I thought we were about to see machine guns and grenades. All I see is two old rusted up single barrel shotguns, and a Daisy Red Ryder BB gun. Man, you're too funny!"

Cheese winks at TC, "Hey, Matt, pick up the BB gun and mash the trigger six times."

"What…?"

"Just do it, and Bones, grab those photos off the table. Leave the bottle, no more booze or weed. If we're going to do this, we need to have clear heads. Okay, Matt, pull the trigger six times."

Matt grabs the BB gun, "Hey this isn't another stupid prank, is it?"

All the guys shout at the same time "Pull the trigger, Yank!"

Matt slowly pulls the trigger the first time, nothing. Then on the second pull, they all hear a click in the wall. So Matt speeds up, click, click, click, click… suddenly the sound of a heavy lock, SHLOCK! They all see movement as a hidden door in the back of the cabinet slowly creaks open.

Cheese steps through and throws a big switch just on the other side. "Follow me, guys, and watch your footing. I haven't quite finished these stairs. One more thing, I have never showed this to anyone. So, if someone finds out about it, I'll torture each one of you, until I find the idiot responsible. Read me, gentlemen?!"

With excitement they all join in, "We've got you, Cheese!"

As they all step through the gun cabinet, their jaws drop when Matt points, "What the heck, Cheese Hound, this is unbelievable!"

They are now staring down at what looks like Batman's Cave. The crew, still speechless, follow Cheese down the long set of stairs. Everyone notices a boat covered with a huge tarp. It's sitting in a dug out section of the bayou, hidden underneath this old rundown camp. The entire left side of the Cajun Bat Cave is lined with stainless steel cabinets.

Bones, curious about the boat, lifts a corner of the tarp covering this 39-foot watercraft. "What you got hiding under here, Cheese?"

"Matt, you and TC grab the corners of that tarp, and roll it back." As this super sport seagoing cigarette boat is unveiled, the crew is overtaken with unbelief.

Bones looks over at Cheese, "Dub, where did you get this thing?"

"Well, a close friend of mine actually left it to me in his will. He was a Navy Seal I met in training, and later on I happened to be at the right place at the right time. I had the honor of saving his life."

"What happened to him, Cheese, if you don't mind me asking?"

"Nah… that's okay. I really don't want to talk about it."

Joey breaks the uncomfortable moment for Cheese Hound. "So what kind of engines has this baby got?"

"Oh, you motor-heads are going to love this. It has dual V-8 engines with a combined horsepower of right around 2600 HP."

"What…?" TC asks in surprise, "You're telling us that boat has 2600 horses?"

"Well if you want to know the truth, you can hook a computer into the system, turn it up, and get more than that."

Matt runs his hand across the slick fiberglass, "How fast have you had it up to, Cheese?"

"When I was bringing it in from Florida I hit some pretty smooth water. I bumped it up to around 160 mph. It was still gaining, but I got a little spooked so I let off the throttle."

Matt shaking his head, "I know I don't want to go that fast on land, much less on the water!"

They all walk back down the dock with TC pointing over at the steel cabinets. "Okay, Cheese, what you got hidden in the cabinets?"

Cheese walks over, reaches inside a mounted alligator's mouth, hitting a button. It magically activates every cabinet on the wall, causing them to automatically pop open.

The dive team all break out laughing with Bones saying, "Cheese Hound, you have totally knocked it out of the park. This is truly amazing!"

They all quietly stand in a row and stare at the different types of weapons hanging neatly inside the cabinets. Ammo belts are hanging in the same fashion. One cabinet is filled with different types of night vision and infrared scopes.

Matt, with a serious look pasted on his face declares, "We are actually going to do this, aren't we?

7

Soldier's Chapel

Over 6,000 miles away Christy Moody slams her locker door as she stands fully dressed in her flight suit. She reaches over and picks up a small satchel from the freshly waxed floor of an empty women's dorm room.

When Christy first arrived at the Akinci Air Base, she found that she was the only woman officer assigned to her sleeping quarters. It made her feel a bit lonely. Still missing her classmates back in Colorado, she would lie in bed and see their faces, one by one, wondering in what part of the world they might have ended up. As her eyes would get heavy before falling asleep, she would capture peaceful moments and think of her mom back in Mountain View. Most nights from all the long hours sitting in an A-10 Thunderbolt pounding ground targets, she would pass out still fully dressed. Sometimes this was on purpose, because she knew the high probability of being awakened in the middle of her slumber for night drills, was likely.

On her second day at the base, Christy walks through the empty rooms of the dorm, observing faded photos and area maps of no personal value to whoever left them hanging on the walls. Not understanding why, she is drawn to one map in particular. She finds herself staring intensely at a satellite map. The area that captures her attention is Syria, near the region of Afrin.

After staring at the map for several minutes in sort of a daze, Christy suddenly has a small vision. It's the face of Ms. Lily, the old flower lady who had the strange dreams and visions back home. Christy quickly steps away from the map and shakes her head. "Where in the world did that come from?" Christy chuckles, "Ms. Lily, what are you doing in my thoughts?"

Not thinking too much of her vision, Christy continues snooping through the dorm rooms, and to her surprise, she finds an old recliner in one of the empty rooms. "Hey what do you know, this might make me feel a bit more at home."

After wrestling the oversized chair to her room, she somehow feels a little less lonely. There is no way she can stand three to four weeks having just a metal chair and desk for the only furniture in her room. Yes, the old recliner is definitely a plus. It must have been her mother's side coming out in her.

So now, after coming in from a hard day of air-to-ground training, Christy would lie back in the worn out, but comfortable old chair. She closes her eyes to clear her mind of attacking ground targets, and just dream of home.

The weeks of final training have passed and now Christy is to report to central command. Over the long grueling days of training, she had often wondered where command would send her. Finally, today is the day she finds out.

After picking up her satchel, Christy heads for the door. On the way across the courtyard, she happens to glance over at a rundown, makeshift chapel. She looks straight ahead, without thought, as she continues on toward her destination. She stops at a crosswalk, having to wait on a small convoy of Turkish guards. Something makes her look back at the chapel once more. Strangely, she sees the face of Ms. Lily as plain as day.

Christy quickly turns back around, now staring down at the concrete walk. "Get out of my head, Ms. Lily. I'm about to do the most important job in my life!"

Unexpectedly, another pilot steps up beside her, "What's that you're saying, Christy?"

"Oh, nothing, excuse me but I have to do something." She quickly turns and heads straight for the little chapel. Muttering, "Okay, Ms. Lily, I'm going. Now everyone on the base is going to think that Lieutenant Moody is losing her mind."

To her surprise when she steps through the door there are three other soldiers kneeling in prayer. They all three turn and smile as she makes her way over to an empty section of the small altar.

One of the three men nearest to Christy leans over and whispers, "We are new here at the base and we're so happy to find they have a chapel. Well, I know you don't have to have a chapel to talk to God, but he says not to forsake the gathering of his people, if you know what I mean."

Christy, taken in by his strong southern drawl and his soft-spoken voice, smiles and holds her hand out. "What's your name, soldier?"

"My name is Brim, pleased to meet you, Miss...?"

As he reaches over, shaking Christy's hand, she can't help herself. "Well, pleased to meet you, Brim. My name is Trout."

They both burst out laughing at the same time, with the two other soldiers holding their index fingers up to their lips, "SHHHH!"

Christy sinks her head down between her shoulders, "Sorry, fellows." With a whisper, "Hey, Brim, I'm from Arkansas, where were you raised?"

"I come from North Carolina."

"Well, good to meet you, Brim, but I guess I need to do what I came in here for, and that's pray." Brim nods in agreement, turns, and bows his head.

After several minutes, they all get up and walk out of the chapel. The first thing they hear is the deafening sound of a C-17 taking off. The three soldiers all stop and watch the giant troop plane as it roars away. Brim looks back at the Arkansas beauty as she heads toward the crosswalk. “Hey, guys, I'll catch up with y'all later.” He suddenly breaks away from his buddies and trots up beside Christy. “Hey, Trout, mind if I walk with you?”

“You do know my name isn't Trout, right?”

“Well, I did happen to catch a glimpse of the tag on your flight suit and it says ‘C. Moody.’”

“Brim, you're pretty observant for a ground guy. Do you look at everyone's name tag, or is it some new hobby you just took up?”

A funny look comes across Brim's face as he stutters a bit. “Ah… I didn't mean to pry, it's just… Ah…, something about you that grabbed my attention.” Brim overwhelmed with the beautiful young pilot, draws a blank as a few seconds of silence passes.

Then Christy smiles. “Well… I'm waiting.”

“I'm so sorry for the hesitation. I was trying to think of how I could explain my thoughts.”

Christy stops walking, “Hey, Ranger, I'm not the enemy. Just speak your mind.”

“Okay, here goes. When I first saw you walk in the Chapel, I knew I wanted to marry you!”

They both burst out laughing as Brim's two buddies walk past. Their curiosity overcomes them, “Hey, you two, what's so funny?”

Christy couldn't help herself, “Your bud just proposed to me.”

The two soldiers join in the laughter with Christy and Brim, as they walk away, shaking their heads.

“Moody, I hope you know I was pulling your leg a bit. It's just so nice to meet another Christian way out here in this godforsaken warzone. One other thing, if you don't mind…”

"Okay, I'm still listening."

"Well, it's just a nice treat, you being from the south. It makes me feel a little closer to home."

Christy smiles, as she looks deep into the light blue eyes of this handsome soldier. She is overwhelmed and a bit intrigued by his taste of childish humor. She's thinking that she had never had anyone propose to her, even jokingly. Still holding the conversation together, her inner thoughts seem to drag her away to something else. *Is there a spark here? Could I have just met someone minutes ago and suddenly have feelings for him?* Christy quickly shakes off her thoughts as she looks down at the gravel walkway. "So… how long have you been in the rangers, Brim?"

"A little over five years now, I've been over here more times than I can count. If it's not here, it's just a country or two over."

"Brim, do you know anything about your mission?"

"Yeah, just a little. I believe we're headed to a place over in Syria called the Region of Afrin-—well just a touch north of there. It's kind of midway between a Turkish border town called Kilis and Aleppo."

"Wow, Brim, that's a couple of hundred miles between the two."

"Yeah, I know. They are keeping our drop zone a secret for now, if you know what I mean."

"Sure, there are a lot of foreigners on this base. Well, that was a stupid remark. We are the foreigners!"

Brim chuckles, "Yeah, I guess when you think of it like that, we are. Hey, Lieutenant, do you think you would mind if I come see you someday? Well, after all this is over, when we're leading a normal civilian life?"

"Sure, Brim, I would like that."

"How will I find you?"

"Just come to Mountain View, Arkansas, and ask just about

anyone where the girl that flies an A-10 Warthog lives."

"So are you going to tell me your first name?"

"It's Christy."

Brim holds his hand out for one more handshake, and before taking his hand, she quickly looks around to see if anyone is looking. Then she stands on her tiptoes, leans over, and kisses Brim on the cheek.

"Well, Brim, this is where I drop off. Remember, Mountain View. Be safe, man with fish name." They both laugh as Christy turns and heads for her Command Center.

Brim continues to stand like a frozen statue with his hand touching his cheek where Christy kissed him. He watches her disappear from sight as the door closes behind her.

Suddenly Brim lets out a long North Carolina yell. "Whaaaahoo! I can't believe what just happened. She kissed me right on the cheek and told me where she lived, whaaaahoo!" Brim turns and takes off in a dead run toward the hanger where the rest of his ranger squad are awaiting orders.

* * *

Christy glances at her watch as she walks through the door whispering, "Perfect timing…"

Silence falls over the room as the HD monitor lights up. The commanding officer (CO) steps up with a laser pointer and begins laying out their battle plans and locations.

"Okay, boys and… girl…" moderate laughter follows, "Hey, I wouldn't laugh too much fellows - she scored in the top three with the A-10 fighter group."

Everyone starts cheering and whistling, with the CO waving his hand in a gesture to calm down. "Well, I guess she has earned her call sign. Christy, the guys and I have given much thought, and it looks like everywhere you go, you seem to be trying to set some kind of a record." More cheering, "This includes throwing your headpiece up on top of a flagpole at graduation. So we finally came up with a perfect call sign."

The CO turns, "Give me that jacket." One of the pilots tosses it over. The CO wads it up and throws it across the room like a football, with Christy jumping up and catching it. "Okay fellows, all together: WELCOME TO THE FLYING 707 FIGHTER GROUP,

POLESHOT!"

Christy quickly stands smiling like a kid at Christmas, giving a few short bows around the room.

"Okay, everyone, let's get back to business. I guess you've seen the troops that came in this morning. Well, they are our mission! We will do everything in our power, and if that's not enough, we will ask our Maker for a little more, to keep those soldiers alive! Do you get me?"

Everyone in the room shouts, "We get you, sir!"

"At 06:00 hours we are moving to an unnamed location on the Syrian border. The runway over there is in rough shape, but I don't think you A-10 pilots will have a problem. You fast movers will have to remain here for now, or at least until we can do a little tarmac maintenance."

The commanding officer slowly turns and points at a detailed map on the monitor. "Intel has informed us of enemy build up, starting here at the border, and up through this area."

The C.O. moves his pointer directly over the town of Kilis as he enlarges the screen. "These criminals have been testing our allies' strength and patience. They've been firing missiles over the border into Kilis.

"At this time we don't believe they've moved additional troops in that close. As I said people, they are testing the waters. The majority are hanging back under the cover of this mountain range. You do not want to get shot down in this area. It's a stretch of around 200 miles. intel has this whole southwest section down around the region of Afrin locked in as a kill zone. They have heavy weapons, ground to air missiles (GTAM) and they even have some old surface to air missiles (SAM). People this report is around six weeks old, so who knows what the heck is waiting on us.

"Ladies and gentlemen, the enemy has so many names, I think they're even confused. So, the Islamic State of Iraq and Syria, better known to you pilots as ISIS, are not going to give up without a fight. I want to let you people in on a little secret. We have a new Commander-in-Chief running the US, and he has put a warhorse in charge of our military. The gloves are off. Do you get me?"

"We get you, sir!"

The CO continues giving his pep talk before handing the meeting over to mission command. Christy leans back in her chair thinking about the handsome ranger she had just met. Suddenly, she has another vision of Ms. Lily. Being totally taken in by her thoughts, the commanding officer recognizes the lost look pasted on her face. He quickly leans in, with his nose almost touching hers, "I hate to interfere with your day dream, but we would all like know: WHERE THE HECK ARE YOU AT, POLESHOT?"

"I'm here captain. I'm listening. You were talking about mountain tops and RPGs."

"That's right, when you people are in those areas beware of your enemy hidden in the rocks. You cannot detect a 16-year-old kid poking his head up blasting your sorry butts out of the sky with a handheld RPG. We've had reports they work in teams and coordinate multiple shots at once. Just watch your six. Do you get me?"

"We get you, sir!"

"I want you pilots to have a PLGR with you at all times. For you people that dropped out of grammar school before the third grade, that is your Precision Lightweight GPS Receiver. If you get shot down, try to get as far away from the crash as possible without being captured. We should be able to get to you by honing in on your handheld GPS receiver. Does anyone have any questions?"

There is light mumbling with sounds of leather pads closing as everyone scans the room for any hands lifted.

"Okay, people, let's make this happen!"

Christy walks across the tarmac, looks over toward the hanger, and notices several choppers taking off heading southwest. She wonders if Brim might be on one, thinking, *I could really get to know him. Mom would fall in love with his manners alone. His charm and sense of humor, and especially his military background, would be a cinch for being accepted with all my brothers. Yes, he would fit in nicely around Mountain View. Wow, what am I thinking? Am I falling in love, and about to crawl into a cockpit of an A-10? Christy, get ahold of yourself, at once!*

Climbing up into the single seat cockpit of her A-10 Thunderbolt, Christy straps in. She then quickly runs through her flight checklist as she has done multiple times with many hours of training. Now these simple tasks have become second nature without any chance of error. She gives her harness another quick adjustment as she feels the vibration of the twin turbofan engines begin to spool up. Looking at the tarmac she patiently watches the ground crew remove the tire chocks, with one signaling to fall in behind two other A-10s, as they taxi over to the runway.

Throttling back traveling down the smooth concrete path only seconds behind the two lead planes, Christy breaks into a subtle smile, thinking back at the expression on Brim's face, as she lightly kissed him on the cheek. She looks over at three more A-10s as they catch up, falling into formation with her and the two other lead planes. As six thunderbolts roar toward a small blip on their inertial navigation systems, Christy continues to think about Brim. Still smiling, at how bold and brave she was to actually steal a kiss from the handsome soldier.

Major Hyde's bold voice rips over the communication system. "Poleshot, get your narrow butt back in formation. What are you doing out there? This is not a vacation or a pleasure flight."

"Sorry, sir!"

Christy quickly brings her jet back into formation. Overwhelmed with her thoughts, she shakes her head. *Now that was embarrassing. Okay, I need to quit daydreaming about Brim. Just wait till I see that guy again. I've only known him for a couple hours and he's already getting me in trouble. What the heck am I thinking? He didn't do anything. I did hear him give out a loud wahoo right before the door closed on the missions building. I think he really meant it when he said he wanted to marry me. Okay, I am totally losing it. Is this how a person falls in love? I've heard of the whole love at first sight thing before… but this is ridiculous!*

Suddenly a vision of Ms. Lily overcomes her. *Ms. Lily what are you doing in my mind again? I need to concentrate!*

Ms. Lily speaks to Christy in her mind as plain as day. *I'm with you child, remember not to have a spirit of fear but of boldness. I'll see you on the other side.*

"What do you mean on the other side? You're alive and well back in Mountain View! Ms. Lily, where did you go?" Christy suddenly realizes her com is hot, on an open channel and she was talking to a vision!

"Major Hyde to Poleshot. Come in Poleshot."

"I read you, sir."

"Who the heck are you talking to over there? Are you losing it?"

"No, sir, I'm fine."

"No you're not! What's going on? It sounds like you've got a ghost in the cockpit. You had better convince me right now, or we'll have to turn this whole squadron around and report you back to sickbay!"

Christy knows she is now busted—caught red-handed talking to a vision in her head. There is no explanation whatsoever. Even if she could suddenly come up with a lie, it would totally go against her beliefs.

"Major, can I meet with you after we land? I think I could explain better if we were face to face."

"Roger that Poleshot, as soon as we land. Do you get me, lieutenant?"

"Yes sir!"

An unknown voice comes over the com, "Panther Claw, calling 707 fighter group. Over."

"Major One to Panther Claw, we read you."

"Major, we've got a large sandstorm just outside of our Forward Operating Base. It looks like your team will have about a 20 minute window to land, so you might want to hurry along."

"Roger that, base. We read you and will adjust arrival time."

The major looks over at Christy and holds his thumb up. "Okay, team, adjust speed to 375 knots and follow me in by the numbers."

8

The Letter

Christy is feeling sick at her stomach having to face the major and explain the unexplainable. She shakes her head in disgust wondering what the whole team must be thinking about her. *They will probably label me as a loony tune that needs to be in a home for the insane. Oh Lord, how could I have been so stupid to talk to a vision out loud over a hot com?*

Christy takes in a deep breath with the tight harness pressing against her chest as she turns and sees the giant sandstorm in the distance. With the rust colored dead ground and the huge dark cloud of sand driven by the parched, dry wind, she wonders why would anyone want to live in this godforsaken land.

Then out of nowhere, Christy begins thinking about maps in her childhood Bible that covered part of this area. As a child, she would lie on the living room floor and stare at the maps, while dragging her finger across the lines. She remembers reading about all the Bible characters and the routes they had taken back in those ancient days. How odd this is… to be flying over the same ground they walked on.

Christy quickly turns her attention back to the job at hand as they make their approach to the dirt runway. Thinking of this sweet childhood memory, a sense of peace floods over Christy as a scripture comes to mind. She reaches over activating her landing gear, while whispering, "If God is for us, who can be against us?"

After the A-10 707 fighter group safely lands, they all walk toward the living quarters with Christy running up beside the major. "Excuse me, sir."

"Yeah, let's hear it, Lieutenant."

"Well, sir, since I was talking over the com and the whole flight team was in on my weird conversation, I would like to address the whole crew, if you don't mind."

"Poleshot, you sure you don't want to explain this in private?"

"No, sir. If I can plead my case to everyone at once, that would keep me from running around trying to explain to all the guys separately."

"Okay then, let's get this over with right quick!" They walk into the mess hall each grabbing a cup of coffee and a few stale cupcakes.

"Hey, fellows, Poleshot wants to address the flight crew. Let's head to the far end."

The screeching sound of metal chairs sliding across the concrete is almost deafening as it echoes through the empty mess hall.

The major sits down, looking up at Christy, "Okay, lieutenant, let's hear it, and don't soften it up. I want to know what's going on, and I believe everyone here would like to know if you are of sound mind. We have to have each other's back out here. In case you haven't noticed, we are in a war zone!"

"Yes, sir, I totally understand. Well, here goes, fellows. We've all been flying together for a few weeks and you know I'm not crazy… but after I share this, you might think I am.

"The day I left Mountain View, Arkansas, we were at church. A sweet 99-year old lady, who our whole town calls the 'Lily of The Valley', came up to me and shared a chilling story. Ms. Lily told me about her dreams and visions, and I was the star of the show.

"You guys please take into consideration that I thought she was just getting old and imagining things. Ms. Lily's told me, in her visions that I would be trying to protect a group of soldiers. With all the firepower I had, I just couldn't save them. She then told me about smoke coming from my plane—that I would be shot down."

The pilots start mumbling, causing Major Hyde to hold his hand up. "Be quiet, guys, let her finish. Christy, is there more?"

"Oh yeah, there's more. Ms. Lily said I would be injured and angels dressed as shepherds would come and save me from the enemy and place me back into the hands of my people. After that, she mentioned not to have fear, and something about the light.

"Guys, after I got over here I was looking around the empty dorm rooms and found myself staring at a map. Her face appeared to me as plain as day. After that I passed by the little makeshift chapel, didn't have plans on going in, but as I stood waiting to cross an intersection on the base, I saw her face again. She was prompting me to go back to the chapel, and I did. The last time she talked to me was on our way here. You know, that's when you heard me talking over the com."

The major asks, "What did she say?"

"Something like, 'I'm with you, child. Remember not to have a spirit of fear but of boldness. I'll see you on the other side.' Okay, guys, you can go get the straight jacket. I'm ready for the loony bin."

Before anyone can say anything, everyone jumps, as the side door suddenly swings open with a blast of heavy wind and sand, hitting the team in the face. Out of the dense cloud of sand a young army private carrying a satchel appears. He quickly gets behind the door and shoves as hard as he can, with the high wind covering everyone with the blistering particles. Two pilots jump up and help the young man secure the door. The major asks, "What the heck are you doing out in that sandstorm, private?"

"Sorry for getting sand in your coffee, sir. Is this the 707 fighter group?"

"Yes, it is."

"Oh thank God! I was hoping I chose the right building. I almost got blown away getting over here. I have mail from the good ole USA."

The flight crew applauds the young private as they begin hitting the poor guy on his shoulders. The sand covered soldier happily dishes out letters from home. "Guys, I guess that's it." Everyone receives a piece of mail but Christy.

The happy group thanks him by patting him on the back as he walks away, heading for the coffee machine at the other end. The pilots feel bad opening their mail in front of Christy, so they kindly fold their letters up, stashing each one in their flight suits.

Christy sadly smiles, "Hey, it's okay. You guys read your letters from home and share if you like. I would love to hear anything about home."

The young private is about midway across the mess hall when he realizes he still has his sand goggles on. He stops, takes off his eye protection, grabs a paper towel from a nearby table, and begins to clear his eyes. "Oh wow, I can see again."

Brushing off both shoulders, he then takes his empty canvas mail sack and turns it upside down over a trashcan. While emptying the last bit of sand from his pouch, a letter falls out. "Well, I'll be dog, how did I miss seeing you?"

The private quickly reaches down inside the metal can taking hold of the lost letter. He uses the back of his fingers as he brushes away the dust, exposing a name. It reads, *To: Lieutenant Christy Moody.* He quickly turns around and yells across the mess hall. "Hey, 707, is there anyone down there with the name Christy Moody?"

The whole crew lights up in cheers and laughter while the private trots up to one happy pilot. "Hey, I'm sorry, Lieutenant. My goggles and bag were full of sand. I didn't see it."

For the moment, the flight team puts Christy's story about the "Lily of the Valley" on hold for mail call. Each pilot walks off a few feet, reading his letters. Some are smiling and snickering with a few hidden tears and quite a bit of laughter.

Christy begins reading her letter in unbelief, with her mouth half open. She quickly scans over each word with a lost look, wondering, how in the world can this possibly be real?

The major notices her countenance has suddenly changed. "Hey, Poleshot, is everything okay at home? You've got a funny look on your face."

"You aren't going to believe this!"

The major takes a few steps closer. "Okay, Poleshot, what is it?"

"If you don't mind, I would really like to share my letter with the whole crew. I truly believe this will either clear things up, and I won't need a strait jacket, or you guys might think my whole family has lost it and have me on the next plane home."

Major Hyde motions for everyone to gather around, as he says, "Poleshot has something she wants to share with us, so everyone listen up. Okay, Christy, you've got the floor. Let's hear it. Tell us what's going on!"

The whole flight team is now mumbling between each other about Christy's ghost. Lieutenant Bailey looks over with a haughty look, "Yeah, give it up, Christy. What are you talking about?"

The major lightly bumps his lips with his index finger, as the chatter abruptly stops. Silence falls over the group, other than the raging sandstorm outside.

Christy takes a deep breath, "I believe this letter from home can help us put this puzzle together, so here goes: 'My beloved daughter, I am writing you today with good news and bad. Your brothers and family are fine and said to tell you they miss you and are praying for safety and blessings for you and your flight team.'"

The guys chatter in the background, "Cool, they're praying for us too."

"Awesome, now that's a good mom, nice family, Christy."

The major butts in, "Settle down, I want to know where she's going with this. Okay, Poleshot, continue."

"Sure, ah… 'Sweetheart, I didn't want to bother you with this, knowing how focused you need to be on your missions. So I fasted and prayed for the last few days. I feel the Lord has given me an answer and has prompted me to share the unfortunate news within this letter with you and your entire team. Let them know we are not some crazy bunch of cult hillbillies from Arkansas! So please share this with them. It could keep them out of harm's way.

"'Christy, my sweet girl, Ms. Lily passed away a few days ago and I was with her holding her hand as she stepped across. Before she died, she had several visions and you were in almost all of them. She claimed she was with you, and the Lord allowed her to lead you to an old recliner in an empty room. She actually laughed and said, "'I know Christy will enjoy the comfort of that old chair.'" She also, urged you to a map hanging on a wall. As you stared at it, she felt like she was there with you, and wanted to hug you so badly.

"'Well, anyway, she said on that map, it showed a mountain range where a great battle will take place. Many soldiers will die and this is where you will be shot down.

"'Tell your people that the enemy has laid a trap and wants to draw them in. She said you are going inside of the lion's den.

"'Sweetheart, I don't have a good way of telling you this, so I'll just say it. You will be mortally wounded near a place called, "The Shadow of the Cross".

"'At this point, she told me not to cry as she continued to share her vision with me. You can imagine, Christy, by this time your mom was a sobbing mess. Lily reached up with her quivering hand and touched my face ever so gently and said, "Be sure and tell Christy not to have fear because by this time, she will be in the hands of the angels."

"'She said this will be a time when you stand in a place between the living and the dead. Sweetie, I didn't really understand what she meant by that. Well anyway, she said two childlike angels, along with a warrior angel, will show you the way, and protect you from the darkness. They will lead you through a portal that brings you into the light and your time there will be for only a moment.

"'Along about this time in our conversation, I actually thought she had suddenly passed away. I felt this way because Ms. Lily stopped talking, closed her eyes, and wasn't moving. I said her name out loud several times, with no response. However, the old girl wasn't finished yet. She lifted her feeble hand pointing at the ceiling and began to sing the chorus to "How Great Thou Art". I actually sang along with her. Well, anyway sweetheart, I wanted to share everything this wonderful old lady from the hills said and did that day.

"'After we finished singing to the Lord, Lily caught me off guard when she suddenly started giggling like she was a young child again and said, "Sarah, are you still here?"

"'"Yes, Lily, I'm here."

"'You tell Christy she has an important job to do for the Lord. She'll be sent back from the gates of Heaven with information for a lost and dying world. Sarah, tell that child, she will be used to help save millions of souls.'"

"'She laughed and said, "Yes indeed, the Lord's going to take back a lot of souls that Satan thinks he's got locked up. Yes indeed, that's gonna be something!"

"'Still laughing, she said something about you meeting a guy in a small chapel with the name of a fish. She said he would be the love of your life. Christy, I thought that was a bit weird; if you've got a boyfriend, you need to let your mom know!

"'Well anyway, she also wanted to inform your flight team that you aren't crazy; because God is about to use you in a magnificent way, and they need to support you and believe in you.

"'As I come to a close, she said to be sure and tell you, "Fear not for The Great I Am is with you."

"'Sweetheart, Ms. Lily squeezed my hand, laughed out loud, and the last thing she said was, "I will meet you at the Eleventh Gate of Heaven." Then she closed her eyes and passed over.

"'My darling daughter, God has given me a peace about this. I know, I was angry with you when you joined the service. However, now I know God has chosen you for this special heavenly mission. I'll be here when you return. I love you, my sweet Christy, Mom.'"

9

Major Hyde and the Great Spirit

Christy slowly folded her letter from home, tucking it away in the front pocket of her flight jacket. Other than the roaring sounds of the sandstorm outside, you could have heard a pin drop.

"Major, I don't know what else I can say in my defense. If you want to know the truth, I was beginning to wonder if there was something wrong with me too. Except now, after tying this letter with these strange visions, I'm beginning to believe it's real. I don't know if y'all are convinced or not, but it sounds like God has allowed this old lady in my thoughts. It seems He's laid out some sort of mission in front of me."

The major spits out a stale piece of cupcake, rinses his mouth out with cold sandy coffee, and turns to look at the pilots. "You guys, take a seat. I want to tell you a little story.

"Back several years ago, I had the opportunity to go on a big game hunt in the Alaskan wilderness. I didn't really care about shooting some helpless animal, but I went anyway. We were dropped off in the middle of nowhere, and to this day, I couldn't tell you where it is on a map. I was totally lost. They flew us in with a small pontoon plane landing on a gorgeous lake, surrounded with mountains and heavy brush. We had a local Indian guide that went by the name, Teeto. He took care of us the whole time we were there. He would catch fish and kill small game for our meals. Oh, this guy was an extraordinary individual. The meals he would prepare would make a New York chef jealous.

"Let me get to my point with this story. My new Indian friend, Teeto, and I became pretty good friends. We spent quite a bit of time together, since I didn't really care about hunting."

The major stops and chuckles, "Oh yeah, one of the first things Teeto asked me was, 'Hey chief, how would someone with the name like Hyde, not be a great white hunter?'" Everyone laughs.

"Well anyway, we would sit around the fire at night and he would passionately talk about the Great Spirit. I asked him if he was talking about God and Jesus. His answer was, 'You speak of the Great Trinity.'

"I said back to him, 'Yes I guess so. The Father, Son, and the Holy Spirit, right?'

"Teeto said, 'Yes, that's right, they are one and the same.'

"I asked him, 'Where did you learn about the Trinity?' That's when he told me a very strange and unbelievable story. He said he had met an elder from a hidden valley near the Mountain of God. This special place is forbidden for anyone from the rest of the world to enter. He said the elder of the village had been in the presence of God and was instructed to seek a stranger out."

Lieutenant Bailey couldn't help himself while snickering, "What did God tell him, Major?"

"Well, this is where you people might think I've lost it. He told me the elder was fishing with God on the Great White River."

Everyone laughs, but Christy. She asks, "What else did he say, Major?"

"He told me God had sent the elder to find Teeto and teach him about the Holy Trinity. Before he returned to the hidden valley, he was told of a certain year, on a certain day, that he would meet a stranger. The elder explained to Teeto, that he would recognize this man to be a servant of God, and would show great compassion for the creatures of the Earth. He would have no interest in the shedding of their blood. This man flew an iron bird that breathed death on the enemies of God. Teeto actually told me… I was this chosen vessel.

"I know this all sounds strange. Just stay with me, it gets better. Teeto went on to say, 'One day in the near future, in the midst of a storm, I would hear a strange story from a woman of war. She would speak of visions from an old lady. The old lady is a prophetess, a woman of great faith. God is allowing her to see into the spirit world.' He also told me that I am to help this woman of war complete her mission."

Bailey speaks with a haughty tone, "Now that's a heck of a tale, Major. So what's that got to do with Poleshot talking to a ghost, and to be clear, I would rather have someone else covering my six, if you know what I mean, sir. No offence, Moody."

Christy responds, "No problem, Lieutenant."

The major stands up, "Bailey, have you been asleep? Haven't you heard anything we've discussed?"

Lieutenant Bailey steps back away from the table, "No, sir, I wasn't asleep. I heard everything. It's just a lot for me to swallow." Bailey chuckles, "This whole story sounds like a spooky novel that someone on drugs has written, and it actually makes it to a grocery store bookstand. You know… that's where all the other sci-fi garbage sits."

The major frowns and is getting angry. "Bailey, when I first heard that Indian guide tell me this crazy story about the elder, the hidden valley, and God's Mountain, I tried my best not to laugh. Now, after hearing Poleshot's story, and then a letter from home mysteriously shows up that confirms her confession—what else do we need to hear?"

Bailey shakes his head, "I still think it's all hogwash."

The major places his hand on Christy's shoulder. "Okay, Poleshot, what about the part in the letter where Ms. Lily talked about a chapel and some guy with a fish name?"

"His name is Brim, sir. He's an army ranger I met back on base at the little chapel."

The flight team is mumbling among themselves when Lieutenant Applegate steps forward, "Major, can I speak freely, sir?"

"Go ahead, Lieutenant, all cards on the table. Let's get this cleared up. I don't want any doubt, confusion, or mistrust out there. Especially after we're in the air watching each other's six."

"Well, sir, I have been a believer all my life."

Bailey suddenly butts in, "Oh, here we go again, another spirit guide."

The major and Christy turn and say at the same time, "Let him finish, Bailey."

The major smiles at Christy then says, "Continue, Applegate, speak freely son."

"Yes, sir. As I was saying before I was rudely interrupted, being a believer, I have never heard of anything quite like this, other than stories in the Bible. No doubt, this could all be coincidence, and I'm sure it could probably be explained away by someone with a higher IQ than I have. Nevertheless, you have to ask yourself, after all this evidence is on the table, and we choose not to believe—and it really is God—well, sir, we wouldn't want to disappoint our Maker!

"One other thing, every time I close the canopy on my A-10, I'm asking for forgiveness for any hidden sin in my life that I might have overlooked. I also ask Him to have mercy on our whole fighter group and that he will bring us all home safe. Guys, I haven't actually spoken freely about my beliefs, but after what it looks like we're involved in, I feel the need to let everyone know where I stand. Saying this, I choose to believe, trust, and help Poleshot. Guys, I support her, and will help anyway I can."

The major holds his thumb up, "Thanks, Lieutenant, and double thanks for the prayers for our crew. Just to let everyone know, I actually do the same thing before we go to battle. The funny thing is, I don't fear the enemy on the ground. I fear God."

Bailey shakes his head in disgust, "You guys have lost it. Applegate, I don't know if my IQ is higher than yours, but I see right through this whole cockamamie story."

The major reaches over and grabs Christy and Lieutenant Applegate on their shoulders while looking in the eyes of the other three pilots, "Okay, fellows, let's all get on the same page here. It sounds like we are in the midst of believers and unbelievers. What I recommend is, we all concentrate on our mission and our mission is to keep those ground guys safe! We can't let our beliefs get in the way of this simple fact. Lieutenant Bailey, are we going to have a problem?"

"Major, considering what I just heard from you three, I have no idea. I mean, I don't know if I can count on Moody keeping her head straight if we run into trouble. What if she starts talking to her ghost and we have a MIG-29 bearing down on us, or an Iranian fighter jet laying down hate?"

"Moody will be just fine, and if it makes you feel any better, from here on out, she's my wingman. Applegate, you okay flying with Bailey?"

"Yes sir, but I have to warn Bailey."

Lt. Bailey with a worried look, "Warn me about what?"

"Well, ole buddy, I talk to God a lot when I'm flying. So if you hear a bit of chatter just relax and know that God is my wingman."

Bailey shakes his head and looks away, "This is just great. So if your God is your wingman, who in the heck is going to watch my six?"

Applegate reaches up and rubs Bailey's head as you would a kid. "Don't worry, friend, I'll ask Him to watch out for you, too."

Bailey, showing aggravation, shoves Applegate's hand away. "Get off me! I don't need a ghost, a god, or whatever else you people are talking about. I depend only on technology, training, skill and fire-power to get me back home."

The major raises his hand, "Okay, let's break this up. I'm craving more sandy coffee and stale cupcakes."

They all laugh while walking back toward the coffee machine, with the major lightly tapping Christy's shoulder, "So, this Ms. Lily said something about you meeting the love of your life at the little chapel?"

Christy blushes, "Yes. sir, I don't know if he is or not, but there was something about this guy that kind of appealed to me. I still have to take into consideration this might all be coincidence. If you want to know the truth, I hope it is just a strange incident. I surely don't want to get shot down."

Major Hyde passes Christy a fresh cup as he says, "On one hand, I feel I should order you to hang back and let us do the majority of hits. However, deep down inside, I have an amazing abundance of faith that we are doing the right thing. It's as if the Lord is showing me… No, it's as if he's commanding me to allow this to unfold. Normally if I had this kind of intel, I would pull the plug, not allowing you anywhere near your plane."

A look of concern comes over the major's face, yet he chuckles, "If Bailey sends in a report about this strange meeting, I will probably get my rank torn to pieces. If I'm lucky, I might get to deliver mail like the young private that brought your mom's letter, however, with the strange information I got from Teeto, my Indian guide, along with this strong desire to be obedient, I have to allow you to go into the lion's den."

Christy suddenly burst out laughing as the major begins to grin with a confused look on his face. "What's the catch? You think I've lost it, right?"

"No Major, just the opposite. That's the exact words Ms. Lily used."

"What words?"

"I have to go into the lion's den."

10

Bar Room Intel

Back down in the swamps of Louisiana, Cheese Hound patiently waits at the top of the stairs. Matt, TC, Bones, and Joey make their way up the rickety steps, leading out of Cheese Hound's secret Cajun Bat Cave.

Cheese turns the light breaker off as the guys crawl through the narrow gun case opening, leading back inside the camp's living room. Joey looks over at the stove, "Hey, Cheese, what about these crabs? I'm a little hungry."

"Sure, bud, we need to eat a bite, clear our heads so to speak."

Matt is at the sink washing his face, "Yeah, I need something in my gut other than moonshine."

Cheese points, "Bones, snag some bowls from the cabinet, and let's dig in. Joey, if you would, look in that oven over there. It's a skillet and a black iron pot in there. One has fresh collard greens and the other has a large pone of cornbread."

Joey laughs, "Cornbread, collard greens, and soft shell crabs; what an odd dish."

Cheese Hound's tone changes, "Well that's all I got, take it or leave it!"

Bones looks over at Joey shaking his head without Cheese seeing.

Quickly letting him know that disrespect is off limits with this war torn veteran.

They all mumble letting Cheese Hound know how much they appreciate his hospitality. "Oh it actually sounds pretty good, Cheese."

Joey jumps in, "You know, collard greens and cornbread is one of my favorite meals."

As they all sit together sharing this strange southern meal, Bones pulls out photos of the Bayou Rose and dishes each one across the table, as if he is dealing cards at a casino. "Guys, these are old photos, but I don't think the inside has changed much, other than the downstairs section Chico told us about." A few seconds of silence fall over the group as they stare carefully at each photo.

Cheese Hound leans back in his chair holding his glass almost straight up for several seconds, insuring he gets every last drop of his buttermilk. He reaches up wiping off his mustache and beard with a small dishtowel, then tosses it on the table. "You guys want to hear what I've laid in bed for many nights and thought about?"

The four divers all have serious expressions, with Joey taking the lead, "Oh yeah, bring it, Cheese."

"The last time I was at the Bayou Rose, they had around six to eight bouncers, four bartenders and a bunch of girls working the floor. All the bouncers and bartenders were armed. Lela told me they have several pump shotguns behind the bar, along with a couple fully automatic weapons.

"Downstairs, where they're processing the drugs, they have a locked cage with a midget inside. This is where they store the finished product. Lela said that this midget that's protecting the drugs is Nikolai's brother. He is an evil rascal. Anyway, she tells me they have surveillance monitors everywhere. This includes a full view of the parking lot, the back side of the building, inside the bar and several zoomed in on the girls cooking the dope."

After hearing how well armed they are, Matt begins squirming in his chair. "Guys, I just don't know if we can pull this off. That's a lot of firepower!"

Cheese continues as if Matt hasn't said anything. "Lela also told me about two detectives and one of the local cops. She said they slide by once every three months to pick up their hush money, along with a hefty percentage made off drug sales.

"Fellows, this is a little more complicated than I thought. Let me tell you why. We know there are several dirty cops involved, including the district attorney, the mayor and the sheriff of Morgan City. I just don't know how deep this sewer of corruption goes, or should I say, who else in positions of power are involved.

"Lela mentioned that she overheard the Russians talking about the mayor and the DA not only getting paid to keep quiet, but they are also involved in moving the drug money through several local banks. From there, the banks electronically transfer everything to offshore accounts."

Cheese Hound chuckles, "The local law dogs' transaction is going down this Sunday morning right around the break of day."

TC couldn't help himself, "Cheese, do you know how much cash we're talking about?"

"I'm not sure. Lela tells me they're covering the whole southern coastline, which includes Florida and Texas. She mentioned new clients popping up from all over the US. It's this new synthetic drug they've designed; people are coming out of the woodwork to get it. So your question about how much… I'm sure it's got to be in the millions, especially if they don't move the money but every three months."

Bones gets up and rinses off his plate in the sink. "So, Cheese Hound, while you were lying in bed thinking about all this, did you come up with a plan?"

"Guys, you know I have never really talked about what my jobs were in the military. I don't want to go into much detail, but when they needed something—what you might call nasty—taken care of, my team would be activated."

Matt leans in with his eyes widened with excitement and respect. "What do you want us to do, Cheese?"

"For right now we have around eight hours before daylight and it's only 20 minutes to the Rose. I want us to roll in as plain ole biker trash, tattoos and everything. We need to ride in separate, two at a time around 10 to 15 minutes apart. When you get there, act stoned but not too much. We'll gather up at a table and honor Chado Cole's 5th year anniversary of his departure to the other side. Let's get loud and act as if we are having a grand ole party in remembrance of our fallen friend. The whole time we will scope out their strengths and weaknesses.

"I'll let you guys know when it's time to leave. Oh yeah, those cameras in there need to see us as five stoned… drunk… bikers."

Joey hasn't said a word the whole time Cheese is laying out the first part of his plan. He looks up with his little gangster smile, "Millions, millions of dollars, untraceable millions…"

Bones pops off, "Don't get ahead of yourself, Joey. We need to hear the rest of this plan. Go ahead, Cheese, continue."

"I don't want y'all to bring anything deadlier than a knife. I'm sure they'll probably frisk us as soon as we walk up to the door. We don't want any suspicion arising of any kind. After I feel we have enough intel, we'll stumble out the door, climb on our bikes, and ride off into the night."

Matt butts in, "I thought we were going to hit that place!"

Bones shakes his head, "Yank, be quiet and let Cheese Hound finish! Go ahead, Dub."

"Well, after we leave the bar, we come back here and stash the bikes. That's when we can sit back down at this table, go over everything we've learned, put on our big boy pants, climb in that speedboat, and go pay these animals a visit. I'm thinking we'll have an hour or so to gear up, jump in the speedboat, and slip in stealth mode."

11

Bigfoot Crossing

The motley crew all head for their bikes parked in the front yard. Matt looks around with his phone light, noticing Cheese Hound isn't walking with them. "Hey, where's the Hound? I thought he was right behind us when he turned out the camp lights."

The guys start laughing at Matt, with Bones mumbling, "Yank, you are a scaredy cat for sure and certain. He'll be along in a second."

As they all stand beside their bikes, a screeching sound of rusted hinges comes from an old shed beside the camp. More noise comes from the darkness, resembling garbage sacks filled with bottles being tossed around, followed by a low tone of aggravation mixed with a few foul gestures.

The silence over the swamp is suddenly interrupted with a loud backfire that echoes across the wilderness. Mumbling with more foul words comes from inside the totally blacked out shed as Cheese makes another attempt. There's a sound of a kick-starter popping back up, followed by another loud boom, POW! Suddenly it's alive, a dim headlight shining in their direction, growing brighter as he revs the engine. Cheese Hound pulls up to the row of customized bikes riding his refurbished World War II 1940 Harley. It even has a rifle holster, shovel, and saddlebags—not to mention it was painted military green with the white star on the tank. Cheese doesn't say a word. He just grins and heads on up the dirt road.

A couple hundred feet before the old rickety bridge, Cheese Hound stops in the middle of the road. Everyone pulls up in a row behind his antique bike. Cheese pulls out a penlight and directs the beam on a hollow tree around 20 feet off the dirt road. "Hey, Matt, be a sport and walk over to that hollow tree. Reach in and pull the top lever. Do not pull the bottom lever. I repeat, not the bottom lever."

Matt laughs, "What happens if I pull the bottom? Better yet, what happens if I pull the top? What the heck am I thinking? Why are you asking me to do it anyhow? This smells like another prank. Get someone else to do it."

Laughter from the crew rises as Cheese replies, "I'm not playing a prank on you. The top lever is to activate the hydraulics on the bridge. This forces big plates up, covering the holes in the bayou crossing. The lower lever blows the whole bridge up." Matt steps off his bike, "You mean like, explosives go 'boom'?"

Cheese laughs again, "Yes, big boom! Now, get over it and go pull the top lever. We need to be on our way, time's running out. Here, take this light if you don't believe me."

Cheese Hound tosses Matt the penlight, "Okay, guys give me a second."

Matt slowly walks up to the hollow tree shining his light inside the dark hollowed out opening. "Well, what do you know, two levers!" He reaches in pulling the top handle. They all hear sounds: click, click, click, click… Matt turns and begins walking back to his bike mumbling, "That wasn't so bad. I just knew you guys were up to something."

Suddenly everyone begins screaming and hollering, "Look out Matt! Look out, behind you!" Matt quickly wheels around facing the woods as he shines the penlight directly into the eyes of this killer monster. It's Bigfoot, and he's coming straight for Matt!

Cheese Hound quickly draws his Colt 45 and starts blasting rounds in the direction of the beast.

Matt is startled by this seven-foot hairy monster and the sound of gunfire causes him to stumble. He lands on his back in a shallow ditch at the edge of the dirt road. Without hesitation, still on all fours he crawls backward like a crab, while facing this fast moving killer. With Matt being very athletic, he quickly twists around, gaining his footing. He then transfers all of his energy from a backward crawl to a full speed sprint, as he runs blindly through the darkness across the dirt road, crashing into his bike. The impact causes his beautiful custom bike to tumble on its side. Matt flies through the air landing completely over into the opposite ditch. This confused and disoriented diver quickly stands, thinking he's still only a few seconds away from getting clawed to death by the hairy beast. He hears laughter, along with the fading echoes of the last gunshot bouncing across the swamp.

Not saying a word, Matt slowly limps back onto the dirt road, reaches down and picks up the penlight. He immediately starts shining the light at his cherished bike lying on the ground.

After everyone finally stops laughing, Bones says, "Hey bud, you okay?"

TC, Joey, Bones, and Cheese Hound all hop off their bikes to help Matt lift his treasured iron horse back to its feet.

"You idiots got me! I can't believe I fell for this Louisiana bull crap again! Cheese, give me your pistol. I'm going to put you hillbilly, Cajun, peckerwoods out of your misery!"

With everyone bursting back out into crying laughter, Cheese pulls his Colt back out and loads a fresh magazine. "Matt, I'll do you one better than that!"

As soon as Cheese Hound chambers a round, he twirls the pistol like a gunslinger, stopping it with the grip facing Matt. The joyful laughter halts and you could hear a pin drop.

Joey stutters, "I… don't know if this is the right time to be handing Matt a weapon? Just saying, if I were Matt, I would probably want to shoot everyone too."

Cheese breaks out in a big smile. "Matt, take it. This whole setup was to let me see another side of you. When we do battle with this drug ring, I need to know if I can count on you getting out of this alive. You see, when it comes time, I don't need you second-guessing. What I need is for you to get low down dirty, with no mercy, no hesitation. You get me, brother?"

Matt reaches out taking the pistol from Cheese, "So what you want me to do with it?"

Cheese pops the kickstand up on his antique bike, backing away. "Hey guys, y'all back up, hit your high beams, and give Matt some room. He's about to let off some steam."

After everyone backs away a few feet, they all direct their lights on Cheese Hound's homemade Bigfoot. This helpless monster is hanging in the center of the road. It dangles from a cable that's attached between two trees, one on each side of the road.

The Hound lets out a long howl, "YAOOOOO… okay, Matt, that monster wanted to tear you to pieces. What are you going to do about it?"

Matt standing only a few feet away from his target, slowly lifts the pistol and points it at the monster.

TC and Joey start cheering him on, "Do it, Matt!"

"Yeah, blast that sucker! Pop him, Matt, he's about to get you again!"

They all hear the hammer click as Matt cocks the dual action auto then suddenly, empties the full clip on this foam-filled monster. As he lowers the weapon to his side, Cheese Hound starts clapping very slowly and loudly. The other divers join in and give out a couple of whistles.

Bones is grinning, "How did that feel, little brother?"

Matt smiles as particles of foam, moss and clothing, along with the smell of gun smoke, hangs in the night air. He looks over at the gang of four, "I don't know why I would thank y'all for causing me to almost break my neck and knock over my bike. However, I think I really needed this. Sounds crazy, wouldn't you say?"

Cheese stops clapping, "No, it's not crazy at all. I've had to face a few monsters in my own life, and I've learned that sometimes you just need to let go and face your fears. Fellows, you can use reason to work some things out; but when you go to war, you just kill it and let God sort it out. That being said, my brothers, I needed to put Matt through this. We have to know if he's ready to go all the way."

Cheese points towards the bridge, "Matt, we are about to go to war with an evil presence just a few miles down that bayou right there. Those sewer rats deal in poison, prostitution, and murder, and we are about to shut it down!"

Matt walks over and hands the weapon back to Cheese Hound as they all crank their bikes.

Cheese jams the Colt 45 down inside his vest, "Hey Matt, stop at the bridge. I want to show y'all something."

They all roll up to the bridge crossing, with Cheese Hound dismounting. "Y'all come over to the edge, you need to see this." As they all five stand near the edge, Cheese shines his penlight through the holes in the bridge floor down at the water.

Before Cheese has time to say anything, Matt pops off, "Hey, I thought you said the top lever back there at the Bigfoot crossing activated the hydraulics for the steel plates?"

"No, Yank, the top lever activated Bigfoot!"

They all burst out laughing, including Matt as he replies, "Now that was a good one, Cheese!"

While they're still laughing—standing at the edge of a 30-foot drop—Bones discreetly takes ahold of Matt's leather jacket; without him knowing it. He then pretends to shove him over the edge, only to quickly pull him back. With this sudden scare, Matt's left foot slips over the railing causing him to fall flat on his butt with both feet dangling over the edge. TC and Joey quickly come to his rescue helping him back to his feet.

Bones, overtaken with laughter from his childish prank, slaps his leg and points, "Now that was a good one right there. I wish you could see the look on your face!"

Matt, being known as a very good kick boxer in his teenage years, smiles as Bones makes the mistake of closing his eyes in uncontrollable laughter. Out of nowhere, Matt swings with full force hitting Bones in the chest, knocking him back a couple of feet. Moving like Bruce Lee, he quickly follows up with a front thrust kick, sending Bones flying across the dirt road landing in briar bushes.

Joey, with excitement asks, "Dang, son, where did you learn how to do that?"

Bones lets out a couple groans, "Someone please help me out of these briars." They all step in grabbing Bones by the arms, pulling him from the brush.

"Hey, Bones, sorry, bud, I didn't mean to hit you so hard. I guess my last nerve got picked on."

"That's okay, Matt, I should've known better. I just couldn't help myself."

Cheese Hound waves the penlight, "Hey quit jacking around! I need to show you this, just in case something happens to me." Everyone sees how serious Cheese Hound is and they all focus their attention on the beam of his penlight. "Okay, keep your eyes on the water." He reaches in his jacket pulling out a remote. "Watch this." Cheese holds the remote up where everyone can see which button he punches. With sounds of screeching steel plates, the water starts moving. As they continue to watch, three huge barricade plates slowly appear as they rise from the bayou.

TC exclaims, "Wow, look at that, Cheese, that's so cool. Now, what are they used for?"

"That's just an extra precaution in case the cops are hot on our trail. We can pass under the bridge, hit the remote and they are shut down."

Bones reaches over and breaks off a chunk of mud from a crawfish hole, tossing it over the edge. "Well, I just hope if they are that close, we won't have to deal with a State Police chopper!"

TC grins, "Well if they do, we can just out run those suckers."

Cheese hits the button on his fancy remote lowering the three plates back down into the muddy bayou. "Remember, guys, this button activates the barricade plates. This one here…" Cheese directs his light at the remote, "…activates the bridge plates that cover the holes. Are y'all clear on this?"

Matt pops off, "Why are you telling us about the remote? Nothing's going to happen to you, Cheese Hound!"

Cheese smiles while sticking the remote into his jacket. "Let me explain something, Yank, if something happens to me, you need to know what to do. When you're going into battle, always plan for the worst or what might happen. Each one of you guys needs to be capable of doing the next man's job. One day it might just save your narrow butts!"

"I understand. Let's just hope we can pull this thing off without losing anyone."

Joey looks at his watch, "Hey, guys, it's a quarter till midnight and we're 15 miles from the Bayou Rose."

Bones laughs, "What are you, Joey, superstitious?"

"No, I just think it's always cool to roll into a place that we're about to send to hell at midnight!"

12

Sandy Kisses

Lieutenant Christy Moody wakes up in her bunk, startled from another strange dream about Ms. Lily. She quickly looks around thinking she is somewhere else. She plops her head back down against the pillow, realizing she is in the middle of a warzone. She places her sweaty palms against her forehead, "Ms. Lily, I wish you would please get out of my head." Now wide-awake, she slips her feet inside her unlaced boots and grabs a sip of water as she heads for the midnight air. Walking past several sleeping pilots, she snags a piece of spearmint gum from a table, making her way out of the barracks.

Christy hurriedly zips up her jacket as she feels a chill in the night air of the desert. Gazing around this forward operation air base, she observes several crews working. Some are running equipment removing the additional sand that had piled up against buildings left from the previous sand storm. Others are busy doing maintenance on their jets. Being overwhelmed with curiosity, she decides to walk out and check the condition of the dirt runway.

An army ranger walks past her not saying anything, just nodding his head in a friendly gesture. Immediately after realizing the rangers were still there she mumbles to herself. "I wonder if Brim is still on base, or is he across the Turkish border in what the major calls the kill zone."

She has to stop and wait at the edge of the runway as a road grader slowly passes by. Stepping over the row of sand left behind from the maintainer, she's surprised at how smooth the runway is. Thinking to herself, *Wow, those Army Corps guys are really good at what they do.*

She turns, plops down on the row of sand, and leans back with both elbows sinking into the soft, cool dirt. As she stares into the heavens, thoughts of her dreams and visions flash through her mind. She whispers a prayer, "Heavenly Father, Lord I feel unsure of myself. I guess… I mean… well, Lord, I don't really know what I mean. I'm truly at a loss on what to even say at this point. Lord, all these weird visions of Ms. Lily, the letter from mom, the major, and his story of Teeto the Indian guide… Could all this be real, and am I about to go through all this crazy stuff? Look at me, Lord, I'm a mess! Half of my fighter group doesn't trust me. Heck, Lord, I don't know if I even trust me."

Christy, looking up at the stars feels overwhelmed with sadness and bows her head. She looks down at the ground with tears swelling in her eyes, when suddenly she catches a glimpse of movement across the runway.

Out of the darkness, a man dressed as a shepherd is heading in her direction. She reaches over for her side arm and realizes she had left her shoulder holster and weapon hanging on her bunk. Christy mumbles, "Oh crud." She looks in all directions for help and only sees a few workers, but they are too far to even hear a loud shout.

Christy, still in a sitting position clinches both hands filled with sand. Her intentions are to throw the glassy particles in his eyes and run away as fast as she can. She has used this technique before and it had worked well against her older brothers back in Mountain

View. The stranger holds his hand out in a gesture of peace, following with a soft-spoken tone, "I mean you no harm, dear child. I am just a traveler in a foreign land."

"You speak proper English, sir. Where do you come from?"

"I speak many languages, and I come from my Father's kingdom."

Christy leans to her left trying to catch a glimpse of his face, but he's still shadowed from the cloth garment covering his head.

"So your father is a king around one of these territories?"

The stranger reaches up to remove his headpiece, slowly looking down at Christy. "My Father is the King of all territories."

Without responding, she stares into his brilliant bluish green eyes and suddenly feels the Holy Spirit flood over her entire body. Christy lunges forward wrapping her arms around his legs and ankles, weeping uncontrollably. "Oh, Lord, I almost threw sand in your eyes."

The stranger places his hands on her head as he laughs, "You know, we have the same name. It's just yours has a 'Y' at the end."

Christy hears voices: "Hey, Lieutenant, you okay? Are you sick?"

As she looks up, the stranger has disappeared and two army rangers are trotting toward her. "Ma'am, are you alright? Do you need a medic?"

Christy quickly stands up, wiping away the tears, and looking in all directions for the stranger. "I'm fine, guys, I'm fine."

She hears one of the soldiers reporting back to base. "Roger base, it's just a pilot out for some night air. We are clear, all good."

She notices two armed Humvees turning around that were headed in their direction. "I guess I'm in trouble for being this far out."

"No Ma'am, you just need to ask for an escort if you want to stroll around, especially at night." The ranger turns and looks at the other soldier. "I'll take care of the Lieutenant, carry on, private." The young soldier turns and trots toward the hanger.

The helpful ranger faces away from Christy as he removes his helmet and face scarf. "Lieutenant, are you ready to head back to the barracks, or would you rather sit for a spell?"

He slowly turns and sees that Christy is still looking in all directions, as if she has lost something. When she finally gives up on catching one more glimpse of the shepherd, she turns and looks into the eyes of the concerned ranger. Christy's mouth flies wide open, "Oh my goodness, it's you!"

She immediately wraps her arms around Brim pressing her face against his, and whimpering like a small child. Brim holds his weapon to the side, placing one arm around her and lightly pats her on the back. He feels the warm salty tears streaming down her cheek into the corner of his mouth.

"My goodness, you look like you've seen a ghost. What's wrong, girl? You're shaking and what's with all this crying?"

"Brim, just hold me for a minute, please just hold me."

* * *

Just around 500 meters away, one of the sniper teams on overlook, spots an odd sight. "Hey, Leroy, you might want to take a look at this."

"What you got, Jake?"

Leroy whispers, "You see where that half-track closest to the runway is parked?"

"I got it."

Leroy directs him, "Okay, walk it south down the runway around 75 meters."

"What the heck, is that two dudes hugging?" They both cover their mouths to muffle their laughter.

Leroy adjusts his scope, "Welcome to the new military, two guys all hugged up way out on the runway. I can't watch it, makes me nauseous and I don't want to throw up. That would mean we'd have to break cover or lie in puke all night."

Jake bumps Leroy's shoulder, "Quit yakking, hand me that spotting scope. I'll zoom in and see who the heck we're looking at. If I know who they are, I'll be jacking with them; they'll never hear the end of this!"

Leroy says, "You better not. Remember the new rule, 'don't see, don't tell', or something like that."

"I ain't worried about that bull crap. They can kick me out anytime they get ready."

"What about your 20 years, Jake?"

"Hold the bus, Leroy, we done jumped to conclusions, brother. Take another look."

Leroy takes the spotting scope, "Well, I'll be. Captain Brim has done found him a fine filly if I ever seen one. Now that's a true Casanova if you ask me. Just think, here we sit, way out here in the middle of hell's creation and Brim snags a chunk of honey right out of the carcass of the beast."

"Hey Leroy, in case you missed it, hell didn't create anything. The truth is, Jesus and all them disciples used to roam somewhere around here."

Jake chuckles, "That was farther south, genius. Put that scope back in the direction of the enemy and leave them two love birds be."

* * *

Christy pulls her sleeves down over her wrists and wipes away the tears. "Okay, Christy, you need to let me in on what's happening.

Is the pressure of flying into battle too much? Is there something wrong at home?" Brim nervously stutters, "Did… I do something?"

Christy holds her hand in the air, "Hang on, Brim. I'm fine. It's just a lot of strange things have been happening lately and it seems I'm caught right in the middle."

"Caught in the middle of what? If there's some soldier out here giving you a hard time, you just say the word. I'll clear that up right quick."

Christy plops back down on the row of piled sand, with Captain Brim kicking a hard clod out of the way, as he sits beside her. She reaches over and places her hand on his knee. "No, it's nothing like that. So far, everyone has been very kind and respectful here on the base. Give me a second, Brim. I don't even know how to begin to tell you what's going on, at least without making me out to look like a Looney Tune."

Brim places his hand over hers, "Take your time, Christy. Truth be known, there's nothing you could say that would ever make me think that you've lost it."

These comforting words cause Christy to lean over and place her head against his chest. Brim slowly lets go of her hand, placing his arm around her shoulder."

"Christy, while you're trying to figure how to fill me in on what's going on, do you mind if I speak freely? Maybe, just maybe what I have to say could help you feel a bit more at ease."

"Sure, Brim, that would be nice."

"Well, as a matter of fact, ever since we met, you're all I can think about. Other than those crazy dreams I've been having."

Christy quickly pulls her head away from his chest. "What dreams are you talking about?"

"Oh, they're so silly. I would be embarrassed to even talk about it."

Christy begs with her tear-filled bloodshot eyes, softly whispering, "Please, you've got to tell me."

"No, first you fill me in on what's got you so upset. By the way, what were you doing on your knees holding your arms out in a circle like position? It looked like you were holding something. "

"Oh, gosh, now I know I'm losing it! Brim, you didn't see the stranger dressed like a shepherd standing in front of me? Please tell me you saw him!"

"A stranger…?" Captain Brim points, "Christy, all we saw was you bent over on your knees, right there."

He shines his hand light at the spot where Christy had knelt down. It was only a couple of feet away from where they were now sitting. "What the heck? Look at that!"

Christy quickly stands, "Look at what?"

"Well, sweetheart, I've been trained in jungle warfare as a tracker. Out here in the desert sand, my blind grandpa could read this!"

"Brim, I'm a pilot. Can you give a mountain girl a quick tracking lesson? Tell me what you're looking at?"

"That road grader went through here and bladed this whole area, right?"

"Right, I stood in this spot and had to wait until he passed."

Brim points, "Okay, those two sets there are good ole army boots. That would be the private and me. These are your tracks, and those two smooth spots are your knee prints where you knelt down. Now my question is who the heck left the sandal prints?"

Captain Brim walks across the runway shining his light all around. He chuckles, "This is pretty strange. I can easily see where he walked across the runway and stood in front of where you knelt. It's like the tracks just end right there!"

They both sit back down on the sand row. Brim jams the stock of his weapon down in the soft ground and sets his helmet on top of the barrel. "Christy, you do know we have several sniper teams located in these surrounding hills on overlook."

"No I didn't."

"Yes, they probably have eyes on us right now and would have seen your stranger. However after seeing his footprints in the sand leading up to this spot and somehow magically vanishing, I guess it could have been a ghost." Brim reaches up scratching the right side of his head while looking up at the stars. "This is a bit strange, yep pretty… strange."

Looking embarrassed, Christy whispers, "Oh, Lord, you mean to tell me someone out there has watched all this? I mean me kneeling and wrapping my arms around the invisible stranger?"

"Don't sweat it, they probably think you have some odd religion and were praying really weird."

They both chuckle, "Brim, you sure have a way of making me feel better. So tell me this; if the snipers are out there, they would have seen the shepherd if he was real, right?"

"Well, I'm not sure, they were probably looking at the same thing I saw, and that was you kneeling alone, praying really weird."

Christy grins as she reaches back over, grabbing Brim's hand. "So, tell me about your dreams."

"Oh… it really wasn't much to them. There was this little old lady that had the sweetest smile. In each dream, she was always digging around in these huge flowerbeds. She would turn and look at me with a kind smile and wave me over. However, when I started heading in her direction, the flowerbeds would vanish, the sky would darken, and the beautiful surroundings would change. The terrain actually favored this rocky, sandy mess we've got over here. The aggravating part was when she led me to a fork in the road. I would lose sight of the old lady and for the life of me, I couldn't ever figure out which road she took. Was it to the left, or to the right?

"Then suddenly your pretty face would pop into my head. In each dream you always seem to be sleeping. I remember touching the side of your face thinking you would wake up, but you just laid there with a strange, peaceful look." Brim stopped talking as he chuckled like a young teenager.

"What's so funny, man with a fish name?"

"Well, each time in this part of my dream, I had a crazy thought. If I could give you a big smooch on the lips, you would magically wake up. You know, like one of those old fairytale movies where the guy would kiss the princess."

"Okay, Mr. Dreamer, don't leave me hanging."

They both chuckle, "At this point, I would lean over with my face almost touching yours and right before giving you a big smack on the lips, I would smell a strong fragrance of the old lady's flowers." Brim suddenly shakes his head as he looks down at the ground. "You think I'm crazy, right?"

Christy elbows Brim in the ribs while smiling. "Heck no, keep it coming, I want to hear every detail."

"Every detail, you say. Okay, right before my attempt to steal a kiss and save the princess, this wonderful fragrance of flowers hanging in the air would draw my attention away from you."

"What did they smell like?"

"I guess if I had to nail it down, jasmine and vanilla."

"What a weird mix."

Well, anyway, each time in my dream when this happened I would look up and see the old lady pointing at a big rock structure that looked like a cross. When I looked back down, you had vanished. Here's the crazy part: after I would wake up, I could still smell those flowers."

"Brim, how many times have you had that dream?"

"You're going to think I've lost it. I've dreamed that same dream for the last several days."

"Brim, you only met me yesterday at the chapel."

"I know I wanted to tell you as soon as we met, but you would have probably turned me in to the psych ward. Now with all this weird stuff going on, I felt it was as good a time as any. So do you think I'm crazy?"

Christy giggles, "This is unbelievable. Brim, what was the old lady's name?"

"She never told me her name. In fact, she never said anything. I dreamed about her so many times that I actually gave her a name myself. That helped when I shared these strange dreams with my buddies. Just to let you know, soldiers have no secrets; we pretty much share everything, sorry."

"Well, what did you name her?"

Brim smiled, "I call her, 'The Lily of the Valley.'"

Christy lies back against the sand pile, laughing and clapping her hands.

"What is it, what's so funny?"

Christy suddenly has a flashing memory of Ms. Lily standing in their church holding a bouquet of flowers, smiling from ear to ear.

"Brim, that's what everyone in Mountain View calls her! She is, 'The Lily of the Valley.'"

"You have got to be kidding me!"

Christy whispers, "So, Lily, you've been inside Brim's head too? Old girl, just what are you up to?"

Brim hears Christy mumbling, "What are you saying?"

"Oh nothing, I just had a memory of Ms. Lily."

Christy stops clapping, sits back up, and raises her hands towards Heaven. "Thank you, God, I am officially not loco."

"Okay Christy, who is the old girl?"

"She was the flower lady at our church back in Mountain View and she just passed away. I actually got the letter shortly after we flew in. My mom gave me the news of her passing.

"Brim, this lady was sort of a prophetess or should I say, she was truly a woman after God's own heart. Before her passing, she was so passionate about some weird journey I had to go on. This included me getting shot down. Oh hey, I just remembered something. You just said in your dream, Ms. Lily was pointing at a rock structure that looked like a cross, right?"

"Yes, she did. In every dream I had about you."

Christy chuckles, "My mom mentioned in her letter that Ms. Lily told her I would get shot down near a place called 'The Shadow of the Cross'. I wonder if that's what she was trying to show you."

"I don't know. It is very strange. Heck, what am I saying? This whole thing is crazy. What else did she say?"

"She said that I would be saved by angels that were dressed as shepherds. They would hand me back over to my people, and somewhere in the mix, I would be involved in saving millions—or maybe it was thousands."

Christy continues, "Well, anyway, she mentioned meeting me at the Eleventh Gate of Heaven and I would only be there for a very short time. Here's another news flash. My commanding officer, Major Hyde, is tangled up in this mystery also. Maybe after it's all over, he can share his Indian story about God's Mountain with you."

"Christy Moody, you have me totally confused."

"Don't feel bad, up until a few minutes ago, I thought I was absolutely nuts."

"So, who do you think the stranger could have been?"

"I think it was Jesus."

"Jesus…? Really? Like Jesus… the Jesus?"

Christy laughs, "Yes, I think so!"

"What did y'all talk about?"

"Not much. He told me our names are the same. It's just mine has a 'Y' in it."

Brim chuckles, "Jesus has a sense of humor? I mean, that's kinda funny."

They both laugh as Christy replies, "I guess it is a bit strange for our Lord to say something so totally off the wall. However, I believe his message wasn't in what he said."

"What do you mean?"

"Well, when I saw his eyes, I went limp as a dishrag and fell at his feet, wrapping my arms around his ankles. There were so many tears coming from my eyes that they saturated his feet and sandals. I guess that's about the time you spotted me holding my arms in a circle."

"I don't even know how to respond, Christy! If that was really Jesus, my goodness, girl! You just touched the Savior of the world!"

This rugged, hardened, tough, army ranger, now with tears streaming down both cheeks, reaches over to take a hold of Christy's hands.

"Mountain girl, this is the craziest set of events I've ever seen or heard of! Come to think of it, ever since the dreams started, I've pondered over these visions and tried my best to understand what they meant. My God, I knew you before we even met. Truth be known, I fell in love with you the second night of my dreams."

Christy squeezes Brims hand, inching closer, as Brim continues.

"All I know, Christy Moody, is that somehow this has to be a part of God's plan. One sure sign is the simple fact that I can't keep my mind off of you. I have never felt such a strong desire to be this close to anyone."

Christy reaches up with two fingers and gently presses both against his lips. "Hush, I have to tell you this. In the letter my mom wrote she quoted Ms. Lily; she said that I would meet the love of my life in a little chapel and he had the name of a fish. Her words have come to pass. I truly feel something I have never experienced. Brim, I don't know when, or if, we will ever get to see each other again, but

I have to tell you this: I have an overwhelming deep love for you."

A sudden burst of wind carries clouds of sand down the runway. This small windstorm covers the entire area like a blanket.

Brim quickly pulls out a rain poncho and covers them both as they continue to sit. Now with his arms wrapped around Christy, she presses her sandy lips against his, underneath the privacy of a sandstorm.

* * *

Five hundred meters away, Leroy talks on the com with two other sniper teams. "Well, if that don't beat all, I just knew we were about to have a soap opera love scene, right there on the runway. I can't see our love birds for that cloud of sand."

"Roger that, I was about to order up some MRE popcorn."

Chuckling comes across the com, "Okay guys; let's give them a little privacy."

"Roger that, looks like the show is over."

"Copy that, we are clear."

"Stay toasty fellows. Watch your six, Snakehead, clear."

* * *

After several sandy kisses, Brim reaches into his satchel taking his goggles and gently places them on Christy.

"I need to get you back. It's past time for me to check in at HQ. Oh, by the way, I believe we're heading over the border tomorrow. So it might be some time before I have a chance to see you again. Whatever happens, we need to lean on God. He set this whole wild journey in motion and I guess we've got a front row seat!"

13

Ancient Language and the Elders

Chado Cole reaches over and dips the quill pen into an almost empty jar, soaking up the last drop of ink. He slowly writes down the final words across the bottom of the second scroll. Just as the last letter was complete, the quill pen was now dry.

Chado looks up to share the good news of both scrolls being completed. His two companions are standing at the base of the cliff wall staring across the cloud-covered lake. The large mixed breed dog hears Chado's whistle. He quickly wheels around and goes into a full speed run across the plateau. Uriel dives off the cliff disappearing only for a few seconds as he flies around and over the tops of the spruce trees, landing a few feet away from the marble table. Chado holds his hand out signaling Buck to stop. A trick he had taught the canine to do back on Earth. Buck comes to a screeching halt, waiting on his next command. Chado lightly taps the side of his leg signaling Buck to drop down on his stomach. Buck obeys and slowly crawls the last few yards.

"Well, Uriel, it's been exactly 21 days and I believe God has shown me everything he wanted me to write in the scrolls. So what do you think? Or should I say, what's next?"

"The scrolls are not complete."

"What do you mean? They have to be finished, I'm all out of words and, not to mention, we're also out of ink!"

Uriel shakes his head, not saying anything as he points to the trail leading back down the mountain.

Buck's ears perk up as they all hear sounds of people humming.

"Hey, Uriel, we got company!"

"Yes, they are right on time, Chado."

"On time for what? Are they bringing more ink?

"I don't think so. God gave me a vision of this while you were writing in the scrolls. He showed me twelve elders from the village across the lake. They have to do something special with the scrolls. So we need to get out of their way and allow them to do God's work."

"Okay, I understand."

"Yes, this will be interesting."

The twelve elders walk past Chado, each one smiling, as they make a complete circle around the table. They are still humming an unfamiliar song. Surprisingly, even with their old age, they are very talented and their sweet harmony is soothing to the ears.

Two of them who look to be the oldest, walk straight up to the table. Both, at the same time, reach out and move the empty ink jars and quills out of their way. The other men all in unison raise their hands to Heaven, while the two elders unroll both scrolls. This humming and praising goes on for several minutes when, suddenly the sky darkens, followed by loud roaring thunder. Heavy wind bends the cedar and spruce trees all around the plateau, but not one blade of grass moves where the elders stand. As the clouds continue to thicken, a heavy darkness covers the entire mountaintop.

The oldest of the elders walks over and takes Chado by the wrist. Still humming along with the others, he leads him near the edge of the table. He then takes ahold of his right and left wrist, forcing Chado's hands to the center of both scrolls.

"Okay, guys, I hope you know, I will need both of those hands back… intact, if you don't mind."

The elder on the opposite side of the table presses down on the back of Chado's hands. He feels the warmth and softness of something in the center of each palm. Only after a second, both elders release Chado's hands, motioning for him to rejoin Uriel.

Chado whispers to Uriel, "What was that all about?"

"I'm not sure. It could be a ceremonial thing or they were marking the scrolls with your palms. Let us just watch. I don't think they are finished yet."

Surprisingly, a small ray of light the size of a needle appears, coming down from the heavens. Its ray is directed at the center of the table. Within a few seconds, the entire table and twelve men are bathed in this bright light.

Uriel nudges Chado, "Let us get a bit closer. We need to see this."

As they peek over the shoulders of the elders, Chado says, "Uriel, look at that. The words I wrote are changing. Does God not like what I've written?"

Uriel smiles, "Pay attention, he is not changing what you wrote; he is changing it into an ancient language. Actually, it is one of the oldest languages in the history of the Earth."

"What's it called? I mean the language?"

"Chado, I think it is Sumerian. It came from a time around 3400 BC. I do not know what God is planning. It is very unlikely anyone on Earth can translate it."

"So, now I am totally confused. If you say there's no one capable of translating, how will anyone know how to read it?"

Uriel shakes his head, as to have figured it out. "It must be a safety precaution. That language is written in such a way that the angels of hell would not have a clue, even if they got their hands on them. Chado, before you ask, hell's angels and demons are going to be hot on our trail wanting to find out what is written in those scrolls. Fear not, Little Soul, God has a plan."

Chado smiles at Uriel as he reaches down scratching Buck's head as they continue to watch.

The ray of light widens, as the language translation in each scroll, seems to be finished. One of the men standing in the circle, steps up to the table with a brass lamp that reveals a small flame. Two other elders gently roll up both scrolls keeping them side by side. The elder with the lamp heats a copper vial that is filled with a dark red substance resembling wax. After heating to a melting stage, he pours this thick liquid over the center of each scroll. The younger of the tribesmen steps forward holding two odd shaped metal objects. He places each on top of the hot liquid. With a quick motion, he presses down, creating a seal onto both scrolls. Each seal favors the other, but differ in a way that is easily recognized.

Two other men from the circle holding leather pouches step forward, and as soon as the seals have cooled down, they place both scrolls, one inside each pouch.

The twelve men step back away from the table, returning to a uniform circle. They drop to their knees while raising their hands to God, and begin to sing. They are praising the Lord in a foreign tongue. "Hey, Uriel, I can understand what they're singing! Wow!"

"Tell me, Chado, what is it you hear?"

"It's right out of the Bible, Psalms 18.

'*I will love You, O Lord my strength.*

The Lord is my rock and my fortress and my deliverer;

My God, my strength, in whom I will trust; My shield and the horn of my salvation, my stronghold.

I will call upon the Lord, who is worthy to be praised; So shall I be saved from my enemies.

The pangs of death surrounded me, And the floods of ungodliness made me afraid.

The sorrows of Sheol surrounded me; The snares of death confronted me.

In my distress I called upon the Lord, And cried out to my God…'"

As the elders are continuing to sing and praise God, the table that had been lowered upon Chado's arrival, now is being lifted back up into the low hanging clouds.

Just as the legs of this beautiful table completely disappear back into the dark haze, the elders complete their song. Rising from their knees, they each walk between Chado and Uriel. All are smiling, and with a gesture of friendship, they lightly touch their shoulders while passing. The last of the twelve walks up to Chado, placing both leather pouches containing the sacred scrolls around his neck. To Chado's surprise, the old man reaches up with both hands, one on each side of his face, pinching the bottom of his earlobes.

The old man gives a polite nod as he drops a small bag on the ground in front of Chado. He then reaches over gently brushing the back of his hand against Uriel's face.

After revealing these strange signs of friendship, the leader of this ancient tribe slowly walks away, heading back down the mountain.

"Okay, Uriel, what was the earlobe thing all about?"

"I believe touching the face of someone is a way of showing deep love."

Chado laughs, "And the earlobe pinch?"

"That is even more special."

"It is more special how?"

"Well first, you have to understand this is an ancient tribe. They seem to have different signs expressing emotion or love. The pinch on both ears is simply telling you, it is an honor to be a part of God's plan. This also shows love toward not only you, but to the millions of lost souls who will be impacted with this mission."

"Wow, you got all that from a pinch!"

"I know, it is a little strange. Would you have rather he reached up and gave you a big smack on the lips?"

They both chuckle. "Heck no, Uriel, I kind of liked the earlobe pinch. In fact, I might try doing that in the future. Maybe I can do it to one of those demons or Satan himself."

Uriel shakes his head. "I don't believe I would try that on either."

Chado laughs, "Okay, maybe I can try it on Summer or Rosie."

"Now you are talking Chado, but enough of this kidding around. We need to head south."

"Hey Uriel before we go, I have to ask; why did the elders press my hands down on each scroll?"

"I believe God marked your palm print. It has something to do with your bloodline. The lines in the palm of your hand are what you earthlings call your lifeline. In this case, God left a print of your lifeline on the scrolls."

"Wow, so the print of my bloodline is on the scrolls. I wonder what all of this means?"

"I am not sure. God will reveal it when He is ready!"

"Cool, so are we flying or going through a portal?"

"Neither! Grab that sack the elder left behind."

Chado picks up the burlap sack and opens it. "What the heck Uriel? It's just some old rags!"

Uriel smiles, "Those are our new clothes."

"My angel friend, I hope this doesn't hurt your feelings, but I believe the old man might have brought us the wrong sack. They smell kind of funky, really stale, a bit of mildew, and I think if memory serves me right, maybe even a little stench of whisky."

"Yes, that is the right sack. Let us get those clothes on."

"So what's going on? Are we going undercover?"

"Yes, my friend. We are now officially incognito! Not even the fallen angels will recognize us. Unless we do something out of the ordinary, we will not be detected. Chado, heed my warning, we are heading into enemy territory and you have to do everything I tell you."

"I understand, but back to my question. When I asked, portal or flying, you said neither. Are we walking?"

"Chado, you do understand we have other ways of travel, here on Earth?"

"Sure, planes, trains, and automobiles," Chado chuckles.

"Little Soul, here on Earth celestials can move from place to place in a blink of the eye. The portals are used to move through the heavens."

"Wow, you can just instantly go anywhere? What about me and Buck?"

"Well…, I will have to help you on this one. Let me show you how it is done. We need to squat down, place your hand on my shoulder, and wrap your other arm around Buck."

Chado, in position, holds on to Buck, "Like this?"

"Perfect! Now close your eyes. Here we go…"

14

Knockout Punch

Chado, Uriel, and Buck suddenly appear in a narrow alley across the street from a pawnshop, in downtown Morgan City, Louisiana.

"Are you okay, Chado?"

"Sure, I actually didn't feel anything. Well, other than leaving the clean crisp air of Alaska, to the heavy humidity of the deep south, now that's a bit of a shocker."

"Chado, look overhead, and also at what is sitting around the parking lot of that bar down the street."

"Look! Demons are everywhere; oh my goodness!"

"This is nothing. Wait until you see where we are going later tonight. For now follow me. We have to pick up a couple things."

The trio walks across the street to the all night Pawn & Party shop.

"Are we getting guns and ammo?"

"Not hardly, my friend. We need a couple of props, so we can really blend in."

As they walk through the door, the store manager, Louie, hollers with a very unwelcoming tone. "You two bums, get out of here, and take that mangy dog with you!"

Chado turns, pointing toward the door and tells Buck where to go sit. The mixed breed trots over quickly sitting down with his eyes fixed on the store manager.

"I said, you guys need to get your broke butts outta here right now. Just look at the way that mangy flea sack is looking at me! I hate dogs and bums!"

Uriel holds his hand up, "Calm down friend. We are not beggars. We just want to buy some of your merchandise."

Louie, the store manager continues to show anger, shouting: "You people stink! What you need is soap, and I don't sell soap."

Chado spots a Martin guitar hanging on the wall. "Hey, mister, how much for the Martin?"

The manager, along with a cop named Billy that had just walked through the door, burst out laughing at Chado. Louie with a disrespectful sneer, "Boy, you can't afford that guitar. That's a D-28 made back in 1938, and today, I'd let it go for around ten grand. Now I've got a $30 ukulele over here that might be more your style."

Chado still having his eyes fixed on the antique Martin, "Hey, Uriel, that looks just like the guitar my Uncle Dobber carried with him when he served in Korea. It was the first guitar I ever held."

The manager and his cop friend are still snickering as they shake their heads.

Chado steps closer, "Hey, mister! Can I hold it, so I can get a feel of the old girl?"

"You're not putting your filthy hands anywhere near it!"

Uriel walks up to the counter rolling two gold nuggets across the glass top. Louie, in unbelief quickly grabs the larger of the two shiny pieces of gold. With a goofy, surprised look still frozen on his face, he reaches for the scales. He weighs the first, then the second. Grinning from ear to ear, he starts juggling both as if he's in a circus act.

"Good Lord, this is a total of five ounces you've got right here, boys! I tell you what I'll do. I'll give you a 1,000 bucks cold cash for both nuggets." He looks over at his cop friend and winks real big.

Billy the policeman decides to get in on the heist. "Yes, sir, that sounds like a heck of a deal. You guys can walk right around the corner and buy enough booze to last you for a long time."

Uriel decides to have a little fun as he displays a bit of humor. Looking over at Chado, he winks real big, just as the store manager had done. Billy and Louie take his wink to mean that these two bums are going for their shady deal. Louie actually starts counting out and shuffling the $100 bills across the counter. "There it is, gentlemen. Just pick it up."

Uriel reaches past the money and tears the nuggets out of the store manager's tightly squeezed hand. "You are a crook, mister!"

"What do you mean?"

"When we walked in here you called us filthy bums and tried to run us out. Just now, you called us gentlemen. What are we? What are you?"

"Now just hold on. I was going to make you a fair deal."

"A fair deal? You weighed the gold and said it was five ounces. It weighs exactly 9.8 ounces. The market price right now is $1,200 an ounce, so that would mean this gold is worth just over 11,760 US dollars. You and your friend wanted to give us $1,000 for both. Not only are you crooks, you are also liars." Uriel turns to the cop. "Shame on you. Instead of you upholding the law and protecting the helpless, you condemn and destroy!"

Uriel has taken both men completely off guard, as silence falls across the room. It is almost like an old west showdown, when Chado breaks silence. "Gentlemen, can we bring it down a notch? I just want to look at that Martin guitar hanging on the wall."

Now angry, Billy, the crooked cop grabs the radio mike pinned on his shoulder and calls for backup. "Officer needs assistance at the Pawn & Party. Bring the dog. Suspect is armed with suspicion of drugs, 54 clear."

The two-way crackles. "Drug Unit, ETA four minutes. Dispatch clear."

The angry policeman pulls his gun, pointing it at Uriel. "Hey Louie, grab that sack of weed I brought you last night and kindly slide it in Mr. Know-It-All's trousers."

Uriel, with a low tone speaks to Louie and the crooked lawman, "I would not do that if I were you."

The cop raises his weapon from Uriel's chest now pointing it at his forehead. "Mister, you need to be quiet, and this will all be over soon. You two will have a nice warm cell, and that mutt over there will hit the incinerator in a couple days; in the meantime, we'll figure out exactly how much that gold really weighs."

Louie and Billy start laughing like two mad men who just won the lottery. Louie spouts off as he walks around the counter, heading for Uriel. "When Lester gets here with his drug dog, that mutt you got sitting at the door might not make it to the incinerator. Yep, the hair is about to fly!"

The policeman changes hands with his weapon, "While we're waiting on backup, tell me this. How did a couple of stinking bums get their hands on them two nuggets?"

Uriel smiles, "Oh… that is not all we have. Take a look in the leather pouch hanging on my right side."

"So what you got in the pouch, boy…? Hey Louie, before you stick those drugs down his trousers, let's take a look-see. Tell me what Mr. Know-It-All is holding in the kitty."

Louie takes the small leather pouch from Uriel's side. "Well, I do believe, it's vacation time. Look what I done found."

Louie, the crooked store manager smiles as he slowly roles out a velvet jewelry cloth, covering the glass countertop. Holding the small sack just above the cloth he lightly shakes it, allowing the contents to be revealed. As the treasures pour out, both men's eyes widen with excitement. Several more pieces of gold larger than the first two, along with several rubies, six diamonds, and a large acorn hit the table.

The cop's laughing stops, as he turns his gun toward Chado. "Okay Mr. Guitar man, let's see what you got in those two leather pouches hanging on your back."

Uriel takes a step to the side shielding the cop's view of Chado. "Those two pouches are of no concern to you."

Cocking the hammer back on his pistol, Billy aims directly at Uriel's head. "I told you Mr. Raggedy Man, this will all be over soon."

The roaring sound of a vehicle pulls up to the front entrance. "Now that would be my buddy, Lester. Like I said, boy, this will all be over soon, and you two can go take a long nap in a nice warm jail cell."

Chado pats his leg signaling Buck to crawl across the floor. Without the cop noticing, Buck is now sitting beside Chado.

The door violently swings open as a huge German shepherd pounces through. He is snarling and pulling against the leash held by a 6'4", muscle bound police officer. "Someone call for backup?"

Both cops, along with Louie, begin to laugh at the two helpless bums and the mangy canine. Louie points at the precious stones lying on the counter. "Look at what we done found. Split three ways, I believe we can all retire a bit early. Lester, when we find out what's in those two leather pouches hanging on that lad's back… well, it might just be a little bonus."

The drug dog violently snarls and pulls hard against his leash. He digs his long claws into the concrete floor, as he lunges toward Buck. Chado reaches down lightly rubbing Buck on the head, "Stay calm bud, I won't let him hurt you."

Lester, the canine cop hears Chado talking to Buck. "Just how you gonna keep us from doing anything we want? We are the law. So take those two pouches off your back and kindly hand them over. You might want to hurry, because my grip seems to be slipping on this leash. You wouldn't want that mangy mutt of yours to be torn to shreds."

With only Uriel, Chado, and Buck having the ability to see into the Spiritual Realm, they witness several demons appear inside the room. Apparently they had smelled the aroma of greed in the air from these evil men; and like a fly to rotting flesh, it drew them in. As the demons swirl through the pawnshop looking for the weakest vessel, they pass over Chado and Uriel. They seem to be fooled by the raggedy appearance of these two smelly bums and a mangy dog. As they zero in on the two cops and store manager, these demons of hell are unaware that standing before them is the mighty Guardian Angel, Uriel.

These spawns of hell immediately swarm the two cops as they coil themselves around these lost men. Their evil presence resembles a nest of snakes. Some are slithering around their legs, others are whispering in their ears, *Take it all for yourself, and look at the luxuries you can acquire. This is so easy, the perfect setup. No one will ever know. You can blame it on the bums. Just look at that treasure lying only a few feet away.*

Without warning, Billy pulls a second gun from his ankle holster. He turns and with no hesitation shoots Louie in the back of the head. Blood splatters across the entire counter.

Lester, the canine cop, is totally surprised by his buddy's actions, "What did you just do? I liked ole Louie!"

"Who gives a crap about Louie, two-way split my friend!"

A wicked silence falls over the room. It is suddenly interrupted with a sick laughter, as if they are both without souls and only darkness rules their evil hearts. The demons seem to be rejoicing along with them as they swirl around Billy and Lester's shoulders.

Uriel and Chado watch as two of the smaller demons drag Louie's soul away from his quivering corpse. These servants of hell proudly laugh as they bathe with pride, over another victory in swaying men to commit murder.

Now with innocent blood on their hands, Lester the canine cop, backs up a few feet and locks the door. "Let's have a little fun with their mutt."

He reaches down unleashing the German shepherd, and as soon as the leash hits the floor, Lester gives a command, "Kill, Brutus, kill!"

This huge drug dog snarls and growls while charging across the room heading straight for Buck. Just as the shepherd is airborne, diving for the helpless mutt, Buck quickly steps to the side allowing the shepherd to fly by, slamming head first into a metal counter filled with power tools. Without hesitation, Buck wheels around and grabs the shepherd by the throat and with one swift motion, snaps his neck.

The canine cop's laughter ceases, "No, no, no, you mangy sucker. You killed my dog!"

He immediately begins shooting at Buck while screaming at the top of his voice, "I'm going to kill you, if it's the last thing I do!" POW, POW… Buck darts behind the counters, dodging each bullet from this mad man. He quickly runs to safety at the back of the pawnshop.

Uriel, still wanting the trio to avoid being noticed by the demonic presence; now has to make a decision of when to strike.

Billy shouts across the store to Lester, "Hey stop chasing that mutt! We need to clean this up before anyone shows up."

Several demons continue to coil around and whisper to both

cops, *Kill them all. Kill the bums first, then your buddy. Do it, time is running out. Look at that, Louie's safe is wide open. Take it all. You won't ever have to work again.*

Lester, the canine cop, kneels down by his dog sobbing with his face pressed against his fur. Billy, hearing the whispers of demons, slowly walks up behind his co-worker holding the snub-nose only inches from his head. POW, Lester's body falls limp, landing on top of his cherished shepherd.

With a sick, lost look on Billy's face, he turns the gun toward Chado, "Give me the two leather pouches, and I mean now!"

As the scene unfolds, only a couple steps behind the gunman, one of the larger demons captures the soul from this fresh kill. He sinks his nasty claws deep within the soul and spirit of Lester. His cries can only be heard from inside the Spiritual Realm, as this separation of spirit and body takes place. Within a few seconds of taking possession of his bounty, they begin their long journey to Hell.

Uriel decides it is now time to end Billy's madness. With lightning speed, Uriel snags the gun from his hand, and with a quick short punch, he knocks Billy out. He slides across the concrete floor crashing into the counter, totally unconscious.

The remaining demons are caught off guard by the speed and accuracy of this street tramp. It causes the leader's curiosity and suspicion to grow. He can also sense the lack of any sin around either of the two bums. This spawn of darkness decides to back away to the safety of the shadows, as he commands the others to wrap themselves around Uriel and Chado. Just as they begin whispering evil thoughts, Uriel makes his move. Without any hesitation, this angel of God unveils his sword from underneath his street garment, and with one swift motion, he slices through every demon but one. Seeing this destruction, the frightened leader makes his escape, quickly disappearing through a back door.

"Chado, grab that Martin guitar and pick out the oldest, worn out case you can find. Oh yeah, and take a harmonica from that shelf over there."

"What about this cop?"

"I will take care of him. You hurry along, because that demon that got away is out there placing us on hell's news network!"

Chado quickly finds an old case, grabs a couple harmonicas, and tosses them in along with the antique Martin guitar. "Hey, Uriel, don't we need to pay for this stuff? I mean we don't want to be labeled as thieves."

"What is the cost of the two harmonicas?"

"Tag says 20 bucks a piece, and the guitar is $11,000."

Uriel walks up to the counter, takes a dagger, and starts peeling off slivers of gold onto the scales. "Okay, there is 40 dollars worth of gold. Now we are covered."

"Well what about the cost of the guitar?"

"When we get through with it, we are giving it back to its original owner. This Martin guitar was stolen several years ago from an old man I know. Chado, it never belonged to these crooks in the first place."

"Wow, how cool is that! Is that why we came to this particular pawnshop?"

"I guess you could say that. Sometimes peculiar circumstances just work out for those who love God. Well anyway, run over there and get the DVD from that surveillance rig and bring it over here."

Uriel picks Billy up from the floor, sets him on the counter, then ties and gags him. He then lightly thumps him on the head several times until he finally begins waking up.

"Hey, Mr. Crooked Cop. Wake up. I want you to see something." Uriel points to the bloody corpse of Louie, the store manager, then over to his friend Lester the canine cop and his dog.

"There are your friends, all lying dead, and over what? Your free will and priorities are all mixed up. You might say you are headed for an eternity of pain and suffering. Let me leave you with a thought. Satan comes to steal, kill, and destroy. Now Jesus on the other hand, came to do the opposite. He came to save the lost, heal the sick, and show us all how to love the unlovable. While you are spending the rest of your life in prison—which may be a very short time because Louisiana has the death penalty—you might want to kick back and read the Bible. It might just lead you to know our Savior Jesus Christ.

"Oh, one other thing, in case you think you are getting out of this mess… Chado, hand me that surveillance disk. You see this Mr. Crooked Cop Man? This video will be in the hands of the state police within a few minutes after our departure. So, if I were you, I would consider taking heed to my words, and maybe you will not spend an eternity in a place, where the worm never dies."

Before leaving, Chado takes a permanent marker and writes across the cops forehead and chest, *I murdered these two men in cold blood. I was under the influence of greed. Please take me to prison. Thank you. Mr. Crooked Cop!*

"Let us go, Chado."

15

The Devil's Playground

The trio steps through a back door of the pawnshop leaving behind a bound and gagged cop, surrounded by carnage. Without being noticed they walk down the back alleys of Morgan City, leading to an all-night diner.

"Chado, do you see those three state police cruisers sitting there?"

"Sure, Uriel, what's on your mind?"

"Well, one of those cruisers has a sticker on the back window you might recognize."

"Oh yeah, it's the sign of the fish. That means one of those three state boys is a Christian!"

"Come on; let us find out if he truly is."

Just as Uriel walks through the door, Chado turns and points, signaling Buck to stay outside. "Sorry, Buck, we smell bad enough and bringing you inside might be pushing it." Buck does his grinning trick as he lies down near the entrance, causing Chado to chuckle as he walks through the door.

Three state troopers dressed in dark blue all turn as they watch the two street bums sit down at a table next to them. Two of the troopers turn their noses up and shake their heads as the fowl aroma infiltrates their air space. They begin mumbling, "Goodness gracious, what a sweet smell. I was going to order up some pancakes, but I believe I'll eat next week after I get over this sick stomach."

The third trooper holds his hand up, "Hang on, guys, lets don't be mean now."

He turns, holding his hand out in a kind gesture, shaking both Chado and Uriel's hands. "Let me buy you fellows a cup of coffee. Better yet, hey, Ms. Linda, bring these two fellows the house special and put it on my ticket."

Uriel smiles at Chado as he whispers. "He is the one with the sticker on his windshield; you know the sign of the fish."

The trooper leans over, "What was that you said?"

"Oh, I was just telling my friend Chado, you must be the one that carries the sign of the fish on your cruiser."

The trooper smiles, "So you fellows know that sign?"

"Yes, sir."

"How did you know it was my car?"

"We see it in your eyes, your face, and your actions. The evidence is clear. You have the love of Christ living within you."

The trooper smiles as his eyes suddenly redden almost to the point of tears. "Yes, I confess. Jesus is Lord of my life."

Uriel smiles as he slides the surveillance disk across the table. "We need to give you this information, so that justice will be served. Do not trust the local cops. View this video and get it to a secure location away from Morgan City."

"What's on it?"

Chado replies, "Do you know where the Pawn & Party shop is located?"

"Yes I do. It's an all-night drug den our people with the DEA have been trying to bust for years. They always come up short. We believe they might have an insider working for the city, because they constantly seem to stay one step ahead."

The waitress slides two cups of coffee in front of the bums, as Uriel leans over looking around the waitress. "Well sir, here is your opportunity. We just left a Morgan City policeman over at the Pawn & Party. I am certain he is one of your dirty insiders. Right now, he is sitting on the counter inside the store, tied and gagged with a message written on his forehead and chest. He is surrounded by dead men. Between this video and his confession, you men can probably do a little house cleaning here in the city."

The trooper takes the disk, slides it into his front pocket as they all stand up in unbelief.

"Are you guys for real?"

Chado replies as the other two troopers quickly head for the door, "Yes sir, we are for real."

The friendly trooper reaches over taking the last swig of his milk. "Guys, I hate to ask you to break off your busy schedule, but you need to wait here. There will be a ton of questions on how you two got this information."

Uriel reaches in his leather pouch pulling out a handful of precious stones. He holds out his hand and the trooper opens his, thinking Uriel wants to shake hands. However instead, Uriel begins dribbling the stones in his palm, as he speaks. "We have journeyed from the other side, friend, and we cannot spare any time. Chado and I are on a mission from God. There will be no delay. Trust me. You have all the information you need."

As the last stone falls to his hand, Uriel looks deep into the troopers eyes. "Take this gift and use it wisely. Be about God's good work, as you go in peace."

The trooper overwhelmed and speechless throws down a $20 bill on the table as he heads for the door.

"Okay, Chado, I guess we are done here in Morgan City. What do you think about attending your 5th year death anniversary party?"

Chado chuckles, as he picks up the old guitar, heading out of the diner. "That actually sounds like it might be fun. What about it Buck, you ready to party?"

* * *

The trio is now standing on the shoulder of Highway 70, watching vehicles as they zoom by. Uriel slowly sticks his thumb out for a free ride.

"Hey bud, why don't we just do your travel zoom thing and just show up?"

"Chado, we are heading into dark territory. The Bayou Rose has an evil presence that dwarfs anything you have seen here. So, we need to show up under the radar, and not allow Lucifer's little helpers to know what you are carrying."

Suddenly a four-wheel drive truck wheels off to the side of the road. It's your typical Cajun monster truck, with all the bells and whistles. Huge tires, with loud exhaust pipes, and sounds of rock-n-roll pouring out of the windows.

A skinny tall kid with tattoos covering his arms, steps out on the running board, and with a heavy Cajun accent, "Hey, you want a ride, shaa? You climb in the back of dis truck. Laissez les bon temps rouler, Beau-frére!" This Cajun language translated to English means, "Let the good times roll, brother-in-law."

As the wild Cajun pulls back out on Highway 70 heading for Belle River, he mashes the pedal to the floor. He is allowing everyone to know his exhaust system is the loudest in Louisiana. Chado holds on to Buck's fur as this wild man blasts through the gears.

Watching the beer bottles and cans sliding around in the bed of the truck brings back to Chado a childhood memory. "Hey, Uriel, this reminds me when we used to ride with my pop. Back then, we had to ride in the bed of the truck everywhere we went. If we weren't going very far, we got to sit on the tailgate. That was so cool, but I think it might be against the law nowadays."

"Chado, you need to drop the childhood memories and focus on what is going on. Like I said, we are heading into the enemy's back yard."

"Yeah, Uriel, I've been meaning to ask you. If we've completed the scrolls, why are we doing this?"

"I am not sure. I just know we are to witness these events and follow whoever the chosen soul is to hell's gate."

Uriel, how will we know who it is? I mean the chosen soul."

"Trust me, God is in control and He will show us. Just don't let any of the fallen angels get their hands on those scrolls."

Uriel reaches around and taps the side of the truck signaling to let them out. The young Cajun wheels his truck over in the parking lot of the Bayou Rose. As they all three bail out and walk by the driver's door, the friendly Cajun rolls his window down. "Hey, shaa, y'all sure you want out here, no? Dis place no good for you, shaa. Bad men run dat place. Maybe you come drink some beer with Thibodaux, no?"

Uriel smiles, "No, sir, we are okay. Thank you for showing kindness and giving us a ride."

"Au revoir, monsieur."

Chado reaches up shaking his hand, "Until we meet again, my friend."

They wave goodbye to the Cajun as he tears out of the parking lot squealing his tires.

Chado and Uriel stand on the edge of the highway looking across a huge parking lot filled to capacity. The heavy bass sounds coming from several different vehicles, vibrate the air around them.

"Can you feel it, Chado?"

"Feel what, the boom boxes?"

"No, the presence of darkness. The heaviness of evil."

Chado looks beyond the parked cars at the huge nightclub. The roof is lined with hundreds of demons. Just above the roof where the outside lights fade into the night sky, several fallen angels are circling, like vultures, overlooking a fresh kill.

"Yes, I feel it, Uriel. It's a dreadful darkness. This reminds me of when I had the conversation with Lucifer at the Portal."

"Shake it off, Little Soul! Remember we have the power and support of God."

Chado smiles as he sets the guitar case down. He drops to one knee reaching his arm around Buck and begins giving him a good ole rub-down scratch. "You ole rascal, I kind of wish I could blink my eyes, ole friend, and we'd be back on the pipeline, camped out somewhere nice. Our only problems might be trying to figure out if we were going to eat spam or beanie weenies for supper. Those were the days, Buck, those were the days."

Uriel makes sounds as if he is clearing his throat, mhmhm. "When you two finish reminiscing, we need to move along."

"Sorry, Uriel. Just thought I'd show Buck a little bit of love. So what's next, or should I ask, what do we do now?"

Uriel smiles, "You see that little grassy spot just this side of the main entrance?"

"Yes, right next to that willow tree… Hey, I see some old metal lawn furniture. Maybe they won't mind if we use it. I've always liked to sit, when I pick guitar. "

"We are going to be right under their noses, Chado, and we do not want them to have any suspicion. So just be yourself."

Chado laughs as they head across the parking lot. "That should be easy enough."

16

Reconnaissance Mission and the Brawl

The dive team stand shoulder to shoulder as they watch the steel plates rise into position, covering the rotten boards on the rickety bridge. Cheese Hound reveals another one of his hydraulic masterpieces. "Pretty cool wouldn't you say. I hired out of town contractors to build all of this."

Matt's curiosity gets the best of him. "Why did you use out of town contractors, Cheese?"

"Yank, you sure ask a lot of questions."

"Well, I was just wondering."

"For one thing, I couldn't have got permits for the barricade plates in the bayou. The waterway commission wouldn't allow it. The other reason, I didn't want anyone around here to know what I was up to. The plates covering the holes under the bridge and the ones in the bayou are meant to stay a secret. So don't go telling anyone."

"No problem. We won't tell a soul, bud."

Cheese straddles his World War II 1940 Harley, "Remember, we need to be seen as a group of bikers celebrating a fallen comrade. Oh yeah, don't forget to stagger; we're rolling in a few minutes apart."

They all head down Highway 70 in single file. Each one over the next few miles are having thoughts, and wondering if they might make it out of this alive. Bones pulls up alongside Cheese, talking loudly over the sound of their engines and pointing, "Hey, bud, is that the bayou we're going to use for our getaway?"

Cheese points to his ears, shakes his head and yells back, "I can't hear you, Bones." He points ahead, "We can talk when we get there."

Not far up the road, they see the lights of the Bayou Rose. Its glow is piercing through the darkness of the Louisiana swamp.

Cheese Hound twists around in his seat, motioning to all four to fall back. He then holds two fingers in the air, giving a signal to come in two by two. They all wave understanding his crude hand signals and at the same time slow their bikes down to a crawl.

Within minutes, Cheese pulls through the parking lot and heads straight over to what the locals had named Bike Alley. He rides his antique up to the line of around 60 bikes. The club has a packed house with hardly any room for more vehicles.

TC and Bones are the first, and within a few short moments, Matt and Joey idle up to the line. As soon as they get off their bikes, Cheese Hound greets each one with a cold beer that he just dug out of his saddlebags. He pops the cap to his brew and turns facing Bones. "What were you asking me back there on Highway 70, Bones?"

Just under a whisper, "I wanted to know, if that bayou that parallels Highway 70 was the one we're going to use for our getaway."

"Yes, that's Belle River. We can use it to go to my place, or if we need to, all the way back through Morgan City. From there we can run out and hit the Atchafalaya River, which leads straight to the gulf. Or we can run the Intracoastal Waterway over to Bayou Chene. I plan on going straight to my place if no one is hot on our trail. Just saying, it's good to have options."

Bones winks, "Sounds like you've thought this thing out pretty good."

Cheese grins, "I've wanted to do this for years." He nods his head in a gesture to follow. “Come on, guys, let’s ease over to the entrance and work our way in.”

The dive team steps in a short line of people near the entrance to the Rose. Matt stops, takes a big swig of his beer, wipes dribble from his chin, as he hears a delightful sound coming from underneath the willow tree to his left. He spots two bums, one playing a guitar, and the other a harmonica. Matt being drawn to this odd music, immediately begins walking in their direction. Joey shouts out, “Hey, Yank, where ya going?”

“I got to check this out; these cats are playing some down home blues.”

“What do you mean down home blues? You’re from Minnesota, Yank!”

They all laugh, as they walk over in front of an open guitar case. Matt, quickly throws a couple of twenties on top of several dollar bills that had already stacked up. His companions, each one following Matt’s generous lead, tosses in a handful of cash.

The four divers and Cheese Hound are totally unaware they are standing within a few feet of Chado Cole. This is the very man they are celebrating, a 5th year anniversary of his death. His appearance as a vagabond, wrapped in rags with a dirty face, hides his true identity.

Chado, now smiling from ear to ear, wants so badly to tell his friends who he really is. As he looks deep into the eyes of his worldly companions, he wonders which one he will meet at hell’s gate. The Holy Spirit suddenly sweeps over Chado replacing this heaviness of fear with an abundance of happiness. It radiates through his fingertips as he bends the strings of the old Martin guitar, bringing sounds to the ears of his friends like they’ve never heard before. Now possessing talents from Heaven and forced emotion from Earth, his playing wins the hearts of now what seems to be over 100 people standing behind the dive team.

As they hit the last note of this unknown song, the crowd goes into a roar. People shove their way to the front to get a better look at these two talented bums, and the mangy dog. Dozens of joyful fans throw loose cash over into Chado's guitar case, to the point of overflowing. Chado, Uriel, and Buck are now surrounded by this happy crowd of music lovers.

Bones grabs Matt on the shoulder. "Hey bud, it's something really familiar with this guy, but I just can't put my finger on it."

"I know what you mean, Bones. It's the eyes. Something about the eyes… is so dang familiar."

Suddenly a loud voice overcomes the happy sounds of fun and laughter. "Break it up, get out of my way. Make a hole. I need to see what's going on here!"

A huge bouncer named Shafer violently pushes his way through the crowd. "What in hell's creation are you two bums coming up here panhandling for? This is private property, and I'll give you about one minute to get out of here alive!"

Two young ladies come to the defense of Chado and Uriel. "Leave these poor guys alone you hateful man. They are way better musicians than your heavy metal band inside."

"Yeah, go hug a refrigerator you big bully! They're just trying to make a living!"

Shafer turns around, grabs both girls by the neck. With his super human strength, he picks them up off the ground. As they're struggling and gasping for air, he shouts at two other bouncers. "Hey watch this."

He tosses both girls in the air and slaps them in the face quickly catching them again before their feet hit the ground."

This awful scare tactic disbursed the once happy crowd surrounding the two blues players. The dive team looks to Cheese Hound for direction, wanting to jump in and rescue the girls. He quickly signals, to back away and they slowly melt back into the crowd undetected.

After this evil man demonstrates his strength and authority to everyone, he hurls both young ladies into the arms of the other two bouncers. "Hey, Shafer, you need any help with the bums?"

"No, I got this."

"What about these girls?"

"Bring them to Nikolai. He might want to hire them out."

The three bouncers begin to laugh, unaware that several demons are swirling around the legs and shoulders of the two young girls.

Chado Cole, with a savior's heart, quickly leans the old guitar against the chair next to him, "Hold up, friend. No need to take those cuties off to work, when we can put them to work right now. What do you say we make a deal?"

Chado was speaking Shafer's language, "What you thinking, raggedy man?"

"Oh, I guess we got a couple grand in the guitar case. That should be worth a few hours with them two honeys."

"You got a deal, raggedy man. However you and your mangy dog, and that harmonica player need to close shop. Y'all welcome to hang around, but no more playing. We need these cattle grazing inside, not out here throwing their money in a guitar case."

Chado continues with his deal making, "Ok then, hand them girls over and you can have at the cash."

The two bouncers hold on tightly to the girls' wrists as they watch Shafer clean out the guitar case. Just before they release the young ladies, who are wrapped in cold fear of being raped by these two nasty bums—something strange happens. Without really understanding… an overwhelming sense of peace comes over both girls. They suddenly feel safe, as they stare into the eyes of Chado and Uriel, feeling an abundance of love and compassion.

Shafer stands up shoving his easy made currency into his front pocket. Grinning like a used car salesman, he displays several gold teeth lined with food particles. This obnoxious man wads a single dollar bill up, and tosses it, hitting Chado on the chest. To further his disrespect, in a very smugly way with his top lip curled up, he says, "Bye…"

Now satisfied with making some quick cash, the three bouncers head back to the nightclub. They leave the girls standing just a few feet away from Chado and Uriel. Without the ladies realizing, Buck crawls on his belly, while doing his grinning routine and is now at their feet. Even though Buck's appearance is that of a dirty mangy street dog, the two girls look down and immediately fall in love with this heavenly beast. They both drop to their knees petting the large head of this mixed breed. As they show love and kindness toward this mutt, and have lost the spirit of fear. The demons slowly drift away, back towards the crowded nightclub.

Chado and Uriel approach the two young ladies and reach down, one on each side, lifting them to their feet.

Uriel with a firm voice, "Do you two have transportation?"

The little brunette, wiping tears from her face, smiles. "Yes, we rode together in my car."

Uriel warns the young ladies, "We have rescued you from the clutches of these evil men. As servants of God, we implore you to leave this place never to return. I say unto you, children of this perverse generation, recognize the danger that lurks upon this unholy ground."

Uriel grabs both girls, holding them within inches of his face and whispers. "Seek the light, in this dark and dying world. The light is Jesus Christ, and the end of time grows near. Go now, children, and never look back."

Both girls with tears streaming down their faces, "Thank you, sir, thank you." They walk away heading for the car, embracing each other as they disappear through the massive parking lot.

"Hey, Uriel, I'm wondering why my buddies didn't jump all over those three bouncers when they were mistreating the girls. That's not like them, especially Cheese Hound and Bones. Back in the day we would fight at the drop of a hat. Especially when it came to defending women being mistreated by some butt-head."

"Chado, you can stop wondering. I believe your old crew is planning something big for this particular night. God sent us here for a reason. So, we need to just watch, stay undetected and see how this all plays out."

* * *

Cheese and the guys split up as they enter the club, with Joey and TC heading for a couple open chairs at one of the bars. Bones and Matt find a small open spot near the 1970's style dance floor. Cheese Hound makes his way over near the stage, where the heavy metal band is playing.

The three guys on guitar, along with the lead singer, are violently shaking their heads up and down, making their long hair flop back and forth. The horrible grunge sound is deafening. The rhythm and timing of this rock band is off, but the audience doesn't seem to mind. The crowd is holding their hands in the air, swaying and jumping as if praising this satanic sound. The eyes of the band members are blood red, sunken in. The dark circles underneath their eyes resemble black paint, but it's not black paint at all. It's the footprint of a horrible new drug that's being manufactured underneath the very floor everyone is standing on. Not only the band members, but also almost everyone under the roof of this hellhole, looks to be hooked on this manufactured poison.

Matt sees Lela standing near the center of the dance floor. He immediately rushes over. To his surprise, when he grabs her by the shoulder and spins her around hoping to see her cute smile, it's just the opposite. She is unresponsive with a lost look pasted on her face. It's like she is looking straight through Matt.

He shakes her, "Lela, Lela, what's wrong with you girl?" He shakes her again, "Hey, sweetheart, it's Matt, your manly man. Come on girl snap out of it!"

Matt holds his fingers in front of her eyes snapping several times. Nothing happens. He decides to make a more aggressive attempt to wake her out of what seemed to be a standing drug coma. With an open hand he lightly slaps her on both cheeks. "Lela, do you know who this is? Okay, girl, I've had enough. I'm getting you out of here, right now!" Matt throws her over his shoulder and heads for the door.

Bones sees Matt with Lela draped across his shoulder heading in his direction. He mumbles, "Oh crap, this is about to get interesting." He whistles over the deafening music, and luckily gets Cheese Hound's attention. Bones points at Matt then holds his hands up with a signal. *What now*?

With a worried look on his face, Matt walks past Bones heading for the door.

Nikolai, the bar owner, and Shafer are sitting in an upstairs office watching the surveillance monitors. "Hey, boss, look at that guy."

Nikolai quickly stands, as he watches Matt carrying Lela toward the door. "Hey, Shafer, send one of your men, see where this biker thinks he goes with my girl."

"Okay, boss."

"Wait, send my nephew Victor. He needs experience."

Matt, with Lela on his shoulder, uses her feet to push the door open. He turns walking through the middle of a small group that's admiring Nikolai's Lamborghini. "Coming through folks, excuse me please. I got a sick girl here, excuse me."

Not far behind, Cheese and the dive team make their way through the crowded bar, knowing Matt is about to be in trouble.

Out of the corner of his eye, Matt can see two bouncers heading in his direction from across the parking lot. He gently slides Lela from his shoulder, placing her on the seat of his bike.

Lela mumbles, seeming to be out of her mind, "Don't make me take the drug, please no more. I promise, I won't try to run away ever again. Please, no more."

Matt grabs her by the face with both hands and lightly shakes her. "Lela, listen to me. It's Matt. I've got you now. You don't have to ever take any drugs, ever!"

Lela looks at Matt as if for a moment she knows who he is. As he stares at this once beautiful Cajun queen, her eyes roll back and she suddenly passes out. Matt shakes his head with anger while he slowly lays her limp body across the wide gas tank. As a precaution he gently ties her hands to the handlebars to keep her hands and arms away from the hot engine.

Nikolai reaches over adjusting the outside cameras, as he zooms in on Matt. "Hey watch this. My nephew is a pretty tough Russian."

Shafer and Nikolai begin laughing as his nephew, Victor, and one other bouncer close in on Matt.

Victor scoffs, "Hey, biker trash, where do you think you're going with Lela?"

Matt turns looking in their direction, "She's a friend of mine and she's sick. I'm bringing her home."

"My Uncle Nikolai says she's not going anywhere. Her shift has just begun and she has a lot of tricks to turn before morning."

The other bouncer spouts off, "Yeah, trash, it's almost time for her next fix."

Victor, the Russian, is holding a syringe in his hand as he shakes it at Matt, "Maybe you need fix too."

Both Russians laugh as they step closer. "Hey, Victor, I bet your uncle will like this bike. Maybe we take bike, take girl, and throw this trash in the bayou."

Without realizing how mad and hurt Matt is from seeing Lela in her condition, he loses control. With all his strength, he swings as hard as he can. This power punch sends the first guy sliding on the pavement. Being caught off guard, seeing his buddy knocked down, Victor tries stabbing Matt in the face with the hypodermic needle. With Matt's cat-like reflexes, he catches Victor by his wrist. He struggles to hold the needle away from his face. The Russian being much larger and stronger overcomes Matt causing him to stumble backward, falling across the hood of a car. After several seconds of fierce combat, Victor has the needle, only a fraction of an inch from Matt's left eye. The other bouncer now back on his feet, steps in to help Victor force the dirty needle into Matt's pupil.

Suddenly the sound of footsteps comes to an abrupt stop. "Yank, you need a little help?"

Cheese Hound, armed with two sets of brass knuckles, hits Victor, crushing his right cheekbone. The sound it makes in the night air resembles a 22 rifle being shot. Cheese knocks Victor out with one punch. His body resembles a wet blanket dropping to the ground.

Bones tore into the other bouncer. He first grabs a handful of his hair, violently yanking his head to waist level, taking him completely off balance. He walks backward, dragging the bouncer across the pavement, as he pounds the guy's face with his free hand. This is a technique Bones learned from Chado, back in the day. Just as he lays the final punch, knocking him out and to the pavement, he grins, "Where the head goes, so will the body follow."

Still angry, Matt picks up the needle, walks over to Victor who is still unconscious, forces his mouth open, and injects the poison into his tongue. "That should heal you right up. Be sure to tip the lady at the front desk on your way to Hell, you Russian dirt bag."

Cheese Hound looks up at the outside cameras, "Hey, Matt, you see that?"

"See what?" Cheese points at the surveillance cameras and waves at Nikolai. "Matt, you might want to quit playing doctor over there, because I think it's a world of hurt about to come down on us. Let's get the heck out of here!" They all fire their bikes off, quickly heading out of the parking lot.

As Matt passes Uriel and Chado, who are still sitting near the entrance, he gives the two bums a friendly wave.

Chado waves back at his friends, who are unaware of his true identity. "Hey, Uriel, do we follow the guys?"

"No, we stay put. This is where the action is at. Look at the sky. That little confrontation has the demonic forces stirring."

Nikolai's security team comes running out, just in time to watch as five bikers' taillights fade out of sight. They begin questioning everyone, including Uriel and Chado, asking if they know who the bikers are. They get nowhere with their investigation.

Victor stumbles up from biker's row, and makes an attempt at talking to security, but his tongue has swollen to the point of filling his entire mouth. The poisonous drug from the hypodermic needle is creating an adverse effect. All he can do is grunt.

After several minutes pass, two unmarked police cars roll in. The detectives remain in their cars until Nikolai and Shafer walk out.

Detective Komo holds his hand out to Nikolai. "Okay, we're here. What's so important you need us here this early? Our pick up time is in three hours."

Nikolai grins, "Thank you for coming on such short notice, gentlemen. I have something I need to show you." Nikolai reaches over handing a computer jump drive to Detective Fletcher.

"What's on it?"

"Take a look. I want you to bring me the five men you see on this recording."

Detective Fletcher leans over in his car and plugs the jump drive into his laptop. "Okay, what are we looking at here? I see a butt kicking. What's he doing to that guy's mouth? Wow, that's a needle." The detective starts laughing. "My Russian friend, that all looks like self-defense, and if you don't mind me asking, what was in the needle?" Nikolai with a loud angry voice, "That's the same product, you and half the police force are getting rich off of!"

"Calm down, ole buddy. What is it you want?"

"Like I said, I want you to either bring them to me, or film their destruction. No one disrespects Nikolai and lives. So, you choose!"

The detective shakes his head, "Okay, okay. We will take care of the biker trash. Now, you feel better?"

"Yes, yes, Nikolai feel much better."

Fletcher zooms in on Matt and Joey's plate numbers, "This should be easy. We are getting a bonus for this, right?"

Nikolai looks over and winks at Shafer without the detectives noticing. "Yes, you get bonus, my friend, big bonus."

Detective Komo grins while patting the Russian on his arm. "Are we still on schedule for 5:00 am pickup?"

"Yes, very good… very good…"

As Nikolai and Shafer head back inside, they glance over at the two bums, "Who is this trash sitting under the willow?"

"Just a couple bums boss, they're harmless. I actually made a few bucks off those two."

"Good… Very good…"

17

Speedboat, Guns and Ammo

All but Cheese and Matt cross the rickety bridge. Cheese pulls his antique Harley over behind a hedgerow of bushes near the highway, laying his bike down on its side.

Matt pulls up with Lela still passed out, draped over his tank, "What are you doing, Cheese?"

"Yank, you get on down to the camp and put Lela in my bedroom. Let her sleep off whatever they shot her up with. I'll be along in a bit. I want to see how bad we stirred up the hornets' nest. That Russian is probably sending his crooked law dogs to hunt us down. You hurry up and get around the bend, so they won't see your lights!"

Just in the nick of time, Matt's lights disappear around the curve. Cheese, now hidden in heavy brush, observes two unmarked cop cars fly by at a high rate of speed. He waits another couple minutes in darkness as he listens closely to the fading noise of the two cars. The sound of radial tires against the pavement is slowly overtaken by the peaceful silence of the swamp.

* * *

Cheese Hound walks through the door of the shack, "I think we're okay. If the Russian showed the cops that surveillance video, it's a good chance they got our license numbers. If that's the case it might be a good thing."

TC mumbles, "How can that be a good thing?"

Cheese grins, "Well all you guys have Lafayette addresses and that means those crooked cops are heading north out of our hair."

With a concerned look on his face, Joey twists around in his chair. "Cheese, if that's the case, won't they come here?"

"Nope, I have a post office box in Morgan City, and this place is registered at the courthouse under my step grandfather. He's been dead for 30 years. I just pay the taxes on this place under a private firm. Trust me. We are off the map."

Matt walks out of the bedroom after tucking Lela in, "I can't believe the law enforcement around here is allowing those Russians to do what they're doing!"

Cheese Hound pulls an old calendar off the wall, spreading it across the table. "Joey, hand me that marker, and let's go over a few things."

Within a few seconds, Cheese draws the entire layout of the Bayou Rose on the back of the calendar. His military training is being revealed as he pinpoints positions of strength and weakness. The short time they were in the bar gave him enough intel to lay out the perfect plan. After lining out the dive team with each having a specific job that will all work in unison, he smiles at everyone. "Remember, guys, timing is everything."

Matt is the first to stand up from the table. "I don't know how to say this, but when you guys first started talking about hitting this place, it totally freaked me out. But after what I saw in that human drug chamber, I want to kill them all!"

Bones, TC, Joey, and Cheese all stand. "Heck yeah, let's do this!"

Matt slams his hand against the table, "Yes indeed. I'm ready! These creeps are so arrogant having the local law enforcement on the payroll, they think they are untouchable."

As they all head downstairs to Cheese Hound's Cajun style bat cave, Cheese lets out a howl. "AOO…, AO, AOOO… untouchable you say. We'll just have to see about that. Bones, hit the latch to the cabinets."

Bones reaches inside the mounted alligator's head, flipping the hidden latch. The doors all fly open on the stainless steel armory cabinets.

Cheese lines out weapons, "Bones, since you're the deer slayer from Grant Parish, you take the 308 sniper rifle. Get the one with a silencer. It drills nails at 200 yards. We need you on over watch."

Bones smiles, "What about this pair of Uzis, can I take them too?"

"Sure, if it will make you feel better. TC, you're a pretty good shot with a rifle. You and I can take the AR's with silencers. Matt, you and Joey grab the riot shotguns. After we kick this thing off, you two can make some racket."

Clicking sounds echo throughout the room as they load and check weapons. No one says a word as they carefully focus on preparing for battle.

Cheese steps away from the cabinets, "Okay, fellows, I've got another little surprise for y'all. TC, look in that bottom cabinet. Let's get everyone rigged out with night vision. Oh yeah, make sure you get extra mags, ammo, vests and a couple handguns. I don't want to be out there with one of you guys complaining like a little girl, screaming 'I'm out of ammo.'"

Matt, stuffing shotgun clips in his vest, "Hey, Cheese, are these ammo vests bulletproof?"

"Yep, the best you can buy. I've always known this would happen one day, and boom, here it is."

The Hound, grabs the corner of the huge tarp covering his speedboat. "Hey, guys, give me a hand."

As they unveil this beautiful coal black powerhouse, the team goes silent. With each standing frozen in their tracks admiring this seagoing masterpiece, Cheese laughs, "What are you deep-sea divers doing? Climb in and let's rock!"

He flips several switches across the control panel before starting this dual engine sea monster. The entire dash lights up resembling a system you might see on a commercial jet. Joey and Bones scramble to untie the bow and stern lines as the massive 3,000 horsepower engines fire off. Matt being concerned with the deafening sound, "Won't they hear us coming?"

Cheese smiles as he reaches over flipping a switch. Suddenly, the loud engines begin getting quieter and quieter, until the massive engines, sound no different from a vehicle motor. "A little something extra I installed. Cool, wouldn't you say?"

Matt with a dumb look on his face, "Cheese, you never cease to amaze me, unbelievable."

"Okay, boys, you might want to turn your night vision on."

Cheese hits a remote turning all the lights off in the camp, and at the same time a hidden door raises just high enough for the boat to idle under.

18

The Take Down

People stumble out of the Bayou Rose as it nears closing time. All other bars in Louisiana by law have to end their night at 2:00 am. The Russian, now having enough dirt on politicians and pull with local law, is allowed to stay open until 4:00 am.

"Hey Uriel, you think anything is going to happen? The night is almost over."

"Have patience, Chado. Did you notice the three security men that just went up on the roof?"

"I did. What are they up to?"

"I do not know. It looks like they are getting ready for something. Maybe a money drop or a drug deal."

"Uriel, I did notice it seems there are more demons and fallen angels than before."

"Yes, it does seem like the presence of darkness is getting stronger. Chado, remember if they come near you, do not look them in the eyes. Just pretend they are invisible, look past or through them. If they realize we can see into the Realm, it will not take long until they figure out who we are. We cannot blow our cover!"

* * *

The dive team and Cheese Hound are like Robin Hood and his merry men on their way to save the princess from an evil king, but they aren't riding stags or carrying bows and arrows. They're cruising down Belle River at 80 miles an hour, armed with military weapons. This is by far not a fairytale. These men have blood in their eyes and are not depending on crooked law enforcement to dispose of this evil. In their minds, they have a moral duty to stop the spread of this new manufactured drug. In doing this, they're saving the entire southern region of the United States.

This awful drug is spreading through communities like an end time epidemic. The locals are calling it, the 'One-Time' drug. The Russian's technique is to give anyone who wants it, a free sample. That one sample is all it takes, and they're chained to it. The victims of this drug find themselves stealing from their families in wicked desperation to get enough money for another fix; but tonight it comes to an end.

They see the lights of the Bayou Rose glowing through the late night fog that's now hovering a few feet above the water.

Cheese Hound throttles down the powerboat. "Hey TC, get off that box you're sitting on and dig the two way radios out, and be careful with that bag, it has the ear bugs in it."

TC hands everyone a radio, "Check, check, can you hear me?"

Bones has a stupid look on his face. "Well I guess so you're sitting right by me, lug head."

With everyone so serious thinking about the mission, they all break out laughing at TC and Bones.

Matt notices something cool, "Hey check it out. The fog is hovering just at the right height over the water to cover the entire boat. Only our heads are sticking up above the fog."

Joey grinning, "Yeah, we can call it foggy camo."

They start laughing again with Cheese cutting their laughter short. "Okay, enough jacking around, Bones we're letting you out about a quarter mile this side of the bridge. You sneak down that levee and find you a vantage point a couple hundred yards from your targets. Make sure you can see the guards on the roof."

"Roger that Cheese."

"Look now, when you get in place let us know. Oh, you might want to pull your mask up. Your white face will glow like the moon."

Cheese steers the boat close enough to the bank allowing Bones to easily jump to dry land. "Later, Bones. Keep your powder dry, bud."

He waves as he turns heading across Highway 70, disappearing into the shaded backdrop of the river levee.

As they near the bridge located across the parking lot from the bar, they hear the jukebox playing. This means the heavy metal band is through for the night.

Cheese kills the engines and they silently coast along for the last 100 feet. Right at the last second, he cuts the long nose of the powerboat to the left. They barely miss the bridge pilings, finally coming to a quiet stop underneath the Highway 70 Bridge.

Joey wipes the moisture from his watch, "Its 3:40, boys. I hope y'all are ready for this."

The sound of several vehicles cross the bridge as the bar continues to empty.

Staring through a thick clump of weeds growing against the bridge railing, they have a clear view of an almost empty parking lot.

Cheese Hound scans the area with his scope and whispers, "Okay, Matt, you and Joey go back under the bridge and work your way down the edge of the bayou. Let me know when y'all are in position."

Without saying anything, they both head for locations Cheese had earlier showed them on the crude map.

A clicking sound from the radio, "Come in, Cheese, can you hear me?"

"Yeah, I got you, Bones. Are you in position?"

"Roger that, I'm a little winded from the trot, but I'm ok."

"Have you got a clear view of the three rooftop guards?"

"That's a big 10-4, Cheese, I'm zeroed in. It looks like they're all standing together smoking crack or something."

"Get a hold on your breathing, Bones. I can hear your heartbeat from here. Try and take some long deep breaths. You need to calm way down. Just think back when you would get all relaxed on a deer hunt."

"Okay, Cheese, just give me a couple minutes to get over my run. I won't let you down. Trust me, I'll be on target."

"You got it, Bones."

TC bumps Cheese on the leg, "Look over there under that willow. The two bums and that mangy dog are still sitting there."

"Yeah, I see them. Man, I was hoping they would be long gone by this time. "Hey, Joey, are you and Matt in position?"

Matt comes back across the two way, "Roger that, we are in position. Hey, Cheese, the two bums are still sitting in the same place they were before we left. You think we need to get them out of there?"

"Negative, just watch your cross fire. We don't want to hurt any friendlies today."

Cheese spots an opportunity. "Hey, Bones, you see that redneck walking toward that old Chevelle?"

"Roger, I see him—nice hot rod."

"That 308 you're shooting has a silencer but it still makes a little racket. So let's time our shots when that guy fires up his muscle car. It should mask the sound. This will be rifles only, gentlemen. Y'all can't let go with the shotguns until after we're discovered. Does everyone read me?"

Sudden chatter, "Roger, we read you, Cheese."

"We are ready, let's do it."

Cheese looks over at TC, "Okay when you hear that V-8 fire off, take out the power lines. Bones, when you see the lights go out nail those three guys."

"Will do, Cheese."

TC rolls over on his side taking close aim at the two overhead power lines and waits. Bones zeroes in on the guy standing alone on the backside of the roof. Suddenly, echoing across the parking lot the hot rod fires off. As an added bonus, two local bikers crank their Harleys.

Bones let go of the first round, blowing the lone guard completely off the backside of the roof. With perfect timing, TC shoots both power lines, cutting the power feeding the club. Having two guards remaining on the roof, Bones quickly turns, and surprisingly, has both guards lined up in his crosshairs. POW! His next round passes through the second and the third guy, dropping them both with one shot.

Within just a few seconds, they had managed to take out every guard on the outside without being detected.

Matt being fixated with anger, runs across the parking lot crashing through the front door. Without hesitation, he begins blasting away at the unexpected bouncers. Joey is not far behind, "Slow down, Matt, you're gonna get yourself killed!"

With the bar room completely dark, the bouncers are easy prey as the team pours over the place using their night-vision. This easy shooting gallery suddenly comes to a slow crawl as the backup generator kicks in. The odds are now even with the lights back on.

After clearing the barroom area, they realize there is a possibility of getting caught in crossfire, between Nikolai's upstairs office and the lab downstairs. Cheese signals Matt, Joey and TC to hold at the cellar entrance. He then motions for Bones, who now has an Uzi in each hand to go with him. Cheese pulls out a grenade and a flash bang. First, he tosses the grenade. It lands directly in front of the locked door to Nikolai's office.

BOOM! Dust, smoke and debris fly through the stairwell. Within a second of the blast, Cheese runs up the stairs, tossing the flash bang through the door. BOOM! Without any hesitation, Bones and Cheese step inside the smoke filled room. They spray the entire office with bullets, almost empting their magazines.

Shafer, being stunned and disorientated cries out, "Cease fire! We give up! Cease fire!"

Cheese, holds his hand up signaling Bones to stop shooting. "Okay, come out where we can see you."

Shafer slowly stands up from behind a desk, with both ears bleeding from the two explosions; he wobbles across the room. Cheese lifts up his pistol, "Hey, Shafer, you remember me, you piece of crap?"

Shafer, showing no signs of hostility, decides to play the part of a humble, innocent, Russian drug dealer. He turns raising his hands in the air, "Your voice sounds familiar, the face, I don't know. You cover with mask. Who are you, friend? Do you work for the syndicate? The money is all here. We didn't pay last quarter because we had problem with Mayor. Don't kill Shafer! We pay now. We clean this up and do business as usual. We never late again, I promise. What you say, deal?"

Cheese quickly sees another opportunity, with Shafer thinking they are with the syndicate. Apparently, there is more to this operation than a few Russians dealing drugs on the bayou.

Bones is startled, as he hears someone digging their way out from underneath a collapsed desk. It's Nikolai, "Don't shoot, it's me, Nikolai. I hear what Shafer say. We have your money."

Nikolai stands brushing off his expensive suit, "Come with me, I show you money. We keep it safe for you. No need for any more bloodshed, my friend. We clean this up. You'll see. Nikolai can fix anything. Just follow me, gentlemen."

As they are coming down the stairs Cheese whispers over the radio, "Hold, we are coming down, do not shoot."

They follow Nikolai and Shafer to a nearby kitchen, where they have two locked freezers sitting side by side. "Just look inside my friends, Nikolai has your money."

They open the two doors revealing six large bales of cash, all having vacuumed seal plastic around each. Cheese, still playing the game, decides to take this to another level. "This is just a fraction of what you owe. Where is the rest, Nikolai?"

"Okay, okay, one more thing I give you." He reaches up taking his gold necklace off, kindly handing it over to Cheese. Attached to the chain is a small gold case. The treasure concealed inside the case, is a 24-gig jump drive. "You see, Nikolai show you everything. You look on computer drive. There you will find bank accounts in Switzerland and Cayman Island."

At gunpoint, they walk back inside the bar near the stairway to the drug lab. Cheese bumps the back of Shafer's head with the barrel of his pistol. "Tell everyone working down there to come out."

Shafer reaches over to a com system on the wall, "Hey, everyone in lab, this is Shafer. It's okay. You come out now."

A dozen naked women walk up the stairs, one after the other, with several of Nikolai's men following close behind. Cheese Hound feeling sorry for the women, escort all twelve to the kitchen. He hands each one a wad of cash as they walk past the freezers.

"Go home and forget what you saw here tonight. Don't come back because this place won't be here."

Some of the women are thanking Cheese; some are just crying as they try to cover their naked breasts with the cash. These women had been turned into slaves, abused, beaten, and raped… but now they are free. Deeply touched from the humility coming from these severely scarred women, Cheese Hound quickly dries his eyes.

After the last girl has left, he walks back inside where the dive team is holding everyone at gunpoint. "Okay, fellows, I need a work detail. Each one of you pigs grab a load of that cash and we'll show you what to do."

* * *

Uriel and Chado notice the naked women walking out of the side door. "My goodness, Uriel, look at the demons swirling around those ladies. Can we do anything?"

"Not now, Chado, we cannot risk breaking our cover. The mission at this point is more important. They are not in as much trouble as you think. Do you see that vehicle crossing the bridge?"

"Yes, it looks like an old church bus."

"Well, watch and learn, Chado, watch and learn."

Suddenly the bus engine starts spitting and sputtering, finally coasting to a stop, just on the bar side of the bridge. An old preacher holding a flashlight is followed by a handful of young adults, as they pile out. The preacher lifts the engine hood, and then throws his hat on the ground, "Lord, you know we are already running late. Why in the world would you let this ole heap of nuts and bolts break down here? Please answer me, Lord, give me a sign or something. I'm getting way too old to be broke down in the middle of nowhere."

The old preacher's wife hearing his moaning and griping to the

Lord sticks her head out the window. "Cletus, you want a sign? Well there's a big sign heading straight at you."

"What are you cackling about woman, can't you see I'm trying to pray."

"Well, can't you see God's trying to answer you? Turn around, Cletus, just turn around!"

"Oh, Lord my God, should I close my eyes or should I run?"

The preacher's wife, with her head still hanging out of the window goes into action. "You kids open those boxes in the back and grab a couple arm loads of those clothes. This is way better than us making money at a flea market. Hurry up now, those girls have to be freezing."

Chado looks over at Uriel, "How many times have we been delayed, broke down or detoured, and it was just God's hand at work?"

"The answer is many, many times during a person's life. You see, Chado, a human's first reaction to disappointment is aggravation, sometimes even anger. Often, it is just God giving an opportunity, just like what we see unfolding right there. I know short delays have kept you out of harm's way, because I was involved in most of your delays.

"Chado, those poor girls have been in bondage and oppressed by these demons for a long time. Just look at how much God loves them. They are walking across this parking lot, into the arms of God's children. The healing of their addictions and broken hearts begins this day. They are naked and he gives them clothes. They are cold and he gives them warmth. They thirst and he gives them living water. Little Soul, where are their demons now?"

Within a few minutes, the sound of the old church bus sputters down Highway 70 with this group of women who once were slaves, but now are set free!

* * *

Cheese and the dive team hold the Russian crew at gunpoint as they carry the bales of money to the speedboat. Nikolai sees the church bus cart away all the girls. "Hey we need to stop that bus. Do you realize how long it takes to train women for drug lab?"

Joey pokes Nikolai in the back with his shotgun barrel. "I wouldn't worry much about those girls. You just set that bale of money over in the bottom of that boat."

Nikolai cuts his eyes toward Cheese, "I believe you men lie to me. You are just thieves, not syndicate like you say, you lie to me!"

Cheese Hound smiles, "We didn't say we were syndicate, Hoss. You and your lead man Shafer said it. Now that we're on the subject, I'll tell you why we're here. You Russians came in here a few years ago and started growing like a stinkweed. Anyone that touched you started stinking. Now you've got the law in your back pocket, now they stink. Heck, you fellows have stunk the whole south end of Louisiana up."

Shafer is so mad, he starts gritting his nasty gold teeth, "If you're not syndicate, who are you?"

Cheese continues, "My Russian outlaws friends, I want you to meet the deep-sea cleaning crew."

The Russians all laugh at Cheese in a belittling way.

Joey whispers to Bones, "The Hound won't take much of that."

Suddenly without hesitation, Cheese swings his AR-15 around. POW, POW, POW! Three Russians hit the ground holding their knees. Cheese snickers as he waves his rifle back and forth, "Now who else thinks this is funny?"

They all look away at the ground except for Shafer. He just can't help himself. "Hey, American, do you realize you just signed your death warrant? One of the men you just shot in the leg is the Morgan

City Mayor's son. When they catch you, the swamp will be your grave. You can't stop what we do here. You just slow it down. We own Louisiana and the southern coast."

Nikolai shakes his head, "Be quiet, Shafer, you talk too much. These Americans need to take their money and just leave."

Cheese points his rifle between Shafer's eyes, "The Mayor of Morgan City, you say. Well isn't this just a cozy little relationship with our elected officials. Hey, Matt, if you don't mind, put Nikolai in the boat, I believe we'll just carry him along with us. The rest of these turds smell kind of funky. I believe they all need a bath. So I'm gonna have to ask y'all to strip down naked, just like you've done those girls that worked in your drug lab."

The evil men start mumbling, "Our people will have your heads on a platter and eat your brains with Russian wine."

Bones steps in front of Cheese now facing Shafer, "Excuse me for a second, Cheese, I need a word with Mr. Gold Teeth."

"Sure, go right ahead, Bones."

"Everybody calls you Shafer, right?"

"Yes, I am Shafer."

"Okay, I just want to make sure I'm talking with the right guy. Do you know a Mexican named Chico?"

"No, I don't know him."

Bones cracks him across the bridge of his nose, as he raises his voice. "You're lying through them nasty gold teeth. You cut him across the stomach and threatened to kill his family, one by one, in front of him, if he didn't sell your poison. Now, do you know who I'm talking about?"

"Maybe I do, but I didn't mean it. I wouldn't kill Chico's family. Maybe, I just scare him."

"Just scare him? Well this is where I have to draw a line. You see, his sister is my girlfriend and Chico told me I might have a kid by her. So I guess that means you threatened my kid."

Shafer holds his hand up, "Wait now, friend, I just wanted to scare Chico a little so he would move product."

Bones continues, "Let me think about your character for a second. Just a little while ago, you had two young ladies by the throat and were going to make slaves out of them. If it hadn't been for those two bums, you would have. Let me see what else... Oh yeah, you poison families with your drugs. Wow, now that's quite the resume. So, Mr. Gold Teeth, tell me something right now that will convince me, to want to be your friend."

Just at the moment Shafer opens his mouth to respond, Bones shoots him in his left kneecap, POW! As Shafer falls to the ground, with split second accuracy Bones buries a thirteen-inch knife blade through Shafer's right ear, killing him instantly. With this evil dead man still on his knees, Bones kicks him in the chest sending his limp body splashing into the bayou.

Cheese smiles at the rest of the outlaws. "Now that my friend has worked out all of his frustration, and has that little problem squared away, it leaves me thinking... Now what do we do with rest of you fellows? Oh yeah, we were talking about a nice cool bath. What do you say we do that? I want you fellows to quit all that mumbling and hand over them clothes. That's right, get'em off, underwear too. Alright now, walk out a few feet in that bayou and start scrubbing some of that funk off. Go on, get on in there."

Three of the six men help the wounded as they slowly walk out into the cold muddy water, each one complaining and still making shallow threats.

Cheese reaches over in the boat, and grabs his combat equipment satchel. "Bones, watch my back, and you guys keep your trigger finger ready. If anyone of these outlaws tries anything, cut them in half. I'll be right back."

He takes off in a hard run for the bar, first trotting by Uriel and Chado, who are now standing near the bridge. "Hey, you guys might want to get out of here. I'm fixing to send this place to hell."

Without waiting for a reply, he runs across the parking lot disappearing inside the bar. Wasting no time, he darts down inside the lab, takes the butt of his rifle, breaking a half-inch flex line that feeds the dope cookers with fuel. Cheese also shatters a few jugs of flammable liquid on his way out.

Exiting the building he glances over and sees the two bums slowly walking toward the levee, out of harm's way. Not wasting any time, he drops down on his knees at the back of the building. He pulls out a long mason bit, and connects it to a high-speed drill. Within seconds he's shoving a tube inside the drilled hole. He then takes out a saw cutting a propane line completely in two. Wasting no time, he then fastens the tube to the propane line. You can now hear the flow of gas being forced inside the building.

Cheese looks at his watch mumbling, "I guess six minutes should be enough time." He pulls out a homemade explosion device and sets the timer as he sticks it underneath a 1,000-gallon propane tank.

Replacing his tools back in the equipment satchel, Cheese Hound mumbles to himself. "Folks are gonna to see this fireball, at least a hundred miles away."

19

Bounty of Demons

Chado and his Guardian Angel, Uriel, stand near the bridge as they witness Cajun justice. The evil men from the bar room are now being held at gunpoint underneath the Belle River crossing. Uriel bumps Chado on his shoulder, "Look back at the bar. The demons are retrieving the souls of the dead."

"I see it, Uriel! Are they taking them to Hell?"

"Yes, Little Soul, they are. Watch the water, where the one they call Shafer lies. They will come for him now. Remember Chado… if they come near you do not let them know we can see into the Realm."

Out of the darkness several demons appear. They quickly swarm around the dive team and the men standing in the water. Uriel reaches over grabbing Chado's arm, "Keep your eyes focused on the men because something else is coming and it's not demons. Don't make eye contact!"

Suddenly the unmistakable sound of wings passes over Chado and Uriel. Its two very large fallen angels, both are displaying a shroud of darkness as though to flaunt it, showing authority over the demons that are busy about their work. These two angels of hell have the appearance of dark warriors, adorned with armor and swords. They both land like giant vultures on the bridge railing, overlooking the scene underneath the bridge. The fallen duo watch, as demons rips the condemned soul out of Shafer's limp body. The two demons blast out of the bayou with water running off their scaly hides. Shafer, now in the Spiritual Realm, suddenly begins screaming as he feels the sharp claws sinking deep into his shoulders. The two fallen angels laugh as Shafer struggles against their demonic grip.

Shafer cries out in agony, "No, no... please let me go! Oh, God, help me! Who are you? Why are you doing this? Oh, God, please, please help me!" Shafer continues to beg and scream as these transporters of hell disappear into the darkness, heading for the nearest portal to hell.

Uriel whispers to Chado, "Something is not right with these two fallen angels. I sense they might be suspicious of our presence."

"What do I do, it looks like they're coming in our direction."

"Chado, clear your mind and stare at the men under the bridge. Or better yet, squat down and act like you're petting Buck. Just do not look them in the eyes."

The two dark angels walk straight up to Uriel and Chado. The larger of the two slowly begins circling them, with his hand draped over his sword. The one in front sticks his face within a couple inches of Uriel's neck. He sniffs like a dog smelling a scent of another animal. Uriel stands firm without budging or changing expression. He moves directly in front of Uriel, to within an inch of his face and continues to sniff.

Uriel, still acting as if he's unconcerned and unaware of their presence, lets out a huge yawn while staring straight through the adversary. The dark angel quickly steps back, almost pulling his sword, alarmed from Uriel's sudden movement. This representative of hell, now irritated and confused, shuffles his wings in a downward motion causing dust to rise from the roadway.

The second of the two is now observing Chado and seems to be curious about the leather pouch hanging on his back. Like the other dark angel, he bends down with his nose near the precious scrolls and draws air through his nostrils. Just as this fallen angel reaches out to touch the leather pouch, suddenly and out of nowhere, two warrior angels pass directly over their heads, landing at the other end of the bridge. However they aren't from hell—they are Angels of God. Irritated by their holy presence, the two fallen lose interest in Uriel and Chado, and return to their vulture like position on the bridge railing, continuing to watch the evil men receive Cajun justice.

* * *

Cheese Hound runs back across the parking lot, sliding down the steep bank leading underneath the bridge. He uses his light attached to his AR-15, shining it into the eyes of the naked men still standing waist deep in water. He then scans across the foggy bayou spotting Shafer's body floating near the edge. "I don't guess Mr. Gold Teeth has said anything since I've been gone."

The dive team chuckles, with Bones saying, "Nope, he's been mighty quiet, Cheese. What now? Or should I say, what do we do with the rest of these guys?"

"I'm not sure. Let me ask them. Hey, scum dogs! If we let you go, y'all gonna start being respectful citizens, or will you run straight to a phone and call your crooked cop friends?"

The Russians and the Mayor's son all start pleading with Cheese, promising they won't say a word.

Cheese turns and winks at the dive team. "Okay, guys, I understand you fellows are just hired hands, and I'm feeling a strong desire to forgive and forget all that evil stuff y'all been doing to our community. So y'all run along, but you got to leave your clothes with us. Go on now. Get out of here before we change our mind."

Matt shakes his head as they watch the group of men hobble off toward the Belle Rose nightclub. "Cheese, I don't think this is a good idea letting these scumbags go. We don't want to be looking over our shoulder from now on."

"Matt, we're going to be looking over our shoulder from now on regardless. You see this jump drive and those bales of money. That syndicate and their hired law dogs are going to do everything they can to find us. We just stuck the cat's tail in the fan my friend."

"Well I still say we need to smoke those guys." Cheese laughs, "Get in the boat, Yank. Grab that roll of duct tape. We need to secure our new Russian friend."

Cheese swings the long nose of the speedboat around and points it back down the bayou toward the camp. Surprising everyone, he reaches over and kills the engine. "Hey, Bones, are they all inside yet?"

Bones stands up while looking through his sniper scope. "Yep, the last one just went through the door."

Cheese Hound pulls his sleeve back looking at his watch, "Hold your ears, boys, we are about to shake the ground."

Within a couple seconds the homemade explosion device goes off underneath the 1,000-gallon propane tank. It immediately ignites the gas filled bar room and basement causing a secondary explosion. The force of the two blasts sends out such a shockwave, it bends over nearby street signs. Everyone sitting in the boat feels the heat and force of the blast as it hits them in the chest. Bones somehow manages to brace himself and remain standing. He quickly looks through his rifle's scope, "Good night, Irene, now that's a fireball if I've ever seen one!"

Matt quickly points in the air, "Look, look, look!" It was the Russian's Lamborghini flying through the air. They all burst out laughing as it breaks through several overhead power lines finally crashing in the middle of the Highway 70 Bridge.

Bones slaps Nikolai behind the head, "You got insurance, knot head?"

The Russian hangs his head and mumbles, "You men will pay for what you have done tonight!"

TC whacks Nikolai on his shoulder with the stock of his gun, "Shut up, you piece of crap."

Matt, with a concerned look, "Hey, Bones, any sign of those two bums and that old dog?"

Bones quickly scans the area, finally he zooms his scope in on the trio.

"Roger that, they're all three sitting on top of the levee watching that hellhole burn. Wow! That was strange..."

Everyone at the same time, "What's strange, what are you talking about?"

"Now I know good and well, there is no way anyone can see us sitting neck deep in fog way off down here in this bayou…"

Joey with expression, "Probably not, so what's your point?"

Bones chuckles, "I could have sworn that harmonica player just looked dead at me and winked."

They all burst out laughing, as Cheese throttles down heading for the camp house.

Moving at a high rate of speed down Belle River, they see flashing red lights, coming from Morgan City. With the bayou paralleling Highway 70, Cheese kills the massive engines to prevent authorities from hearing their escape. They safely coast past several emergency vehicles, including dozens of cop cars, undetected. The giant sea-going speedboat is hidden under a blanket of fog. This gang of modern day outlaws witness what looks like the entire police force, and fire department, heading for the orange glow of what used to be the Bayou Rose.

Within a short few minutes, Cheese Hound hits the remote as they all watch the heavy camouflaged door, rise out of the muddy bayou. He turns the long nose of the speedboat around and backs this massive beast into its stall. Now safely back at the Cajun Bat Cave, they unload the bales of money placing them in plastic seal tight containers. Cheese smiles, as he walks over to what looks like a rock wall, beneath the stairwell. Showing off more of his hidden engineering skills, he kicks one of the stones near the bottom several times. Suddenly, sounds of gears turning and stone rubbing together, and to everyone's surprise, part of the wall opens up to another room. Still filled with adrenaline, they quickly stow away the containers filled with cash.

Cheese turns to TC and Joey, "Let's get our Russian friend out of the boat, and find out just who's involved in this syndicate they've been yapping about."

Matt, with a concerned look on his face, "Hey, Cheese Hound, does your TV work? I'd like to see if they have anything about the bar on." Cheese tosses him the remote for the big screen TV hanging on the wall.

"Yank, I got all the channels, but you might want to flip over to 31. That would be your local."

Near the boat stall door, Cheese lowers an overhead electric wench line. "Hey, Mr. Nikolai, this is for you."

With a nervous voice, "What you do with wench? I make deal. Nikolai make good deal, I tell you, no need for torture."

"Oh… calm down now, all we need is a little information. You can avoid any more violence if you just come clean."

"I come clean, you don't have to do anything, I tell you all I know."

"My new Russian buddy, let me fill you in on what's about to happen, just in case you decide to leave anything out. You see, I have an old friend by the name of Little George. He lives out there in the swamp. That rascal and I became friends about 25 years ago. You see, I had just come in off of active duty, where a few of my close buddies had gotten killed while we were defending a small village. You know, come to think of it, those villagers actually hated us and our country, but we followed orders and protected them."

The Russian butts in, "What this have to do with Nikolai?"

Cheese waves his hand as he stops the wench line just above the floor. "Hold on now, I'm getting to the point. You see after all that, I was pretty bitter, and pretty much withdrew from the world. But one day Little George came into my life.

"Nikolai, I was running hoop nets not far from here, and when I raised my last net, there was a baby gator trapped and almost dead. My first impulse was to crack his head on the side of the boat, but something came over me. For the first time since my buddies got slaughtered, I felt like giving mercy. So I decided to bring Little George home and nurse him back to health. Now wasn't that a nice story?"

"Yes, yes... good story. Does he still live? Where is Little George now? "

Cheese reaches over sliding a dive harness over Nikolai that's already attached to the wench line.

"What are you doing? I said, I tell you everything!"

Cheese activates the remote wench and they all watch as Nikolai swings out over the water.

"Well I guess, I should answer your questions in order. Little George is alive and well, and he lives in this boathouse. Actually, you're hanging right over the very spot where I feed him. But here's the kicker. I always wanted to see just how big a Louisiana gator could get, if they didn't slow down in the winter and could have a nice warm area with plenty food. I believe Little George finally topped out and is now a full-grown gator. He's just an inch or two under 20 feet in length. Mr. Drug Man, I don't think he's getting any longer, but he makes up for that in weight. He's well over 1,200 pounds. Saying all that, I haven't had time to feed him over the past couple weeks, and I would imagine he's a bit hungry. So I'm thinking it's time to share a little information about your gang."

Hanging from the cable, suspended over the water, Nikolai resembles a floating parade balloon. He slowly spins, as he stares down at the water with fear in his eyes. "Okay, I give you everyone's names. I don't like any of those guys. I tell you all I know."

Cheese turns to Joey, "Take your phone and record this. Okay, Nikolai, let's hear it."

"I start with top and work my way down. The headman in Morgan City is Mayor Dalton, and then you got the District Attorney, Phillips. Next one is City Police Chief Lewis. That's it my friend."

Cheese bangs on a piece of metal, signaling Little George that it's feeding time. "That can't be all, if the mayor, DA and the police chief are involved in all this, they have to have a ground crew doing the dirty work."

Suddenly thousands of tiny bubbles come up underneath the dangling legs of Nikolai. "What makes the bubbles, is this alligator?"

Before Cheese could answer, Little George barely pokes his huge head out of the water, with only his eyes and the tip of his nose exposed.

Nikolai spots George and quickly picks his legs up as high as he can, quickly continuing his confession. "Yes, yes… they have lots of dirty cops working for them. They have parish and city cops on my payroll. We pay them lots of money to run business."

Matt reaches over jiggling the cable that holds Nikolai above the water, "We need names!"

"I don't know all, just two more. They are detectives Fletcher and Komo. I don't like either one. They make me give them much more than the original deal we make. Okay, get me away from Little George. I don't like the way he looks at me."

Cheese smiles at the crew, as he gives them a devious wink. "Okay, Nikolai, you done pretty good. I guess we can get you out of that harness. Help me out here fellows."

The crew pulls the Russian over the dock, lowers the wench line, and takes off the dive harness. Nikolai starts smiling, relieved he's no longer in danger of being eaten. "I knew we could work things out. We make lots of money and you can have all the Cajun women you want."

At the very second of his last comment, it struck a nerve with Matt and Cheese. Without hesitation, they both use a front thrust kick to his chest, sending a surprised Russian through the air landing directly in front of Little George.

The rest of the dive team quickly step up to the edge, as they all silently watch Little George have his first Russian meal.

20

Snakehead

Just a little less than 6,000 miles away Lieutenant Christy Moody, along with five other A-10 pilots await take off orders. Their location is a temporary runway codename, Panther Claw. This hidden location is twelve miles inside the country of Turkey, near the Syrian border. Their mission is to assist and protect US ground troops. These army rangers, along with air support are to push back and destroy ISIS fighters that have been attacking citizens of the border town Kilis, Turkey.

As Christy stares down the dirt runway, a sense of fear comes over her as she remembers Ms. Lily's visions. At the thought of being shot down mixed with anxiety of her first real combat mission, Christy suddenly feels an overwhelming need to pop the canopy and run away. She takes her fingertips off the controls and stares at her hands. They are shaking uncontrollably, "What's wrong with me?" She quickly pulls her gloves off, clapping them together, then shaking each in an attempt to overcome the jitters. "Oh, Lord, help me overcome this anxiety attack. God, this isn't like me. I've never had the shakes like this." Lifting the shield of her flight helmet, she leans back taking a long deep breath as she wipes her sweaty palms against her legs. "Okay, I have to think of something else, anything but Ms. Lily and getting shot down, now let me see..."

Suddenly a sense of peace surrounds her heart creating a subtle smile on Christy's face. Sweet memories of the night before stream through her mind like flowing water. This instant replay seeing the face of Jesus, and feeling his garment touch her face sends the Holy Spirit flooding over her body. As she remembers wrapping her arms around the Savior of the world, Christy realizes the shakes and anxiety are completely gone. "Oh, Lord, I haven't thanked you for allowing me to see you in person last night! Also, thank you for removing my fear through these comforting memories. I love you, Lord."

Sudden chatter over the radio, "KTK6686, we are ready in three minutes. Do you copy, FG707?"

"We copy KTK, ready in three."

Without realizing, Christy breaks out laughing over an open mike remembering the sweet sandy kisses from her new beau. *I can't believe my handsome army ranger, Brim, stole a few kisses from underneath his poncho.*

Major Hyde with a rough voice, "Who the heck thinks that's funny?"

After a few seconds of silence, Christy confesses. "That was me, sir."

"Poleshot, are you okay back there?"

"I'm fine, sir. I just had a funny thought about last night, sorry, sir."

"Roger that. You guys get your head in the game. No time for reminiscing."

"KTK to FG707, you are clear for take-off?"

"Roger, KTK. We are green light. I say again we are green light."

Six A-10 Thunderbolts take off heading toward a mountain range southwest of Aleppo, Syria.

"Panther Claw to 707, come in Major."

"Go ahead PC."

"Major, we just got word from HQ. You need to split your fighter team into three groups."

"I read you, Panther Claw, three two man groups."

"Roger that, Major. Send two, east toward Euphrates River, sending new coordinates now. Ground team needs assist."

"Roger, PC, we are receiving new coordinates."

The major looks through his canopy over at Christy and sees her give a thumbs up. He shakes his head no. "Come in Bailey."

"Go ahead, Major."

"Bailey, did you receive new coordinates for ground assist?"

"Yes, sir, I have it."

"Take Leadfoot with you."

"Roger that, sir, we are on our way." Bailey and Leadfoot peel out of formation heading northeast to the Euphrates River basin.

"Panther Claw, we are ready to receive second location."

"Roger, Major, sending coördinates now."

"Thank you, Panther Claw, we have it; I repeat we have new location."

"Major, HQ had three F-18's tear a few holes in the Aleppo Air Base earlier this morning. They want to send in the A-10s to do a little more cleaning."

"Roger that, Panther Claw. Stand by; Applegate, you and Jaywalker take care of it."

"We won't let you down, sir."

"Don't worry about letting me down, just watch your backs."

Flying just off the major's wing tip, Christy gives out a hand signal letting the major know she wanted to go on either of those missions. He waves back and signals, *go to private channel.*

Christy reaches down twisting the dial of her com system.

"Hey, Major, are you there?"

"Poleshot, before you even ask… I told you guys back at the base that you were now my wingman. You know Lieutenant Bailey doesn't trust you after what happened back at the base. Heck, after what I shared about my Indian friend, Teeto and the whole Mountain of God thing, he probably doesn't trust me either."

"No, sir, I guess not."

"I know you're anxious to get in the fight, but our orders are to recon a mountain range southwest of our location. No more, no less."

"Hey, Major, you being a believer, what's your take on us fighting right here in the same area, John wrote about in the Bible, in reference to the end times stuff? You know, every time I hear someone talk about the River Euphrates, I think about the Book of Revelation."

The major chuckles, "No doubt, it is kind of strange being anywhere near where the final battle of Armageddon will be fought. Oh yeah, and not to mention all this crazy stuff we've got going on with the old lady's dreams. What was her name?"

"It's Ms. Lily, sir, the town folk at home call her, 'The Lily of the Valley'. Jed, my brother, calls her a prophetess. All I know is that mom told me, I need to take her dreams and visions very serious."

"Well, there you go. Between her and the encounter I had on my hunting trip with the Indian Guide, Teeto, we could very well be out here mixed up in the final battle stuff. Saying all that, God might just have some other plan going on."

"Hey, Major, look down there, is that our guys?"

"Yes, that's the 1st Ranger Battalion. I saw them move out at 3:00 am this morning. The mountain range we're doing surveillance on is where they're headed."

"Roger that. I pray God's protection over those soldiers down there and that everyone will return home safe."

"Amen, sister, Amen."

Christy and the major dip their wings a couple times as they fly over the convoy as a friendly hello.

"Hey, Christy, have you seen any visions of Ms. Lily since we all met in the mess hall?"

"No, sir, but I did see Jesus on the runway last night."

"Do what…? You're pulling my leg!"

"No, sir. I wouldn't dare say anything like that about our Savior, if it wasn't true."

"You mind telling me about it?"

"Not at all, I was sitting out on the runway last night watching a road grader level it out, and he just walked up. At first I was scared to death, and then I saw his face. Major, it was unbelievable. I immediately fell to my knees, and began crying tears of joy. Oh yeah! I hugged his legs and dripped tears all over his feet."

The major starts laughing, "Did he say anything?"

Christy snickered like a young child, "He just said our names are the same, except my name has a Y in it."

"That's so strange. So that was all he said to you?"

"Yes, sir, that's it. That's all he said."

"Well, Poleshot, back to what we were talking about earlier, and taking everything that's happened to both of us as fact, we might just be about to go into the final days."

"Hey, Major, is this the mountain range our army rangers are headed for?"

"Roger that, kiddo, we need to keep a sharp eye out. Scouts reported a few weeks back these hills are contaminated with those cockroaches."

"Yes, sir."

"Poleshot, switch back to open channel."

"Roger that, switching back to open channel."

The major and Christy approach the foothills of a long mountain range that parallels the coast line of the Mediterranean Sea. From north to south this mountainous region spreads from Turkey down in the heart of Syria. They are traveling at Mach 0.72, just under 450 miles per hour, and have to adjust altitude due elevation change of terrain. They level out at 1,800 feet above the surface.

Christy remembers her training as she continually glances back and forth. First down at her instrument panel then back through the canopy. She carefully searches the rough terrain for the enemy, but without any signs of life, or the absence thereof, it almost makes her feel cheated. She knows the other four pilots are probably blowing up tanks and she's looking for ghosts.

Suddenly they hear signs of life over the radio. "Snakehead to A-10s, do you read me?"

The major answers, "We read you, Snakehead. What's your location?"

"We see you coming straight for us. If you adjust three degrees southeast you will fly directly over us."

"Roger that, Snakehead, adjusting."

"You are over us in 4, 3, 2, 1 mark."

"Snakehead, my call sign is Major Hyde, and we have your location son. What is your status?"

"We are good, Major."

"Roger that, Snakehead. I wasn't informed we had friendlies in this area. Over…"

"Yes, sir, we've been crawling around up here for the last six days… glad to see something with the USA stamped on it."

The major and Christy laugh as they circle this sniper team's area.

"Snakehead, have you seen any movement in your grid? Our intel is three weeks old; do we have targets in this area?"

"Well, up to a few days ago there wasn't anyone out here but us chickens. The last three days, we've seen beaucoup movement, especially to our northwest. You birds might want to stay frosty."

"Roger that. Hang tight, fellows, you got a convoy of rangers bearing down on your location. They should be here by nightfall if they don't run into anything heavy."

"Major, is this your turnaround point?"

"Negative. Poleshot and I are doing a little reconnaissance mission. We are heading a little farther southwest from your position."

"Roger that. Hey, Major, pay attention to the narrow canyons. We've seen several combatants armed with RPGs a few clicks south. They are hard to spot as they hide in the clefts of those rocks. So you and Poleshot tread lightly."

"Copy that. We are southbound. Keep your heads down, Snakehead, A-10s clear."

"Thanks, Major. Snakehead is clear."

21

Ambush Canyon and The Lion's Den

Several miles north, the 1st Ranger Battalion consisting of 450 soldiers approach a narrow canyon of the Shesla Mountains. Two helicopter gunships fly ahead of the convoy giving the rangers a green light to pass through the canyon.

After the last soldiers enter the seven-mile long canyon and make their way a few hundred yards past the narrow entrance, they have no idea they are standing in the mouth of the beast. The well-hidden ISIS fighters have set explosives overhead and along the floor of the canyon, even going to the extreme of drilling holes deep into the cliff walls, then lowering dynamite down inside each one. This technique is used in a way to shear off the entire walls of the overhead cliffs, crushing everything below. The ISIS fighters have spent months preparing for this battle.

The two attack helicopters buzz back over letting the 1st Battalion know everything within the next few miles looks clear, and are heading back for fuel.

ISIS commanders watching from a distance, patiently wait before giving orders for attack. They are in fear of the deadly firepower of US helicopter gunships, so they delay this slaughter until the choppers are completely out of sight.

Using hand held electronic devices, the enemy triggers a sequence of explosions. Having carefully marked certain locations on the canyon floor, their timing is perfect. The first four explosions shear off sections of the rock cliffs, taking out three Bradley armored vehicles along with two M1A2 tanks. The mighty force of the heavy rock walls crushes everything in its path. Within seconds, several more explosions behind the American soldiers completely block the exit back out of the canyon. The 1st Battalion is now trapped in a maze of boulders, with no way out and no air support.

Second Lieutenant Gordon, shielded between two large boulders, survives the blast. Now stunned and choking on smoke and rock dust from the explosions, he pulls his face scarf up over his nose then slides on his goggles. With the heavy dust trapped in the narrow canyon, visibility is only a couple feet. Still disoriented from the concussion of the blasts, Gordon struggles just to stand upright. The ringing in his ears is so intense it affects his equilibrium in such a way it causes him to fall back to his knees. This brave soldier knows if they don't receive help soon, the ISIS fighters will swarm in to finish off the entire Battalion.

With all the strength he can muster, he begins crawling in search of a radio. After only a few feet his clothes and hands feel wet. He reaches up wiping the heavy dust from his goggles and suddenly realizes his hands and chest are covered in blood. Lieutenant Gordon had just crawled over several dead soldiers. Overcome with sorrow and despair he lays his face against the rocky ground as to give up. Suddenly, to his surprise the ability to hear returns as the high pitch ringing is being replaced with voices of other survivors. Looking up, Gordon discovers the heavy cloud of dust is now clearing. He can see an overturned Humvee that is only a few feet away. After a short crawl, he grabs a radio mike. "Mayday, mayday, does anyone copy? Mayday…!"

"We hear you, mayday, this is Snakehead, come back."

"Snakehead, we just got hit. I repeat we just got hit. We need medevac and air support."

"You are breaking up, repeat, low signal, please repeat."

"This is Lieutenant Gordon of the 1st Ranger Battalion. We just got wiped out. Send everything. Broken-arrow, I repeat, broken-arrow!"

"Roger, Lieutenant, we will relay, Snakehead clear."

The spotter of this forward operations sniper team uses their satellite phone to call headquarters, while his marksman uses the radio to contact the two A-10s for close air-support.

"Snakehead to Major Hyde, come back."

"Go ahead, Snakehead, we read you."

"1st Ranger Battalion needs assist. Broken-arrow, I repeat, broken-arrow! It sounds like they are getting hit hard, sir."

"Roger that, send me a fix for TIC assist."

"No need for that Major. Just look northeast of my location. You can see the dust cloud. They are definitely in a hot zone, sir. We heard several large explosions and can now see the smoke."

"We see it Snakehead. I repeat we can see smoke."

"Major, we could barely make out what they were saying. Their radio was breaking up pretty bad. When you get a little closer you might establish contact."

"Will do, Snakehead, we are clear."

The major and Christy push their A-10s to max speed as they race toward the ambushed 1st Battalion.

"Christy, remember your training. It won't let you down."

"I'm good, Major."

As they race toward the rising dust and smoke cloud only a few miles away, Christy glances over to the northwest and is suddenly startled. Staring through the tented canopy of her jet, she focuses in on a rock formation resembling a cross. With chills flooding over her entire body, Christy tries to talk over the com system, but can't seem to say anything. Flying just off the major's wing, she throttles a few feet ahead, bobbles her wings then slows back down. The major looks over at her with curiosity.

"What are you doing, Poleshot?"

She points down at the rock formation and finally is able to blurt out a few words, "Look… Major, it's a cross. Just like Ms. Lily described. Oh my goodness, this is really happening!"

"Calm down, Christy, I see it, but it could just be the angle we're flying that makes it look like a cross."

"No, Major. Unmistakably, that rock formation looks like a giant cross. Just like her dream."

"Okay, I tell you how we're going to handle this. You hang back and I'll go in and see what we have on our plate. You copy?"

"Yes, sir. I copy."

Major Hyde passes over the deep canyon and has a clear view of the destruction below. At least 75% of the 1st Battalion is wiped out from the fallen rock walls and secondary explosions. ISIS fighters were scattered on top of the cliffs, armed with RPGs and small arms. Further south, inside the canyon, more combatants are advancing on the Battalion's location armed with heavy guns and artillery.

As the major attempts a flyby to pinpoint US soldier's position, several ISIS fighters imbedded in the rock walls take pot shots with RPGs narrowly missing his A-10.

With the heavy dust and smoke he can barely distinguish exactly where the rangers are located. Now with a fairly decent fix on 1st Battalion, the major realizes this is too much to handle for one jet.

"Come in, Poleshot!"

"Go ahead, Major."

"I know I told you to hang back, but our boys are dying down there. They need help. So follow me back in. Let's see if we can take out that convoy south of our boys. On our way in, let's light the edge of that cliff up on the southeast side. Guns only, no heavy stuff, we don't want to lose any more of our soldiers today."

"Roger that, 30 mm GAU on the southeast wall."

"Poleshot, we've got to fly down inside this canyon to see the enemy and they are behind every crack with RPGs, so go in hot."

As the major takes the lead, midway through their first attack his plane is struck several times with heavy machine guns damaging his left engine. He pulls out of the canyon still getting peppered with small arms fire.

Christy makes a clean run taking out three light duty pick-up trucks and one flat track armored vehicle. With her accuracy it causes the rest of their convoy to stop and seek shelter near the walls of the canyon. As she goes into a climb above the canyon walls preparing for another pass she realizes the major has been hit. His A-10 is moving very slowly with smoke pouring out of the left engine.

"I'm done, Poleshot, heavy stick, sluggish controls, and my left engine is shot to pieces. I think it's best if we head for base."

Christy quickly flies up alongside and does a visual inspection, "Major, you're shot up pretty bad, but I believe the ole girl will get you home."

"Roger that. So let's get the heck out of here!"

The major looking through his canopy sees Christy shake her head no, as she says, "I'll be staying, Major. I can't leave these guys. Besides that, Ms. Lily described my plane with smoke coming from the engines. I believe she might have been mistaken and saw your plane in her vision instead."

"Poleshot, as your commanding officer, I would normally order you to follow me in, but I believe, I would be getting in the way of whatever God is up to. I still say you should wait for backup before you make another run like we just made."

Christy bravely replies, "Negative, sir, I'm going to try to save as many lives as I can."

Christy banks her jet away from Major Hyde and heads back toward the canyon. Without warning she has a vision of Ms. Lily. As plain as day Ms. Lily is standing in the forks of a dirt road holding a baby lamb in her arms. *Oh, child, we are waiting on you.*

"Good Lord, Ms. Lily, this isn't the best of times for you to be in my head!" *Remember, Christy, fear not for the Lord Thy God is with you.*

A strange silence overtakes the cock-pit, as Christy zones in on her chosen entry point to the canyon. Even the sounds of her jet engines become a quiet purr in her mind, as she intensely focuses on the attack. Without hesitation, she dives over the edge of the cliff like a mighty eagle, releasing the power of her A-10s arsenal. She sprays the cliff walls with the 30 mm cannon fire, mowing down target after target. The US soldiers hidden in the rubble below stand up and cheer, as they watch Christy lay down fury upon this horrible enemy.

After several attacks the A-10 is now taking heavy damage as she flies through the narrow pass. She hears multiple rounds hitting the fuselage. Christy suddenly laughs out loud in a crazy sort of way, then, begins talking to Ms. Lily, "Now don't those bullets hitting my plane remind you of popcorn popping in a microwave? Where you at, Lily? Are you still with me?"

Knowing she is short on precious fuel, she unloads the rest of her payload saturating the entire area of the enemy convoy.

"Okay, you suckers, get some, here you go, see how you like a few sidewinders. Oh, that ain't all… Chew on this 500 pounder, you jug-headed monsters."

As Christy pulls up into a hard climb, she banks to the left looking over her shoulder. She witnesses almost total devastation of the enemy convoy.

She decides to make one last pass over the 1st Battalion's area, possibly taking a few photos for HQ. She dives over the cliff wall slowing her A-10 down flying only a couple hundred feet above the surface. Christy, having never seen this kind of carnage up close, immediately feels sick inside. She wonders if her new boyfriend, Brim, could be one of those poor soldiers.

As she nears the end of the canyon she hears and feels the impact from three separate explosions. The ISIS fighters hidden in the rocks manage to hit her plane with multiple RPGs.

The A-10 electronics and hydraulics are both failing. Christy pulls back as hard as she can, barely clearing the top of the canyon walls. Almost completely out of control, the A-10 slowly drifts back to the southeast, as though it is flying itself. She looks back over her shoulders and sees the black smoke coming from both engines.

"So, Ms. Lily, it looks like your visions are on the mark."

Christy's jet continues to lose power, and is flying only a few feet above the jagged mountaintops, she has to make a quick decision—eject or crash land. Knowing she is entirely too low for a parachute, the only other option is to find a smooth grassy area for a crash landing.

Fear like never before washes over her as she has to face facts. "I'm about to crash in the middle of enemy territory; Oh Lord God, help me survive this. Please, dear Lord, save me from dying out here all alone."

Suddenly Christy remembers when she was back at the base and met Jesus on the runway, and how when she looked into his eyes, she fell at his feet.

Out of nowhere, she hears a soft still voice.

"Sweet child, you are not alone."

"Lord, is that really you?"

"Behold."

Christy, overwhelmed with the Holy Spirit and blinded with tears, reaches through her open shield clearing her watery eyes, and the first thing she sees in front of her is the giant rock formation Ms. Lily called 'The Shadow of the Cross'.

"Well, Lord, I guess you've got me!"

22

Burn It Down

Back in Louisiana, Chado Cole, his dog Buck. and Uriel, sit on top of the Belle River levee at the Highway 70 crossing. They watch the Fire Marshal along with several detectives as they sift through what used to be known as the Bayou Rose. This once thriving bar and drug lab is now no more than a smoldering pile of splintered lumber.

The modern day vigilantes responsible for this destruction are undetected and safely hidden just a few miles away.

Several ambulances back into position as the EMTs along with the coroner move in with stretchers and body bags. One after the other, they roll body after body to their vehicles.

The local news team arrives and starts following the EMTs in an attempt to get a shot of the scorched bodies. They eventually work their way around until they get close enough to ask the Parish Sheriff for a report. "Sheriff Bradford, Sheriff Bradford, do you mind answering a few questions, sir?"

"No, I cannot answer any questions. However, I will give you a very short statement. As of right now, you know about as much as we do. We're waiting on the Fire Marshall to give us his findings on what caused the explosions."

The news journalist butts in. "You said explosions, was it one or two?"

The Sheriff, staring across the crime scene, says, "Our 911 dispatch reported that several locals called in and stated it was two very loud explosions. So, I guess we can safely say there were at least two."

"How many were killed, Sheriff?"

"We don't know at this time."

"Was there foul play?"

"Ma'am, I told you I wouldn't answer any questions about this case. We need our facts."

"Yes sir, we understand."

"I tell you what, since me and your daddy used to go frog hunting together back when we were kids, I'll give you what us Cajuns call lagniappe—just a little extra. The Coroner just told me that he believes some of those men died from gunshots. From their charred bodies it is hard to tell here in the field. At this point we believe there could be foul play."

"Sheriff, could you tell if there were any women that may have died in the explosion? I knew a few of the girls working here.

"No, Ma'am, we don't think so. That's all I can tell you this morning. We'll give an update later this afternoon. You folks need to get back and let our detectives do their work. Tell your folks Sheriff Bradford sends his love."

"Thank you, Sheriff."

* * *

The heavenly trio stands on top of the levee, watching from a distance.

"Hey, Uriel, you think the Sheriff is mixed up with those crooked detectives?"

"No, Chado, he actually just got elected. He is a just man who loves the Lord. Your friends that destroyed this place may have saved that Sheriff's life."

"How's that, Uriel?"

"Chado, do you see those two detectives sifting through the rubble?"

"Yes, they are the same ones that visited with the Russian last night."

"Yes, and those same two have been ordered to kill Sheriff Bradford. They tried first to bribe him, and he turned away from their wicked offer. So now he is on their hit list."

"Who ordered the hit, Uriel?"

"The ones giving the order are the Mayor of Morgan City, the City Police Chief, and District Attorney Phillips."

Chado shakes his head, saying, "That reminds me of a scripture."

"Please tell me, Little Soul."

"Okay, here goes: Genesis 50:20, *You intended to harm me, but God intended it for good, to accomplish what is now being done, the saving of many lives.*"

"I like it, Chado, it is fitting for this entire event. Speaking of events, we need to go."

"I'm ready. Where to, Uriel?"

"Hold onto my hand, Chado. I've got Buck."

"Okay Uriel, you mind giving me a hint where?"

"It is a mountain range near the Mediterranean Sea."

"Isn't that in the country of Syria?"

"Correct. Are you ready, Chado?"

"Let's do it."

As the morning sun is peaking over the cypress trees, Sheriff Bradford notices two men and a large dog sitting on the levy. "Hey, Chigger, who are those people on the levy up there?"

Deputy Chigger raises his hand shading the glare of the rising sun. "I don't know Sheriff. I'll go check."

Just as the deputy takes a few steps in their direction, the Sheriff and the deputy are blinded by a flash of light. The young deputy stops in his tracks. "Hey, where did they go? They couldn't have just vanished!"

The Sheriff looks over at his surprised deputy and starts laughing. "Now that was strange, I'm telling you right now, as sure as God made little green apples that was strange. You run on up there and see if maybe they played a trick on our eyes."

23

Jagged Rocks and Canyons

Chado, Uriel, and Buck appear just a few feet outside an abandoned shack sitting on a small plateau overlooking the Shesla Mountains.

Chado staring over the jagged mountain terrain mumbles, “So this is Syria.”

“Yes, Chado, we are standing in northwest Syria.”

“Well if you ask me, it’s not much to look at. Our mountains back home are way prettier than this.”

Uriel smiles, “Is the home you speak of Louisiana or Heaven?”

Chado laughs, “Hey that’s right, I have a new address.”

Suddenly the sound of jet engines popping and sputtering are echoing across the mountainous terrain and it gets louder and louder.

“What the heck is that, Uriel?”

The angel points, “Look behind you, Chado, we are right on time.”

Chado’s mouth flies open as he watches an A-10 Thunderbolt heading in their direction. The jet engines are struggling to keep the plane just a few feet off the ground.

“Goodness gracious, Uriel, who is that?”

“My friend… behold, that is our mission.”

"Our mission, what are we supposed to do? Rescue the pilot?"

"No, Chado, we are to only observe. Fear not. She has a guardian angel, who is protecting her."

"The pilot is a girl?"

"Yes. Her name is Christy Moody. She is one of the chosen instruments of God."

"What do you mean a chosen instrument?"

Uriel doesn't answer Chado as the deafening sound of the war torn plane passes directly over their heads. Tons of black smoke, belch out of both engines as it flies only a couple feet above the jagged rocks.

* * *

Christy is doing everything she can to keep the A-10 in the air. "Oh, God, please let me find a smooth piece of ground to set this plane down on."

Knowing if she ejects this low to the ground, her odds of survival are slim to none. She stares through the canopy and can't see anything ahead that resembles something to land on, when she hears the word, *Canyon*.

"Was that you, Ms. Lily? Did you just say canyon?"

To her surprise, a few hundred yards ahead she sees what looks like a narrow ravine.

"Will this work? Is it deep enough that I might survive? It has to be, this is my only chance."

Just as the bullet riddled A-10 approaches the edge, she hears the voice again. "Get out, Christy, get out now!"

Christy reaches down with both hands activating the ejection system. Within a split second, she flies through the air like a rocket directly over the narrow canyon. Just before experiencing blackout from the G-forces caused by the ejection system, she catches a glimpse of her plane crashing into the cliff wall only a few hundred feet away. She feels the heat from the giant fireball as she passes out completely.

With the extreme depth of the canyon her parachute system has time to activate properly. Christy is now drifting out of control, at the mercy of the mountain winds. As the heavy ejection seat sways back and forth like an old swing hanging from a tree, she narrowly misses the cliff walls.

Christy regains consciousness and screams out loud when she almost collides with the jagged rocks on the east side of the canyon. The odd wind suddenly changes direction just before slamming her into a rock ledge. Still disoriented and confused, she quickly looks from side to side. The steep cliff walls remind her of the Grand Canyon as she seems to be caught in some kind of wind tunnel. The strong winds are not allowing her to get any closer to the surface. Instead, this strange wind is dragging her at a high rate of speed farther down the canyon. She notices in a short distance what looks like an opening. Yes, it is the exit out of the canyon. The hard wind is now calming, gently allowing Christy to finally land.

Now in fear of the enemy discovering her location, Christy quickly hides her chute, and rolls the heavy ejection seat over between two boulders. Following her survival training she takes the small satchel from the seat and straps it over her shoulder. After tossing her flight helmet behind the shaded rocks, she looks back down the canyon at the black smoke coming from the crashed plane for a brief few more seconds. "Okay, Lord, you saved me from sure death. Please help me make it back to base."

She wheels around and in a fast pace, heads for the mouth of the canyon. Only after taking a few steps, Christy comes to an abrupt stop. Frozen in her tracks not believing her own eyes, she is standing at the base of a giant rock cross. It's the rock formation that Ms. Lily had told her about in her crazy vision. Now she stands in the shadow of the cross.

"Oh, Lord God, is this really happening?"

Suddenly feeling defeated, Christy drops down on her knees in the soft sand of the canyon floor. "Ms. Lily, I wish you had never told me about any of this. At least I would have hope of getting out of here."

With her face and palms down in the sand she drags her fingertips through the dirt, "This can't be real, Lord. I'm getting out of here right now!"

Just as she gets near the canyon entrance she hears sounds of vehicles heading in her direction. Christy runs over quickly diving behind a small pile of rocks just in the nick of time. Not being very well hidden, she lies perfectly still and watches as they pass.

She's lying so close to the enemy as they drive by, she hears their laughter and cheering. It sounds like they're celebrating victory over the 1st Battalion and shooting down an A-10.

While the combatants all focus on the smoke coming from the crashed plane, no one notices a female pilot lying within a few feet of their path.

Being undetected, as soon as the last vehicle disappears around the bend, Christy makes her move. She heads northeast, hopefully away from hostile territory. As she jogs along she remembers what Major Hyde mentioned back at base. *Get as far away from the crash as possible, and make sure you have your precision lightweight GPS receiver activated. We will find you.*

* * *

Uriel and Chado find clothes that someone had left behind at the abandoned shack. They can now blend in as common shepherds. Shaking the dust away from their facial scarfs, they quickly make their way along the cliff walls observing Christy from above. At their vantage point they can still see the ISIS fighters sifting through the wreckage of the downed aircraft looking for the charred remains of a pilot.

It doesn't take the ISIS combatants long to figure out the pilot has escaped the crash, and still has to be in the area. As they huddle around their vehicles, the leader sends half of his men farther up the canyon and the other half back out toward Christy. Swarms of demons hovering over these evil men split off following each group in hopes to be involved in another slaughter.

Suddenly out of nowhere, the sound of wings comes from behind Chado and Buck. As the canyon winds clear away the dust stirred from his mighty wings, Uriel quickly reaches up grabbing Chado's shoulder, "Fear not, Chado, I want you to meet Haniel. He is assigned to Christy."

Without saying anything, Chado slowly holds his hand out in a gesture of friendship. The warrior angel looks over at Uriel with a stern look on his face. He hesitates for a few seconds before submitting, and allowing a touch from this immortal.

Chado, now feeling very awkward and out of place, almost pulls his hand away, but then he notices, the huge angel gives in to a subtle and kind smile.

You can hear the sound of Haniel's armor rubbing together as he reaches out with his large hands, grasping Chado's. "So you are the one they call, Little Soul?"

"Yes, sir, but you can call me by my earthly name, Chado Cole, if you like."

"I believe I will stick to Little Soul. It is what the Great I Am calls you."

"That's fine with me, Haniel," Chado stuttering, "It's… is a pleasure to meet you, sir."

Haniel steps over to Uriel holding his arm up as they bump the back of their wrist together, "Unto God, my brother."

Uriel replies, "Unto God!"

Haniel dives off the cliff wall heading in Christy's direction.

"Wow, Uriel, that was intense."

Uriel holds his hands up, "Before you ask. Yes, we are all of the same brotherhood. It is the Brotherhood of Warrior Angels, and yes, we are of the same status in Heaven. We all serve God in the same capacity."

"Uriel, I still can't get over being able to witness everything that's going on. I mean seeing into the Spiritual Realm. My goodness, I just shook hands with another guardian and witnessed that pack of demons swirling around those ISIS fighters."

"Little Soul, you have not seen anything yet, just wait."

* * *

Christy trots along a narrow goat trail already feeling exhausted and thirsty. She looks back over her shoulder to make sure there is no sign of the enemy. Remembering her survival training she peels off the rocky path and seeks shelter.

She knows priority at this time is to hydrate and get a fix on her location. She ducks behind a cluster of dried brush. As she leans back against the trunk of the bush, she lets out a small giggle. This crooked dead bush reminds her of a west Texas deer hunt she went on with her dad the year before he got killed. As they sat waiting for a deer to come out, her dad told her all about the mesquite bushes.

Her countenance suddenly changes from a giggle to tears running down her dusty cheeks. "Oh, Dad, I wish you were here with me, or better yet, I wish we were sitting underneath that stupid mesquite bush over in Texas."

She reaches up wiping away the tears then takes a few more sips of water. As she replaces the water container back in her satchel she feels around for her hand held GPS.

Suddenly she feels her blood pressure spike as it causes her scalp to tingle. Her heart sinks in fear. Quickly turning the bag inside out, dumping everything on the ground, “My GPS, where is my GPS? Oh no!!” Thinking back to where she could have possibly dropped it. *There is no way anything could have dropped out of a sealed bag. It had to have been taken out on purpose. But who would do something like that? The only one coming close to this act of evil would be Lieutenant Bailey. He hates my guts. Surely, he wouldn’t stoop that low! Well, I guess it could have been one of the locals back at the base…*

Christy looks at her compass, gets a bearing in the general direction of the base and takes off walking. Within a short distance she sees several rescue choppers heading for 1st Battalion’s position, due west of her location. She knows if she tries to signal with a flare from this distance, the only ones who will see it are the ISIS fighters that are searching for their trophy pilot.

With the sun almost setting and the cool evening air hitting her in the face, Christy decides to seek shelter for the night. After a few hundred yards, she spots an old dilapidated building near a dirt crossroad.

Christy carefully lies out in the bushes for over an hour watching the building to make sure there is no sign of the enemy. After convincing herself that it looks safe enough, she slips in through a side door. She digs two old mattresses from out of the debris. Placing one up against a wall behind a pile of trash, and the other on top, where it doesn’t look suspicious. Underneath it creates a small space just large enough for her to fit.

As she crawls in between the smelly mattresses, Christy can’t help but giggle as she has a silly thought. *I just made a mattress sandwich. I hope I don’t get eaten by an evil giant.*

Before falling asleep the sounds of bombs exploding in the distance along with an occasional fighter jet flying past, somehow makes Christy feel a bit safer. "Oh, Lord God, I pray they got all the wounded out of that dreadful canyon, and I pray for Brim's safety too. Lord, I really like him." Overwhelmed from total exhaustion within seconds of her prayer she falls asleep.

24

Shepherds and Angels

Within 20 miles of Christy's location, the 1st Battalion with the help of air support has driven ISIS fighters back into the mountains. Rescue choppers, along with troop choppers, airlift all the wounded along with the fallen soldiers back to a Combat Support Hospital at Akinci Airbase.

Word quickly spreads through the base, how a crazy girl A-10 pilot flew through the canyon time after time attacking the enemy, until finally getting shot down behind enemy lines. They are saying if it hadn't been for her brave efforts, the entire 1st Battalion would have been totally wiped out.

A large group of army rangers gather outside the situation room trying to find out any information on the downed pilot.

The colonel's private aide says, "Okay, okay, you guys make a hole. Let Colonel Walker through!"

The colonel holds his hand up, "Hang on, Private. Let's see what this ruckus is all about. Okay, Rangers, tell me what's going on."

The men all go silent, looking around for someone to speak up and plead their case.

The colonel getting impatient, "Let's go, I don't have all night."

Captain Brim steps forward, "Can I speak freely, sir?"

"Go ahead, Captain, let's hear it."

"Well, sir, we got our butts handed to us today and there was a pilot who got shot down behind enemy lines. We want to be the ones who go back in to get her. Her name is Lieutenant Christy Moody; the other pilots call her Poleshot."

"I'm aware of Lieutenant Moody's situation, and we have Search & Rescue already trying to find her. You men need to stand down and get some rest."

"I don't believe you understand, sir. If it hadn't been for her we wouldn't be standing here."

"The rescue team will find her; y'all need to stand down."

Colonel Walker turns away as if to reject the ranger's request. Just as he is about to enter the building, Captain Brim quickly trots up behind the Colonel, lightly grabbing his shoulder. "Please, sir, Military Police told us a private found Lt. Moody's GPS in a trash-can near the runway."

Captain Brim humbly pulls his hand away from the Colonel's shoulder. The Colonel's face turns blood red as he takes off his hat rubbing the other hand across his flattop haircut.

"Well, Captain, my first question is how do you know it was her GPS? My second question, if it is hers, what in the heck was it doing in a trash can?"

"Sir, the Military Police (MP) has already run the serial numbers, and it is definitely attached to her A-10. The why, we just don't know, sir. We believe someone might have taken it out of her plane, and it could possibly be foul play."

"Captain, you don't think this pilot just dumped her GPS, and went on some kind of a crazy suicide mission, not wanting to be found?"

"Absolutely not, Colonel. I know her personally, and she's just not that type of pilot."

"So, Captain, you and your men feel like we've got someone on this base that would pull a stunt like that?"

"Yes, sir."

"Well, I'll have the MPs wrap her GPS up. I'm flying back tonight and I'll have prints pulled off of it. If there are any prints to be found, maybe we can get to the bottom of this."

"Colonel, please let us back in the fight. You know there's not a snowball's chance in Hades those flyboys will find her without her location device. It's going to have to be boots on the ground. Colonel, in all my years of service, I've never asked for anything like this. I say again, please… let us go in and save the life that saved us!"

The Colonel reaches up placing his hand on Brim's shoulder. "You know, I could have you thrown in the brig for grabbing me like you did?"

"Yes, sir, please forgive me. We are just desperate to save this pilot's life."

"Captain, we need to give Search & Rescue a crack at it. So like I said, get some rest."

Brim turns, slowly walking away with his head lowered when he hears the Colonel, "Hey, Captain, I don't understand it, but I just had a strange feeling that came over me." The Colonel hesitates as he looks down at the sidewalk shaking his head, "Well anyhow… what do you need to go back in to get this pilot they call Poleshot?"

"Yes, sir, thank you, sir! All we need is two six men teams with transport."

The Colonel turns to his aide, "Give these men everything they need and be quick about it!"

Just before Colonel Walker walks into the situation room he held both hands in the air with his thumbs up. "HOOAH 1st Battalion, HOOAH!"

* * *

Sitting only a few hundred feet away from the building that Christy is sleeping in, Chado lies back on a huge flat rock underneath a crystal clear night sky. Staring into the heavens he can't help himself, "Hey, Uriel, how far would you say it is to Heaven from here?"

Buck whimpers and stares at Uriel, like he would like to know also.

Uriel takes a deep breath then let's out a long sigh. "Little Soul, would you like that in miles, kilometers or light years?"

With excitement, "Light years? You mean it's that far away?"

"I actually have no idea how far it is to Heaven. Angels do not think about distance. It is of no use to us. Our means of travel is not measured by length, width, nor depth. We have the ability here on Earth to move from place-to-place in the twinkling of an eye. Now space is a little different. We use portals. If you would like to know the exact distance, you might ask God, if we make it back to Heaven."

"What do you mean 'if' we make it back to Heaven?"

Before Uriel can answer; out of nowhere Christy's guardian angel lands directly in front of Chado. He folds his mighty wings behind him and points to the south.

As Chado and Uriel turn to look behind them they spot the lights of a single vehicle heading in their direction.

Chado jumps up with excitement, "Should we warn Christy?"

Haniel places his hand on Chado's back, "No, Little Soul, we wait."

Two young ISIS fighters slam on the breaks sliding their truck within a few feet of the rock. They point Russian made weapons at Uriel and Chado as they start asking questions in their foreign tongue. "American pilot, American pilot, where is American?"

Uriel smiles and offers them wine from a goatskin pouch, "No American here, you want wine?"

The young ISIS fighter shakes his head no to the wine. Then pointing his rifle at the guitar case, "Open case, shepherd, we see what is inside."

Chado being able to understand their dialect slowly reaches over and opens the case, while smiling at the young man. To everyone's surprise, this confused young teenager no more than 16 years old, smiles back while motioning for Chado to play a song.

Chado looks over at Uriel as to ask for permission. "Go ahead, play something."

He reaches in taking hold of the antique Martin guitar and of all things, starts playing the melody of "Amazing Grace." As Chado's fingers so delicately touch each note, the two ISIS fighters slowly lower their weapons with a sudden change in their countenance. They now have a look of peace over their faces.

* * *

A few hundred feet away, Christy is still well hidden and wedged between two mattresses. Exhausted and sound asleep, she is unaware the enemy is nearby. She tosses and turns having a strange nightmare. In her dream she is lying in an ant bed franticly rubbing her arms and her legs to fight off the ants, when she suddenly awakes and realizes this isn't a dream. She is covered in some kind of biting insects that were all over both mattresses. She jumps up in total darkness, strips down to her underwear, swatting and rubbing against her legs and arms. After shaking out her clothes she quickly gets dressed then feels around in the darkness to find her satchel. Taking out a small penlight, she finds an old wooden chair. Just as she sits down to put her boots on she hears a familiar sound. "Ms. Lily, are you playing mind games with me again? Because, I hear someone playing 'Amazing Grace', and I know these ISIS fighters aren't capable of that."

Christy slips out of the building and creeps through the brush hoping to see a few rangers playing and singing around a campfire. She gets within 50 feet and realizes it's just a couple friendly shepherds, a sheep dog, and two teenagers. She thinks to herself. *Surely, they have to be Christians, they're playing worship music.*

After watching a few more minutes she decides to take a chance. She walks out from behind a cluster of dead brush, "Hello there, guys. I'm an American and need help."

Chado stops playing the guitar as silence falls over everyone. Christy makes another attempt to make new friends. "Hey there, do any of you fellows speak English?"

The two teenagers almost fall off the hood of their truck, as they direct their weapons over at Christy.

Uriel looks at Chado whispering in his thoughts. *Be still Chado, do nothing.*

Chado answers with thought. *We can't just let them take her, they'll bring her back to their leaders and you'll see them cut her head off on the internet!*

Chado hears Haniel's thoughts, *Do nothing, Little Soul, this is all part of God's plan. Have patience and watch.*

The two ISIS teenagers load Christy in the back of their truck, wasting no time heading south.

Haniel reaches down grabbing Buck, spreading his mighty wings, "Follow me, Uriel!"

Uriel takes hold of Chado and they are now flying just above the enemy's vehicle, twisting and turning down the rough rock roads heading straight back toward the Shadow of The Cross.

Both angels, at the same time, fly over to the left side of the ISIS vehicle. Suddenly an F-16 fighter jet sends down a sidewinder missile cutting the truck in half. As the front section of the vehicle explodes it kills both ISIS fighters instantly.

The bed of the truck flips catapulting Christy through the air. Her limp unconscious body flies through the air resembling a rag doll. Upon impact she looks lifeless.

The F-16 pilot buzzes back over his handiwork not realizing he has possibly just killed one of his own.

As the black smoke bellows off the burning vehicle, other ISIS fighters a few miles away hear the explosion and see the fire. Immediately, they are on their way to investigate and won't take long to get there.

Uriel and Chado land next to Christy where Haniel already stands with sword drawn, watching over her soul.

Several demons swarm around the dead soldiers, as they look over at Christy. They know they are no match for the Guardians, but they snarl and hiss as they squirm through the brush and rocks, making sure they stay just out of reach.

The two demons turn their attention back to easier prey, as they freely dive in to strip away the ISIS fighters' dark souls. The young fighters immediately start screaming as their eyes are open to the Spiritual Realm. The demons' dreadful appearance along with the pungent smell of sulfur causes them to struggle even harder against the sharp claws that are dug deep into this fresh kill. The dreadful sounds of their screams continue as they disappear out of sight.

Like angels of peace, three shepherds step out of the darkness. The light from the burning vehicle causes their faces to glow in a strange way, and it is evident, they are men of peace. Each one smiles as they all three walk straight up to Christy, with one leading a small donkey.

The colt is light grey with a black cross directly over his shoulders. This type of donkey is called the Jerusalem Donkey. Another small colt with the same markings across its back once carried Jesus on Palm Sunday through the streets of Jerusalem. Now this one is to carry Christy away from the clutches of the oncoming enemy.

With gentleness, the three shepherds drape her over the little donkey and begin to disappear back into the darkness.

From out of the night sky two fallen angels of hell, land within a few feet of the burning vehicle. With wings almost touching the flame, they step forward a couple of feet. They look directly at Chado, and he unintentionally makes eye contact with the fallen, and they ask, "How is it a mortal sees into the Realm and dares to look upon the servants of Lucifer?"

Chado whispers to Uriel, "Sorry, bud, I guess I just blew the whole undercover gig. I looked right into his eyes."

Uriel steps in front of Chado, "Fear not, Little Soul. We knew it was bound to happen. I guess now is as good a time as any."

One of the two fallen angels laughs, "So this is the one they call Little Soul. Satan has cried out your name from the Throne of Hell. He told us he visited you as a child and also spoke with you on the Mountain of Tabula Rasa. You turned away from his generous offer and now here you are, standing on Earth dressed as a common shepherd. As I gaze into your frightened eyes, I sense you hide something even now! Is it the girl the shepherds just carried away? Or could the answer be hidden inside the leather pouch you carry on your back? We only seek the truth, Little Soul. Tell us of your journey and its purpose."

Chado leans around Uriel like a kid looking around his dad, "Our journey is none of your business, angel!"

Both fallen angels laugh, "Our demons just informed us there were two strangers standing with an angel way out here in the middle of Syria. How odd, I guess you could say it is our lucky day."

The smaller of the two, places his hand over the handle of his sword. "Immortal, we know the Creator is desperate to win back the souls of the lost. Any attempts to change the hearts of mankind will be met with the fury of hell!"

Uriel takes the last comment as a threat and quickly steps forward. Within a flash, the raggedy clothes Uriel is wearing rips into threads as he exposes his mighty wings and armor.

Haniel also advances. This show of force frightens the two fallen in such a way they both quickly disappear back into the darkness.

Chado is concerned for Christy's safety, "Hey, guys, don't we need to catch up with the shepherds and Christy?"

Without saying anything, Haniel leaps into the night air flying in their direction.

"Let us go, Chado. We need to get out of here. I see the headlights of the ISIS fighters and they are getting close."

25

Lambskin, Trail of Blood

The three shepherds lift Christy off of the back of the Jerusalem Donkey. They carry her inside a small adobe shack, laying her down on a narrow table. One of the men carries in water and rags as the other two begin to wash the blood away from her injuries. After what seems like a close examination of the damage, the leader speaking in an ancient dialect gives each one a task.

The youngest of the three walks out to a small pen taking the smallest baby lamb over to a rock table. He raises his hands to Heaven in prayer, turns, and with a sharp knife takes the life of the baby lamb. Not wasting any time he takes out the stomach and begins cleaning it. After a thorough wash, he hands the stomach lining over to the oldest of the three.

With gentle hands the old man takes sections of the lamb's stomach lining carefully covering several injured areas on Christy's body. The final piece is wrapped around a deep laceration to her right temple. After the shepherds finish they gently lay her on a small bed.

Chado slowly walks through the door and he's met with kind smiles from the three shepherds. They each take a step back allowing Chado a clear path to Christy's bedside.

Chado falls to his knees, reaches up placing his hand over her bloody wrist. "Oh, dear God, I pray your healing hands upon this young lady and your protection from the enemy of this rugged land. Precious Lord, give us power and wisdom as we help protect her from those angels of hell. We love you, Jesus, Amen."

Chado slides his fingertips around her wrist searching for a pulse. "Oh, Lord, don't let her die. Please, God, help her."

He places his hand on her neck, pressing down with the tips of his fingers discovering a very weak heartbeat.

As Chado stands, he discovers all three shepherds are on their knees in prayer. He slips past these men of God, being very careful not to disturb them. He meets Uriel and Haniel just outside the shack. "I don't know if she's going to make it, guys. You can barely feel her pulse. If we don't get her to a hospital, I mean now, she is going to die."

Uriel interrupts, "You need to slow down, Chado! Take a deep breath… just think about what is going on. I know you feel compassion for the girl who is near death, but you need to just take a step back and watch the power of our Maker unfold."

* * *

Seven miles away from the shack, Captain Brim along with two six men teams, are traveling in Humvees toward the Shadow of The Cross. They also have two Apache gunships riding shotgun overhead. In addition to this frantic search for the downed pilot, they have two other rescue choppers running search patterns from the crash site, working their way back north.

Captain Brim, sitting on the passenger side of the lead vehicle, suddenly starts having thoughts of the old lady he had dreamed about in the past. He grins as he looks over at his driver.

Sergeant Baker smiles back, asking, "What are you smiling about, Captain?"

The men have to speak loudly over the noise of the Humvee. As they bounce down the rough rocky road, Brim answers, "Oh, I was thinking about those dreams I told you guys about."

Sergeant Baker replies, "I remember those wacky dreams you had. Didn't you give the old lady a name?"

"Yeah, I call her Lily."

The Sergeant laughs. "Lily, that sounds like an old western dance hall girl's name."

"Trust me; she wasn't that kind of a girl. As a matter of fact, if you won't tell the rest of the guys, I'll let you in on a little secret."

"I'm in, let's hear it."

"This pilot we're looking for knows the lady in my dreams."

"No way… what are you saying?"

"What I'm saying is, Lieutenant Moody and I were sharing stories and I told her about my dreams. Then she told me about her having visions of this same old lady. She said she knew her from home. Folks around Christy's hometown called her, 'The Lily of The Valley.'"

"That's freaky, Captain. What do you think it all means?"

"I don't know exactly, but there has to be something to it."

After a couple more miles the rangers arrive at a crossroads.

"What direction, Captain? You want to go left, right, or straight ahead?"

Without answering, Brim gets out and motions for the team to gather up. He spreads out a satellite map of the area and places his finger on their location. "Okay, fellows, we are standing right here. Moody's downed jet is here inside this narrow canyon." He slides his fingers across the map, "With her training she would have probably headed northeast, back in this general direction. Our rescue choppers are searching all this open terrain, so I feel like we need to split up and cover the foothills surrounding this area they call 'The Shadow of The Cross.'"

A private reaches over Brim's shoulder pointing to an area further north, "What about this section, Captain?"

"Remember, she's on foot and may very well be injured. I don't think she could have made it that far yet."

The private speaks up again, "The enemy might already have her."

Captain Brim raises his voice, "Shut your pie hole, private! We heard back from a sniper team this morning that's imbedded back in that canyon. They said it looked like ISIS fighters were searching for her too. So let's find her before they do. Okay listen up! I want three trucks with me. You guys take the other three and head southwest of that rock formation that looks like a cross. We'll cover the southeast side. If you run into trouble call in air support, kill them all. Hooah, gentlemen!"

All the men in one accord shout, "Hooah!"

Captain Brim, along with five other soldiers, bounce along on a one lane rocky road, as each man carefully scans the terrain for Christy, and possible enemy combatants.

Suddenly Brim starts thinking about Ms. Lily again. Just like a movie, his dream plays out in his mind. Brim shakes his head, pulls off his helmet, takes a bottle of water and pours it over his head. "You okay, Captain?"

"Yeah, I'm fine. I just keep thinking about the old lady in my dream. I keep seeing her standing at a fork in the road and then she vanishes. I'll be fine, keep rolling."

"Hey, Captain, you got feelings for this pilot?"

Just before Brim answers the Sergeant, the soldier manning the 50 cal turret gun slaps the cab, "Hey, Captain, I see something up ahead!"

The Captain wipes the water off of his face replacing his helmet. "Hold up right here, lets walk it in."

The Humvee comes to a stop as they all cautiously get out and scan the rocky foothills.

The Captain looks back toward the truck, "Stay on the 50 cal private! Hammer, you take point!"

"Yes, sir."

As they all approach the smoldering vehicle, Brim feels something familiar about this place.

Hammer reports back, "It looks like one of our fly boys did a number on these two guys. Wow, that airstrike cut their truck in half!

The Captain, still having déjà vu, walks a few yards past the destroyed vehicle, as if walking in one of his dreams. The sergeant notices this lost look on Brim's face. He quickly trots up to the Captain, and with a low whisper, "Hey, bud, you okay?" Brim doesn't respond as he continues to stare at the fork in the road.

The Sergeant hits him on the shoulder, "Captain, snap out of it. Where are you, Brim?"

Brim slowly raises his hand and points, "Sergeant, you see that split in the road?"

"Yes sir, what about it?"

"You see the one to the left that looks more like a goat trail than a road?"

"Yes, sir, I'm still with you."

"Sergeant you might think I have totally lost it, but that's the exact spot the old lady I told you about stood in every one of my dreams."

"Wow, Captain, I just got cold chills from one end of me to the other! Do you think Ms. Lily was showing you where our pilot is located?"

"I don't know, Sergeant, but we are going to find out!"

The Captain swings around, "Two of you men stay with the trucks. The rest of y'all come go with me. Hammer, stay on point."

Within a few feet up the goat trail, Hammer finds drops of blood. "Captain, we have a blood trail, and whoever it is, won't last long before they bleed out."

In fear of it being Christy, Brim passes Hammer in a fast run.

"Slow down, Captain, we don't know what's up there. You could run right into an ambush."

With no fear, Brim runs completely out of sight leaving his men behind. He notices it's getting harder and harder to see signs of the blood trail. Being so sure from the many dreams of Ms. Lily showing him this trail, Christy has to be up there!

The Captain begins hearing the sound of sheep and goats scattered all over the hillside. He comes to an abrupt stop as he can see an adobe shack with three shepherds standing in front of the door, waving him over.

The Captain almost totally out of breath from the uphill sprint leans over placing his hands on his knees. Gasping to catch his breath, due to the thin mountain air, he's finally able to shout out, "American pilot, have you seen an American pilot?"

Without saying anything, the shepherds move to the side and point at the shack door.

The other soldiers top the ridge just in time to see the Captain enter the shack.

Brim runs in expecting to see his Arkansas beauty, but to his surprise, he's met with an unrecognizable, unresponsive, bloodstained body.

He quickly steps back outside just as the men arrive. "We got her guys. We got her. Call it in, Sergeant, we need a medevac chopper, and I mean now. She's in a bad way."

"Roger that, Captain."

The Sergeant calls in for the chopper with each one taking defensive positions around the shack. Just before Brim walks back inside he looks around for the shepherds, "Watch out and don't shoot those friendlies."

Hammer laughs, "What friendlies would that be, Captain?"

"There were three shepherds standing right here when I walked in the shack."

"No, sir. We had eyes on you when you went in and we didn't see any friendlies. We had a clear view of at least a hundred yards in all directions."

"What do you mean you didn't see anyone?" Brim says with concern, "They were right here!"

Hammer replies, "They must have been ghosts, sir!"

26

Portal of the Eastern Winds

Within minutes the medevac chopper sits down in a small goat pasture near the shack, while two Apache Gunships hover a short distance away on over watch. Captain Brim gives orders to round up their team and head back to base. "Hammer, I'll be riding in with Lieutenant Christy on the chopper."

"Roger that, Captain."

As soon as they lift off, the medics begin doing everything possible to save the Lieutenant's life.

Brim holds Christy's hand while whispering a prayer as the morning sun peeks over the mountain range, while on their way to the Akinci Air Base. During the flight, Brim notices one of the medics as he sits back against the wall of the chopper, shaking his head as though he has given up.

Brim reaches over grabbing the medic by the collar shouting over the high pitch noise of the chopper, "What are you doing?"

The young medic shakes his head again and with a somber look on his face, "It's no use, Captain. We can't get her back."

The Captain removes his dark shaded eye protection as he glares at the medic, "For your own good, Mr. Medical Man, you better not be giving up on her!"

"She's gone, Captain. She's gone…"

"I don't think you understand. God is involved in this one. If you don't get back to doing whatever it is that you do, I'm going to make sure you meet him today. Do you get me?"

"Okay, okay. No need for violence."

With both medics working feverously to keep Christy alive, the UH-60 Black Hawk hits max speed heading toward a combat support hospital some 140 miles away. Both medics have low confidence in saving the Lieutenant's life.

The determined Captain Brim displays in his own rugged way, a deep faith in her survival. He holds both medics almost at gunpoint forcing them not to give up.

* * *

Christy opens her eyes and experiences a strange sensation as though she has just awakened from a deep sleep. She is suddenly standing near the door of a moving helicopter looking out over the rocky terrain below. She can hear the sounds and feel the forward motion of the chopper. Being totally confused of where and how she got here, she begins to concentrate on her most recent memories. Thinking back, she remembers being captured and forced at gunpoint to ride in the back of a truck. From that point until now is totally blank. Not really understanding, she decides this has to be part of a crazy dream. Christy looks back to see whom else might be riding with her in this wild dream. A sense of peace sweeps over her as she recognizes the Captain.

"Hey, Brim, where are we headed?" Without answering or even looking in her direction, she shouts a second time, but a bit louder. "Hey, Ranger, where are we going?" She notices his full attention is focused on a wounded soldier two medics are working on.

Just as Christy reaches over to tap Captain Brim on the shoulder, she feels someone grab her left hand and whisper, "Hey, Christy, we shouldn't touch the living."

Startled at what she had just heard, Christy turns toward the voices and to her amazement, standing right behind her are two beautiful childlike angels.

Before having time to respond, she feels the touch of the second angel. With a slow gentle movement they seem to fall backward out and away from the chopper, pulling Christy along with them. This freefall reminds her of how much she enjoyed dive training, but the only problem is she doesn't have a parachute. As they are falling, she glances at the helicopter zooming away, then back at the ground. "Oh Lord, what's happening?" As she squeezes the hands of the angels, they suddenly begin to slow down. At last, they are hovering just above the sandy ground below.

"Christy, we would like to introduce ourselves. My name is Allayer and my friend is Nipper. We're here to take you on a magnificent journey, so hold on and enjoy!"

"Wait, guys, I have a question. I actually have lots of questions. Am I experiencing some crazy dream, or am I dead?"

Allayer smiles, "You're not dreaming."

"So, I guess I'm dead!"

"Well… kinda sorta. You're caught between the living and the dead."

"What do you mean? Like an out of body experience?"

Nipper laughs, "We hear the mortals use that term all the time. I guess you could use it as a type of description, surrounding your circumstances."

"Okay, guys, let me get this straight. My spirit is floating out here over this desert? So where's my body?"

Allayer points at the helicopter that's now almost out of sight.

"You mean that soldier the medics are working on is me?"

Allayer shakes his head, "Sorry, kiddo, your body is headed for a combat support hospital along with your sweetheart, Brim."

"So, neither Brim nor the medics could see us standing in the chopper?"

Allayer shakes his head again, "I'm afraid not. Mortals can't see into the Spiritual Realm. We can see them, but they can't see us."

"Wow, I can see into the spirit!"

Nipper smiles as he points behind Christy, "Take a look, kiddo. You see those six men and that dog standing way out there in that rocky desert?"

"I do, who are they?"

The one on the right adorned with armor, well he's your Guardian angel. His name is Haniel. The three shepherds on the left are also angels. They were assigned to help keep you alive until your friends came to rescue you."

"Nipper, that's only four. Who are the other two guys standing by the big dog?"

"The one standing to the left of the dog is another Guardian, and the one on the right is a chosen vessel who is involved in the Almighty's plan. I'm almost sure you will get to meet him later."

"Okay, guys, now that I kind of understand, what is it exactly that God wants me to do?"

Allayer squeezes her hand, "Have patience; everything will be revealed to you. We need to hurry along, so just hold our hands and enjoy the ride."

Christy looks back over where the six men and the dog stood. "Hey, where did those angels go?"

Allayer and Nipper laugh, "Well, your Guardian angel is hovering above us. He will be watching over you every step of the way. As far as the others, we don't know, they could be anywhere."

"One more question, fellows. Could this all be tied in with Ms. Lily's visions?"

Nipper with excitement, "With God, it's all tied together. Everything in the past, present and future is part of his plan. Trust us, you're about to see the mighty hand of God at work!"

Allayer chimes in, "Remember the scripture, Philippians 1:6, '*Being confident of this, that he who began a good work in you will carry it on to completion until the day of Christ Jesus*'. So young lady, we believe God has included you in this work, and you need to have faith throughout this journey he has laid out before you."

"Thanks, Allayer, that's an awesome scripture, but why in the world would God pick me to be in the middle of all this?"

"Sorry, we don't know. His ways are not our ways."

Within seconds the two angels and Christy are standing in front of a strange rock formation known as, The Portals of the Eastern Winds. They walk down the cobblestone path that leads to three separate stone doorways. This tourist attraction located in Egypt is surrounded by an ocean of sand. The rolling hills stretch out for hundreds of miles in each direction. With the setting sun, heat devils rise over the parched sand creating a mirage resembling a gold colored lake.

The angelic trio walks through a small group of tourists that are taking photos of the peculiar rock doorways. Christy hears a professor in a small group of students, giving his theory of what these rock doorways are doing out in the middle of the Sahara Desert. He points at the odd markings as he continues to explain how old they are. His students follow him as he circles the stone doorways, writing every word he speaks in their notebooks.

Christy hears Nipper chuckle, "What's so funny, Nipper?"

"Oh, it's just these college professors. They think they've got a handle on everything. They are so far off base with all their theories.

I wish God would allow them to see us walk through this portal. Those students would probably throw their clipboards at him."

Christy smiles, "Yeah, I was kind of wondering if they could see us."

Nipper continues explaining, "Nope, they have no idea we're standing right here in front of them. It's just certain times when God allows mortals to see into the Spiritual Realm."

"Hey, fellows, I remember Ms. Lily telling me she would see me at the eleventh gate. Is that where we're headed?"

Allayer smiles, "Yes, Ma'am, that's our destination."

Just before walking through the portal Christy looks back over the small group of tourists and she spots Haniel her Guardian angel standing in the midst of the people.

Christy points, "Hey, guys, I see Haniel. Why doesn't he just come up and join us?"

Allayer grabs her by the hand, "Guardians usually are a bit stand-offish. I believe it's probably just their way. Don't you worry; he'll be with us the whole way."

"Well, you two aren't like that. You guys seem to be very friendly and socially balanced to the point it seems we've been friends for years."

Nipper grabs her other hand, "Thank you for the compliments, but his job is a lot different and tougher than ours. He's a warrior angel who's committed to protect you for life. Allayer and I, well... we are different kinds of angels. Our job is to comfort and transport. We usually stay away from the spiritual warfare. However again, thanks for the kind words."

Haniel walks past Christy stopping in front of the portal.

"Hey, guys, what is he doing?"

Allayer smiles, "He is about to ask God to open the portal."

In silence, they all three watch Haniel take his sword and stab it in the soft sand. He then kneels down draping his hands over the handle, bowing his head as if praying. Suddenly the portal opening looks to have a watery, iridescent membrane covering the entrance.

Allayer squeezes her hand, “Okay, Christy, are you ready?”

She nods as they all three walk through the Portal of The Eastern Winds.

27

The Eleventh Gate

Chado Cole, Uriel, and Buck step out of the portal, facing the stairway leading up to the Eleventh Gate of Heaven. Chado's eyes glisten as the light of Heaven reflects against the golden walkway. This beautiful path leading up to the base of Heaven's mountain is so spectacular, the Saints ahead of the trio are raising their hands and shouting praises to God.

Overwhelming joy of being back on the Planet of Heaven causes Chado to quickly turn, wrapping his arms around his lifelong guardian. The mighty angel opens his wings and slightly raises his arms, allowing this unexpected contact from Chado. "Little Soul, what is this all about?"

"I'm sorry, Uriel, I just felt the need to hug you and tell you how thankful I am that you've watched over me my entire life. Without you, I might not be here seeing and experiencing all this."

The mighty warrior slowly lowers his wings and gently wraps his huge arms around Chado, while lightly patting him on his back.

"Well, Chado, I am touched by your emotion and compassion, but I stand only as a servant to the one who has united us. Remember, Little Soul, it is God himself who designed the heavens. He also designed the story of your life. I am just a small piece of your story. I watched as you took your first breath of life and as you left the womb of your mother. I also watched as you took your last breath as a mortal. Now we walk together as immortals, bonded as brothers through Christ."

Uriel steps back placing his hands on Chado's shoulders, while staring deep into his eyes, "Little Soul, as your guardian, I see God has given you a heart filled with love and compassion for the lost and the fallen away. So, let us now continue this mission set before us. We will follow the will of God and steal away as many souls from Satan as we can."

They both hear Buck barking, as he stands at the foot of the giant stairway. Chado laughs, "I guess Buck wants us to hurry along."

"No, I think he is just excited to be back in Heaven."

"I believe you're right. So, Uriel, what's the plan? Do we head on up to the gate?"

"No, let us take a seat over on the side near the bottom step and wait."

Chado suddenly bursts out laughing again as Buck snuggles in between his legs.

"Little Soul, what causes you to laugh?"

Chado reaches up scratching the huge canine between his ears, "I guess I'm just overwhelmed with how cool this is. In a million years, could you ever imagine we would be sitting on the bottom step of a stairway leading up to the Eleventh Gate of Heaven? Not to mention having one of my favorite dogs with me. Oh, and that's not all. Sitting only a couple feet away is a mighty angel of God. Now if that don't tickle your funny bone you probably don't have one!"

With Chado's contagious laugh, Buck joins in as he begins to howl. "Hey, Uriel, you want to hear something funny?"

The huge angel leans over placing his arms over both knees. "Okay, Chado, tell me your story."

"You're going to love this. In between pipeline jobs when I was home, I had to babysit my three kids while my wife attended nursing school. With having little to no experience dealing with three babies still in diapers, I learned to improvise. It took me a while to get the hang of changing out sagging, wet, nasty diapers. Well anyway, I would sometimes delay the whole process. When they all three would start crying ready for a change, I would grab my guitar and start playing a crazy blues rhythm. Each time this would happen, they quickly stopped crying and began dancing to the music. As their sagging diapers would sway back and forth with all three in perfect time, Buck would get into the action and start howling along with the music. Yes, sir, that's a sweet memory. Forgive me, Uriel. I guess with me feeling so happy about being back in Heaven, and with Buck's howling it just brought on those old memories."

"Little Soul, there is no need to apologize, you forget, I was there when you wrote that song... you named it, 'The Diaper Rash Blues.'"

Chado slaps his knee, "Hey that's right. I keep forgetting you were there with me the whole time."

Uriel gives Chado a small grin as they continue to watch the flow of saints coming out of the portal. This line of happy believers slowly moves in their direction.

He bumps Chado's leg then points. "Look, it is Haniel, Christy's guardian."

Haniel is easily recognized from a distance, due to his size. The immortals get a close look at a true warrior angel walking in their midst. Just a few feet past the Portal, he steps to the side and plunges his sword into the soft ground. Now standing near the edge of the golden path, he drapes his wings behind him with only the tips touching the ground. Resembling a statue, Haniel stands at attention and waits.

"Hey, Uriel, what's your buddy Haniel doing?"

"He will wait there at the portal until it is time for Christy to return to Earth, and then continue his mission as her guardian."

Out of the corner of Chado's eye, he notices a very old black lady dressed in a beautiful white cotton dress coming down the steps. "Who do you think that is, Uriel?"

"I do not know. I have never seen her before."

"Uriel, I see the girl pilot, I mean Christy. Hey, those two little angels look familiar! Wow, that's Allayer and Nipper! Let's go over and say hello!"

"Hold up, Chado, you will get to say hello before they leave. Just watch for now and enjoy."

* * *

Christy slowly walks within the line of saints, who are all carrying a look of wonder. This infilling of amazement is painted on everyone's face. The deafening silence of voices is replaced with sounds of the gentle breeze flowing through the giant live oaks that parallel the golden pathway. Overtaken with this indescribable beauty they feel a weakness at the knees, almost like a child taking its first baby steps. Now they're taking their first steps on the Planet of Heaven.

With Christy so caught up in admiring her surroundings she doesn't notice the old lady standing to the left side of the path, waving. This sweet lady, realizing Christy didn't see her, makes her way through the crowded line, quickly catching up to the unaware pilot. Unexpectedly, Christy feels someone's hand on her shoulder. Without turning around, she reaches up touching the old lady's hand, kindly patting her, thinking she's just another saint.

The old lady speaks softly, "Child, I've been waiting for you."

Christy stops in her tracks. Without a doubt she recognizes the voice. Quickly turning around she embraces the old lady as tears of joy fill her eyes. “Oh… Ms. Lily, it's you. It's really you!”

“Yes, it's me, sweetheart. I sent word through your momma to let you know I would meet you at the Eleventh Gate.” Ms. Lily laughs, “Here we stand, child. Well the gate is up those stairs, but I would have to say, this is close enough.”

“Ms. Lily, I still can't believe this is all happening!”

“Oh… it's definitely happening. Child, you are so blessed to be a part of God's plan. Speaking of God's plan, we need to get on up those steps. Remember my visions back on Earth. You can only stay for a short time.”

“What if I don't want to go back? I'd rather just stay here with you, Ms. Lily. I don't want to go through dying again.”

“Well, sweetie, technically you're not dead yet. Back on Earth your new boyfriend, Fish…”

Christy laughs, “You called him Fish in your vision. His name is Brim.”

“Like I was saying, your new beau, Brim, and a handful of soldiers are helping load your body on a transport plane, right now as we speak.”

“How would you know that?”

Ms. Lily chuckles, “I've got connections. Well anyway, they're headed for London, England. The field doctors pronounced you dead a little while back. Brim, Major Hyde, and the survivors of the 1st Battalion all caused such a fuss they stuck you on life support and headed for some high-end hospital over in England. They had to get special permission from a Colonel Walker.”

“I wonder why they made such a ruckus and didn't just let me die in peace.”

“They claiming you're some kind of a hero the way you kept attacking the enemy over and over, until you're poor plane just wouldn't fly anymore.”

"Well, actually, I just ran out of bullets, Ms. Lily. I got hit trying to take photos on my last pass through the canyon."

"You know, in my vision, I thought all the soldiers you were trying to save got killed. I missed that one. I'm glad I was wrong."

"Me too, Ms. Lily, me too…"

Just before reaching the top of this magnificent stairway to Heaven, Lily takes Christy by the hand as she kindly steps to the side allowing the continuous flow of saints to walk past.

"Sweetie, I want to show you something. When I first got here, I stopped at this very spot and just stood here for a short spell. The overwhelming beauty just blessed my soul. So, I feel like this would be a good place to share a little something the Lord wanted me to tell you. Child, while you admire this small piece of Heaven, I'll inform you on what he said."

She continues as she points out over the landscape. "Sweetie, when God sends you back, you'll be carrying something of great importance with you. This is a gift to some and damnation to others. It will open the eyes of millions who have fallen away from their faith. He says their minds are filled with lies and deceit. This nourishment of unbelief has to be stopped, and God has chosen you to help deliver this final message. He said that among these millions of lost souls, there are some who once believed but have turned away, and others that have never believed. The message you carry, along with your testimony of what you see here, will be a weapon against the dark prince of the earth, Satan.

"Christy, in the eyes of your soldiers, you have become a hero for what you've done in battle. Sweetie, now you have been chosen to be a soldier for God. Your battle is not against flesh and blood, but against principalities, against powers, against the rulers of the darkness of this age, against spiritual hosts of wickedness, so be strong, and know that God is with you."

"Ms. Lily, what is it that I'll be carrying back?"

"Sweet child, I'm actually not sure what it is. All I know… it's very important."

"Did God say anything else?"

"Not really, but I have a little advice if you don't mind it coming from an old lady."

"Sure, Ms. Lily, I'm all ears."

"You're about to see something that's going to make you want to stay. However, you need to prepare your heart and be strong, because we both know you have a mission, and I'm pretty sure the Lord won't let you out of it."

"I'm good with it. I mean there's nothing that will keep me from completing God's mission."

"Okay then, let's climb some more steps."

"On a lighter note, Ms. Lily, I have a few questions."

"I'm listening."

"You're still old. I thought when we get to Heaven we would instantly be young. Oh yeah, and you smell like those yellow roses you used to bring to church."

Ms. Lily bursts out laughing, "Let me start with the smell. At the moment you pass through these clouds we're walking in right now, your clothes are instantly changed into these beautiful pure white cotton gowns."

Ms. Lily holds her sleeve up to Christy's nose. "Take a good whiff, sweetie. It's my very own favorite smell."

"Wow, Ms. Lily, that scent is just like those yellow roses you grew back home. I remember that sweet fragrance filling the sanctuary on Sunday mornings."

Ms. Lily let out a small giggle, "The blessings here in Heaven can't be measured. You'll see."

"What about the age thing?"

"Well that threw me for a loop. I just knew when I got here, I would instantly be around the age of Jesus when they killed Him on the cross. Which I think was around 33 years old. Well, I had to ask someone and here's what I found out. First, I have to tell you, time is different here than it is on Earth, so I'll explain using seconds, minutes, and days."

Lily continues to explain, "Now back to the thought of instantly becoming young. It does happen, just not like we thought. Sweetie, when we get to Heaven every second that passes we begin to get younger. At first, I was a little disappointed. However, after a while I realized instead of one surprise, instantly becoming young, God gives that happy experience over and over. Look at it like this. Say you look in the mirror and you're instantly changed. You would jump for joy, rejoicing for a while and then soon after, you would accept it and then move on to other things. Then, say you look in the mirror and see your face becoming younger each passing day; it would make you want to do a happy dance every time."

"I love it, Ms. Lily. That sounds so awesome. Younger every day! Wow, God is so cool! Well, what about the little ones, do they get to grow up in Heaven and have a childhood?"

Ms. Lily smiles, "I believe we need to wait, you'll have an answer to that one shortly."

"Okay, hey I see some of the saints getting their white cotton gowns and mine isn't changing, and I don't smell my favorite scent."

"Sweetie, I don't think you'll be getting those blessings yet. You haven't passed over, so to speak."

* * *

Christy and Ms. Lily step off the landing from the stairway into the courtyard of the Eleventh Gate. Overtaken by this scene, Christy is completely speechless as they slowly walk between the two rows of warrior angels; seven on each side of the gate entrance, each are facing the courtyard. Their silver colored wings are closed, as to be resting their metallic tips against the golden cobble. As these angels stand just a few feet away from the wall, the reflection from the brilliant white pearl gate and the silver-laced gold cobble, creates an array of different colors. It seems to continuously change with each step Christy takes.

She briefly stops, as she stares across the courtyard and notices that the golden cobble takes on the appearance of water. Ms. Lily lightly squeezes her hand, "I know child. It looks like the floor moves."

"Yes, isn't it beautiful? It looks like it's covered in flowing water."

Ms. Lily smiles as she reaches up wiping away tears of happiness from Christy's cheek. "Sweetie, on the other side of this gate awaits a land of blessings, love, and happiness beyond all comprehension. What you're feeling right now is only the beginning of joy. Come with me child, let us step through together."

* * *

Slowly walking behind the many saints, Ms. Lily and Christy witness lost loved ones being reunited with family and friends. Christy smiles as she hears the happy voices from so many reunions.

Her eyes widen as she notices a gorgeous waterfall coming out of a rock formation in the center of the street square. This crystal clear stream flows down the center of the golden street. Weeping willows, along with beautiful aquatic plant life are growing down each side, as if to be manicured by God himself.

"Lily, this is so gorgeous. I can't believe the water is flowing right out of solid rocks."

"Yes, it's beautiful. Everything here in Heaven has meaning. This particular scene you're witnessing represents something you've probably read about in scripture."

"Is it the one about Moses striking the rock with his rod bringing forth the water?"

"No… I don't think so. If you remember, God had told Moses to gather the congregation and speak to the rock. Moses didn't do as the Lord commanded. Instead, he showed anger with the children of Israel by hitting the rock twice. This got Moses and his people in trouble."

"So what scripture represents this beautiful waterfall and stream?"

Ms. Lily smiles, "Christy, it is written in John 7:37–38, '*Jesus stood and cried out saying, 'If anyone thirsts, let him come to me and drink. He who believes in me, as the Scripture has said, out of his heart will flow rivers of living water'.*'"

"Ms. Lily, I do remember reading it, not to mention hearing my brother Jed using this very scripture in some of his sermons. You know, I wish mom could see all this."

"She will, don't you worry. She will."

They continue to walk along admiring the breathtaking beauty in every direction. Christy realizes that she doesn't recognize anyone. Suddenly an overwhelming feeling of sadness washes over her. "Ms. Lily, has no one come to meet me?"

Without saying anything, she points down the street at Allayer and Nipper; the same two angels who brought Christy to Heaven. "They've come to pick you up, sweetie."

Christy quickly stops as she reaches up touching Lily on the shoulder. "But I'm not ready to go back! Please let me stay just a little longer. Please, Ms. Lily."

A thousand butterflies are fluttering in Christy's stomach as she awaits Lily's reply.

"Sweetheart, it's not in my hands regarding how long you have here in Heaven. It is our Lord who guides our footsteps. Be at peace child. *Trust in the Lord with all you heart, and lean not on your own understanding; in all your ways acknowledge him; and he shall direct your paths.*"

Christy turns to see the two childlike angels approaching. "Okay, Lily, I guess it's time."

Allayer and Nipper both walk straight up to Ms. Lily each giving her big hugs. Nipper, noticing Christy having a look of sadness, feels the need to shed a bit of cheer. "Now, now… No need to be so sad, Christy."

"I know, I'm standing in Heaven for goodness sake!"

Nipper continues, "Well, are you ready to go?"

Christy gives a bit of a subtle smile, "Do I have a choice?"

"Nope, sorry kiddo, we are on a schedule. So this is what I want you to do. Place both feet together, close your eyes, click your heels three times, and say there's no place like home."

Ms. Lily and Christy burst out laughing with Allayer immediately butting in, "Nipper, you need to quit playing around!"

"Well, I got her to laugh!"

"Christy, pay no attention to my silly companion. This is by far not the Land of Oz."

Christy takes up for Nipper, "Well, he did lighten the sadness of leaving Heaven."

Allayer smiles, "Who said anything about leaving? We need to show you something very special before we bring you back. So close your eyes, take our hands, and hold on."

Christy quickly embraces Lily, kissing her on the cheeks several times before letting go. "Enjoy Heaven, Ms. Lily… enjoy Heaven."

28

Secrets Unveiled

Allayer and Nipper take hold of Christy's hands, and as soon as she closes her eyes, they vanish. Within what seems like a blink of the eye, they are now hovering over a beautiful mountain range. Nipper chuckles, "How was that for quick transportation…, oh yeah, you can open your eyes now."

Christy opens her eyes to discover they are floating a few hundred feet above the surface. "Wow guys, I'm home, I can see the White River and the foothills of Mountain View, Arkansas. I'm really back home."

She hears both angels giggling like two small children. "What's so funny?"

"Allayer, you tell her."

"Well… Christy, this looks a bit like Mountain View, but it's not."

"What do you mean? Where the heck are we?"

"I tell you what; let's get our feet on the ground and walk a while. It's probably easier to show you rather than trying to explain."

As soon as they touched the ground, Christy turns into a chatterbox. "Okay, we're on the ground, so let's hear it. Where are we? Are we still in Heaven?"

Nipper trots ahead, turns, and starts walking backwards while talking. “Slow down hero, like Allayer said, it’s better you see for yourself. Just have a little faith and trust us. You’re going to love this.”

Christy smiles, “Okay, guys, I get the picture. It’s a surprise.”

Nipper and Allayer both hold up their thumbs in agreement as they walk for a short while.

Christy, now focusing on her surroundings, realizes this in fact couldn’t be the White River back home. This one flows a bit slower and even looks narrower but displays more beauty. The colored rock formation along the shore is laced with streaks of gold and silver.

The strange plant life and different kinds of birds are unfamiliar to Christy. “Hey, guys, we’re still in Heaven, aren’t we?”

Nipper and Allayer reply at the same time, “Yep, we are still in Heaven.”

“I thought Heaven was like a giant city.”

Nipper tells her, “Okay, Christy, here’s a little Heaven 101: Where we just came from was the City of The Eleventh Gate. There are twelve gates along the great walls of Heaven, each having its own city. The main city where the Throne of God sits is located in the center of Heaven. The location we’re at right now is located outside of the walls of Heaven.”

“So how is that possible? Well, what I’m trying to say is, I have been under the impression that Heaven hovers out in space somewhere.”

Nipper grins, “Listen, silly willy. Don’t you remember coming through the portal and walking up the stairway to Heaven? Don’t you remember looking out over Heaven’s creation while you and Ms. Lily stopped midway up the stairs?”

Allayer smiles, “Maybe this will help. Think back to the Bible where God said he created man in his own image. We believe he created Earth in the same image as the planet of Heaven. It’s just the planet of Heaven is much larger. I wish you could have seen Earth a few thousand years ago. It was something really spectacular.”

Nipper chimes in, "Yes it was, until mankind began the earth's slow death. The last few hundred years we've watched as it took on the stench of industrial disease."

"Calm down, Nipper, God's about to fix all that."

Christy widens her eyes, "What do you mean, Allayer? Is the world as we know it about to come to an end?"

Without answering, Allayer points up ahead at a beautiful home-place sitting near a slow bend in the river bottom.

"Who lives there, guys?"

Nipper shoves her from behind, "Let's go find out!"

They all three continue in the direction of the homestead. After only a short distance, Christy notices two men and a huge dog standing at the crest of a hill to the right of the house. "Who are those people?"

Nipper out of the blue claps his hands together in a happy gesture. "They, my dear, are two friends of ours. The very tall gentleman on the left, well… I wouldn't say he would fit in the gentleman category, that's Uriel. He's a guardian angel similar to the ones you saw standing at the Eleventh Gate. The fellow to your right is Chado Cole. He was a human mortal like you, now he's an immortal. The dog, well, I'm not sure. Chado didn't have a dog with him when we dropped him off here in Heaven."

Christy says with excitement, "Hey, those two look familiar. I remember back when we bailed out of the chopper I saw six men and a dog standing out in the desert. You said five were angels with one of those being my Guardian angel. You never told me who the guy was. You mentioned he was a chosen vessel, and I would meet him later on. So is this later? I mean, is that the guy?"

Allayer nods his head, "Yes, he's got something very special that's to be passed on to you."

"So that's the one we've come way out here in the middle of Heaven to meet with?"

Without answering, Allayer and Nipper continue following Christy as they approach the beautiful homeplace. Uriel and Chado both give out a friendly wave as they make their way down the hill.

To Christy's surprise, she spots the front door of the home slowly open with a little girl peeping around the edge, and then slowly closing it back. They hear the pitter-pat of her feet running through the house, "Pawpaw, there's some people in our yard. Come see!"

Christy laughs at how precious the little girl sounds calling for her Pawpaw. "Nipper, who is that little girl, she is adorable."

Without any response from Nipper, they all watch as Buck trots up within a few feet of Christy. He drops down and does his crawling trick, grinning the whole way as he approaches. "Well, hello, big guy. Now you are for sure a big ole handsome dog."

Christy, distracted with petting and hugging Buck, doesn't realize the tenants of this home are now standing on the porch only a few feet away. Still smiling as she wiggles the loose skin around Buck's forehead, "You big rascal, you want to go home with me? Yes, you are a sweetheart, and such a pretty puppy."

Christy feels Nipper tap her on the shoulder, "Hey, kiddo, you might want to look over at the porch."

She quickly turns having to hold her hand over her eyes to shade the setting sun. The silhouette of a tall man comes into view. Still not making out who she's looking at, she stands up taking a couple steps closer to the porch when she hears a soft familiar voice, "Hello, Short Stuff."

Christy falls back to her knees, "Oh, Daddy… is it really you? Tell me I'm not in some crazy dream. Is it really you?"

Christy's eyes suddenly fill with joyful tears. Everything becomes a giant blur as she reaches up using her sleeves to clear her eyes. She notices a little girl peeking around the leg of her father. Then suddenly another glowing face appears from the other side. Christy, still whaling with joy, asks, "Who are the little girls hiding behind you, Daddy?"

Before answering, he takes a few steps closer, dragging the two girls along as they seem to be glued to his pants legs. He gently squats down picking both girls up. Now with one under each arm, he sits down on the edge of the porch, placing them on his knee.

"Christy, I want you to meet Chris & Jessie. They are your two daughters."

From out of nowhere total shame and humility overcomes Christy, forcing her to fall on her knees once again. She slowly bends over placing her forehead to the ground. Using her outstretched arms, she drags the loose soil near to her face.

The angels, Chado, and Christy's family silently watch as she continues to display a depth of regret by sprinkling hands full of dirt over the top of her head. Chado remembers reading in the Bible how in ancient times, people with great sorrow would act in this same manner. Out of a kind heart and wanting to comfort this poor girl, he advances. Before taking a full step, Uriel quickly grabs Chado's arm and whispers, "Be still, Little Soul, and watch."

Christy continues wailing with tears of regret as dreadful memories come crashing down. Thinking back to a little over five years ago, how she was coached into an abortion. She remembers how the school counselors were so kind and persuasive as they directed her to a pro-choice group. This led to the worst mistake of her entire life.

Deep down inside she remembers feeling the conviction of the Holy Spirit and knew it was wrong. Nevertheless, along with counselors, convincing her that this unwanted pregnancy would surely destroy any plans of her entering the Air Force, she decided to harden her heart and not listen to the soft, still voice of God.

After walking out of the abortion clinic, Christy had a feeling of relief, and believed this mistake was finally behind her. She could then move on, continuing with her plans.

Her days were full of activity, swallowing up any thoughts of regret, but at night when she would lay her head on the pillow this great sin would haunt her every thought.

Crying herself to sleep most nights she would reach out to God in prayer. For over a year she begged God for mercy by night, only to bury her feelings by day. This emotional rollercoaster tore a hole in her heart, but she knew living as a Christian, if this dark secret should ever come to light it would crush her family, especially her mother. With much practice over a period of time she was able to tuck it away so deep that it became invisible, even to her.

Today, upon this revelation of having aborted not one child but two, fractures Christy's hidden vault.

With her face pressed to the ground in humility, her emotions pour from her heart like a river of sorrows. Seeing these two beautiful twin girls and knowing she allowed them to be destroyed in the womb is more than she can take. Christy leans back on her knees with her hands lifted, "Dear God, take my life away. Let me die, Lord. I don't deserve to even look into their eyes. Just take me, God." Christy slumps back over with her forehead touching the ground, "Just kill me, God. Please, just let me die…"

A silence falls over the homeplace with only the sound of a stranger's footsteps, when one of the twins points, "Look, Pawpaw!"

Christy's dad pulls Jessie even closer, as they sit side-by-side, "Shhh… be quiet."

With Christy still begging God to destroy her, she suspends her prayer of destruction, as she hears a familiar voice. "Yes, our names are spelled the same. The only difference is that yours has a Y in it."

Christy looks up, but is almost totally blinded from the tears and sand in her eyes, "Jesus, is that you?"

Without answering, he kneels down beside Christy and with the hem of his garment he gently begins wiping away her muddy tears. As her vision begins to return, she sees the beautiful smile of Jesus appear. "Jesus, how can you still love me after what I've done?"

"Christy, when you made the awful decision to allow someone to take the lives of these children, you dampened the flame of my Holy Spirit. With this act of sin, you felt that I had abandoned you. Sweet child, I have never left you nor will I forsake you. As you cried out in the night, and bathed in the sickness of your conviction, I was there... and I wept with you."

Jesus reaches up brushing her hair away from her face, "Christy, I forgave you the very first night you asked. I know your heart, and I know you would never allow this to happen again. It is Satan himself that hands out the seeds of sin. With freewill, you fell into his trap. His seeds brought forth a harvest of condemnation. With this harvest, he stole away your joy, and replaced it with sorrow and regret. After a period of time, you learned how to bury this pain down deep, even hiding it from your own conscience. Behold child, as you gaze upon these two children your heart is lanced, and it now pours out and reveals your brokenness. This sin has been given back to Satan; it is of no value. It is forgotten and replaced with a love that only comes from the Great I Am."

Jesus motions for Chris, Jessie, and Christy's father to come forward. They all embrace Christy, with Jesus standing over them. Within a short time, Jesus pats Jessie and Chris on their heads, "It is time, children…"

Without hesitation, both kids, along with Christy's father, sit back down on the porch. Jesus holds his hand out, "Chado, bring the scroll."

Chado takes off the leather pouch, and reaches in, taking out both scrolls. "Which one do you want, Lord?"

"Little Soul, you choose."

Chado stares at both scrolls, knowing they are identical, but can't seem to make his mind up. Nipper and Allayer chuckle at Chado as he struggles with a simple decision, "Hey, guys, give me a break. God might have some hidden message that's in one or the other, special for Christy."

Jesus pats Buck on the head, "Help him out, old friend." Buck swiftly trots over, sits down in front of Chado, and begins whimpering. Then, with his paw he taps the scroll in Chado's right hand.

"Thanks, Buck, your guess is as good as mine."

Chado hands Jesus the Scroll and they all watch and listen.

"Christy, I want you to take this scroll back with you to Earth. It is to be shared with the believers and the unbelievers alike. This scroll is of great importance and holds the mysteries to my Father's final warning. Christy, you will be mocked and persecuted, but know this, I Am with you."

"Lord, is the end near? I mean, is it really the time of your coming?"

"Child, this revelation is a final warning for all who dwell upon the face of the earth. It is near the end of the age. Remember, the message in this scroll can only be revealed through the bloodline of the one to whom God chose to write it. Within his bloodline, there is a child. He alone holds the key to this scroll, and he alone, will be the only one capable of the interpretation."

"Lord, who is this child? How can I find him?"

"His name will be revealed at the appointed time."

Jesus reaches over to place his hands on Christy's shoulders. "As you share your testimony, tell them the last thing you heard Me say: Woe to those who have eyes and choose not to see. Woe to those who have ears and choose not to hear. Blessed are those who believe and receive this final message, as it pours from the lips of a child."

Jesus smiles as He stares deep into Christy's soul. Gently placing his left hand on her forehead he whispers, "Fear not child. The Father, Son, and the Holy Spirit, We are One and We are with you."

As gentle as a butterfly barely touching her face, Jesus slowly moves his nail-scarred hand down from Christy's forehead, gently closing her eyes. Suddenly, within a twinkling of a star, she disappears.

Chado catches a glimpse of Christy's guardian, Haniel, as he vanishes. He also notices Jesus raising his hands and smiling. "What are you two waiting on? Do you not have a mission to complete?"

Chado steps forward, "Lord, can I ask a favor?"

"I am listening, Chado."

"Well, I've been lugging this old Martin guitar around ever since we left that horrible pawn store in Morgan City. I'm wondering if someone might take it to its original owner."

Jesus laughs, "The owner, well, that would be your Uncle Dobber. I'm sure he will be thrilled to get it back, but I recommend you hold on to it for now... and, Chado?"

"Yes, Lord?"

"I am sure he will enjoy it more if you were the one who presents it to him. You probably do not realize, but it can be used as a weapon against the dark forces. Trust me; it will 'come in handy', as your granny use to say."

Just as Chado begins to respond, Jesus disappears. "Wow, I guess I'll just have to hang on to it a little while longer."

Uriel bumps Chado on the shoulder, "Yes, it seems so."

"Hey, where did Allayer and Nipper get off to? I wanted to visit with them for a spell."

"They left with Christy. You and I need to do the same. We need to get back to Louisiana."

29

The Infilling

Christy slowly opens her eyes thinking she is still in Heaven talking with Jesus. To her surprise, she's staring into the bright lights of an operating room. Suspended in midair, she hovers over a team of surgeons who are franticly operating on a patient. "Could that be me? Oh, God, please let me go back to Heaven."

Without realizing their presence, she feels the two childlike angels squeeze her hands. "Allayer, Nipper, I'm so glad you're here. I thought I was all alone, floating like some ghost."

They both laugh, "You're not alone. We are here with you, and Haniel your guardian is with you. Behold, child, look right above you."

Christy smiles as she gazes at the huge guardian just a few feet away when she hears Allayer whisper, "He loves you and will always watch over you. Oh, and you also have others. Hold on to our hands and we'll show you."

They slowly move across the operating room passing through a glass observation window. The entire window is covered with young medical students as they all focus on the surgeons below. They hear the students chattering, "Some say she was a pilot and was severely injured in battle."

"Hey, I overheard some soldiers talking in the cafeteria and they were saying she is some kind of a hero."

"Me too, I heard the same thing. They said she saved a bunch of guys, but they don't think she's going to make it."

A young Korean girl holds her clipboard to her chest and looks over her horn-rimmed glasses, "Oh, that so sad. Maybe we see her die."

Most of the students get quiet hearing the morbid comment from the Korean girl, except for a British kid. "Well if that wasn't right out of the loo. I'm personally not giving up on her. As a matter of a fact, would anyone consider placing a wager?"

Nipper tugs on Christy's hand, "Come along, and pay no attention to those students. They're blessed with high IQs, but are in dire need of respect."

They float down the hall turning onto a wide corridor. From this vantage point Christy spots several soldiers all standing in a circle.

Allayer whispers, "You see, you're not alone. Those soldiers are boldly standing in the midst of this room full of unbelievers, praying for you right now."

"Can we move closer? I'd like to see who they are."

Allayer shakes his head, "Sorry, Christy, we are out of time. We have to rejoin your body, soul, and spirit."

Without any reply from Christy, they all three float back to the surgery room. Now hovering a few feet over her body, Allayer and Nipper place their hands beneath Christy's legs and back. Together, they both tilt her back into a lying position. She quickly glances back and forth looking into the eyes of these beautiful angels. "Wait, will I ever see you again?"

"We're almost certain. Now close your eyes and dream of Heaven."

Allayer and Nipper gently lower her soul and spirit, as they display this wonderful miracle of God, in the rejoining of the body, soul, and spirit. With the breath of life, Christy is now whole once more. "Goodbye, Christy, goodbye."

* * *

The head nurse over the surgery room notices a change in pulse rate and blood pressure. She whispers to the lead surgeon, "Dr. Wise, we've got a jump in pressure and pulse rate."

"Well, it sounds like we might save this young lady after all. Dr. Miller, would you mind closing? I have a three o'clock tee time on the golf course with two very impatient lawyers, and I want to spend a few minutes on the driving range before they get there."

"Sure, Dr. Wise, I would be happy to."

Dr. Wise with curiosity asks, "Oh, before I forget, did we ever find out what that strange membrane we removed from her wounds could have been?"

Nurse Carlson quickly pulls up information from the surgery room computer, "Perfect timing, Dr. Wise, they just loaded information from the lab. Wow."

"Wow, what? Carlson, let's hear it."

"In all my years of nursing, I've never seen anything like this used to save someone's life."

Dr. Wise tapping his fingers on his clipboard, "I'm waiting."

"Sorry sir. It says here, the membrane was the stomach lining of a lamb."

Wise laughs, "Those guys down in the lab must be high! Whoever heard of someone using a lamb to save a person's life? There has got to be some kind of a mix-up. Hey, Dr. Miller, have you a word on this matter?"

"Well, if you think about it, whoever pulled that little trick off actually saved this pilot's life."

Dr. Wise, being an unbeliever, smirks, "I guess she was saved by the Lamb."

The nurse's aide chuckles as Dr. Wise continues, "Are you a believer, Miller?"

Dr. Miller ignores his question as he focuses on the patient. "Nurse, clean her up and get her to ICU. I'll come through and check on her in few minutes. "Now what was that you asked, Dr. Wise?"

"I asked if you are a believer. You know, all that God and Jesus stuff."

Dr. Miller answers, "Actually, I am a believer."

Dr. Wise takes a step back, "Really, I would have never thought of you as a Bible thumper."

"Wow, Dr. Wise, that was a low blow, wouldn't you say?"

"Oh… I mean no harm. I just think it's funny hearing people talk about all that voodoo."

"It's not voodoo, Dr. Wise. It's actually plain ole simple faith and a belief in a higher power."

"Well, if you say so, Miller."

Dr. Miller smiles, shaking his head as he watches Dr. Wise walk out of the surgery room. "Nurse, I almost forgot. We need to take another look at her right arm. Before surgery I noticed contusions and swelling, so let's get another x-ray around that area."

"I'll get right to it, sir."

The nurse and two aids carefully pull back the surgery cloth covering Christy's right side. Suddenly Nurse Carlson's mouth flies wide open. "What in the world is that?"

Dr. Miller, scrubbing his hands at a nearby sink, turns to see what the excitement is all about; "What's wrong, Nurse?"

"Dr. Miller, you need to see this."

The doc reaches over, grabbing a hand full of paper towels as he makes his way over to the operating table. "What in the world is that in her hand?"

Nurse Carlson rolls her eyes, "It looks like a scroll of some kind."

Almost speechless, the doctor takes Christy by the wrist, lifting her arm to get a better look at this object clinched in her right hand. "This is really strange; I just wonder who could have put it in her hand. This is a sanitized surgery room. Whoever the idiot may be, chances are they probably won't be working here any longer if they're found out!"

Dr. Miller turns, almost stuttering to a male nurse, "Go… catch Dr. Wise and tell him to get back down here. He has to be the one that set this up."

The male nurse shakes his head, "I don't think so, Doc. I was with him during prep and I didn't see Dr. Wise with any scroll. Well, I guess what I'm trying to say—I helped get her ready for surgery and she did not have anything in her hand. I swear, Doc, on my mother's grave."

"Well, go get him anyway. This is too strange not to inform Dr. Wise, so scram!"

The male nurse turns, and in a flash runs through the surgery room doors. Dr. Miller, still confused with this new mystery, happens to look up at the observation window. "Oh crap, those medical students just witnessed this whole fiasco, and almost every one of them has their cell phone cameras pressed against the glass. It looks like this event is going viral, folks."

A concerned nurse pulls her surgery mask down. "Doctor, if this gets on social media, will we be in trouble?"

"It's probably already being passed around to a few thousand. Within a couple hours it will be in the millions. Your question of being in trouble; I don't know, Nurse. I just don't know."

When one of the nurse's aides reaches over to touch the scroll,

Miller quickly grabs her hand. “Don’t touch it. I want Wise to see exactly what we are seeing. In fact, go get my cell phone. It’s in my locker. The combination is 4,3,2,1. I want to take a few photos, prank or not.”

Within a couple of minutes, a disgruntled Dr. Wise bursts into the surgery room. “This better be good! I’m already late for my golf game.”

Standing between the scroll and Dr. Wise, without saying anything, Miller slowly steps to the side and points to the scroll.

“What the heck is that?”

“Well, Doc, we know it’s some kind of a scroll. Before you ask, we have no idea how it got in this patient’s hand. We were all hoping you might shed some light.”

The nurse runs back into the room, “Dr. Miller, here’s your phone, sir.”

“Yes, thank you Nurse.” Miller turns and attempts to take photos as Dr. Wise quickly places his hand in front of the camera. “No, no. Put the camera away Miller, we need to keep this between us. From here on out there will be no photos, and no talking beyond this surgery room. We could all lose our license to practice medicine, not to mention being hit with a law suit from this girl’s family.”

Dr. Miller and two of the nurses start laughing at Dr. Wise. “What, you people think this is some kind of a sick joke?”

Without saying anything, Miller slowly points up at the observation window. Dr. Wise angrily looks up, only to be faced with several cell phones pointing down at the room. “Oh crap, I forgot we had that group of students here today. Double crap, well, I guess the cat is out of the bag. Miller, take as many photos as you like.”

Dr. Miller takes several shots from different angles while Nurse Carlson holds Christy’s arm in an upright position.

Miller slides his cell phone over on the counter, “Okay, ladies, let’s see if we can pry it from her hand.”

Just as Miller takes hold of the scroll, Christy loosens her grip allowing him to easily retrieve it. "Hey, did you see that? She's still fully sedated and it was like she knew when to let go."

The disgruntled Dr. Wise shakes his head, "I believe you people are sedated. We need to get to the bottom of this and find out who placed it in her hand."

Miller pats Dr. Wise on the shoulder, "Well, I would suggest viewing the hospital video. If there is any foul play you can bet it's on that disk."

As Miller closely examines this ancient scroll, he feels a strange sense of peace sweeping over him. "Wow, guys, this isn't just some dime-store scroll. I believe this is the real deal. Look at this paper. It looks really old to me. Take a look at that seal! Yes! I think this thing is hundreds of years old, maybe even thousands. What do you think, Dr. Wise?"

"I have no idea. I'm a surgeon, not an archaeologist. If it is some ancient scroll, why would a priceless artifact end up in the hand of a pilot?"

Dr. Miller continues to examine this strange parchment, "What if no one from this world put it in her hand, what if it's from somewhere else?"

"What are you saying, Miller?"

"I'm saying, when they brought this girl in here she was actually dead. She was totally dependent on life-support. What if her soul was somewhere else?"

"Okay, I've heard all of the foolishness I can stand for one day. I'm going to try and salvage what's left of my golf game."

"Well, what should we do with it? By law it belongs to this pilot."

"Miller, do whatever you like. I absolutely could care less at this point! Oh, and don't call me if you need me."

Dr. Miller shakes his head as he turns to the nurse, "Okay, guys, for now I'll call hospital security and have them lock this thing up in our safe, at least until we can view the disk and talk to this young pilot. So let's get her through x-ray then straight over to ICU."

30

Lawless

Back down in south Louisiana, Chado Cole, Uriel, and Buck sit on the steps of the Morgan City Courthouse, as they watch the morning sun peak over the cypress trees. The city streets come alive with the noise of vehicles and people as they all rush to their jobs. Unconcerned men and women walk past the two raggedy bums and the mangy dog as they make their way up the courthouse steps. One or two out of dozens give them any attention. Most act as if they are invisible, possibly in fear they might feel obligated to toss the less fortunate a couple bucks for a hot breakfast.

It's been three days since what the locals are calling the Bayou Rose Bombing. This violent action has caused a wave of anger, not only coming from a drug syndicate, but also from politicians and several civil servants that are embedded with the Russians. The surrounding communities are suffering as it affects almost every family in some fashion, whether it's been immediate family members or distant relatives. Drug overdose in the entire Pelican State is giving funeral homes more business than ever.

The local buzz around coffee shops and restaurants show that the residents are celebrating the destruction of the Bayou Rose and its employees. They are calling this modern day gang of outlaws responsible for the bombing, "Cajun Heroes."

* * *

Chado, becoming impatient, slaps his knees with the palms of his hands, "Okay, Uriel, what are we doing here at the Morgan City Courthouse?"

"My friend, we are doing a little surveillance."

"I'm in, who are we watching, bad guys and crooked cops?"

"I do not know if you would call your old dive crew, bad guys."

Chado grins, "Surely, they won't show up here. I bet they're hiding out down on the bayou somewhere."

"Now, that is where you are mistaken. Do you see that white van pulling up in the parking lot?"

"No way… is that Joey driving the van?"

Uriel brushes Chado on the knee, "If that surprised you, look who is coming out of the Courthouse."

"Now that is a sight. I've never seen Cheese Hound in a suit. Uriel, what was he doing inside the courthouse?"

"I believe they might be doing their own surveillance."

Cheese Hound walks straight up to the two bums with a huge smile on his face as if he had just won the lottery. Without saying anything, he wrestles with taking off his tie and jacket while digging around his trouser pocket. "You two look like you're a little down on your luck. This jacket might fit you better than it does me."

He tosses the new jacket and tie into Chado's lap along with a big wad of cash. "If you don't mind, fellows, don't tell anyone where you got the loot."

Chado and Uriel smile as Cheese turns heading away when he

suddenly stops and stares at Chado. "Hey, Mister, have we ever met? You sure look familiar."

Chado stutters not wanting to tell a fib, "Maybe… so, friend."

With a confused look on his face, Cheese swiftly snaps his fingers. "Oh… I know where I've seen you fellows. It was at the Bayou Rose a few nights ago. No… that ain't it. It's something about your eyes... friend. I believe I know you from years back, I just can't place where."

Chado wants so badly to tell Cheese who he really is, when Uriel takes over the conversation, "My friend has what you might call a familiar face. You've probably got him mixed up with someone else."

"I don't think so. I never forget a face. If y'all don't mind me asking, what names do you go by?"

"Well, my name is Uriel, and my dear friend here is called Little Soul, and of course our canine, we call Buck."

Cheese laughs, "Forgive me, but who in the world would ever name their kid Little Soul?"

They all three hear a loud whistle. It's Joey waving at Cheese Hound.

"Hey, I've got to go fellows. Y'all buy that mutt some flea shampoo with the money I gave you. Catch ya later."

As Cheese trots away, Chado chuckles, "That was a close one! I just knew our cover was blown."

* * *

Just a few yards away, Joey, TC, and Cheese are in the back of Cheese Hound's homemade surveillance van. They are preparing to find out what Mayor Dalton and his associates are planning.

Joey, sipping on chocolate milk and eating powdered donuts gazes at the weird electronics attached to plywood hanging from the walls of the van. "Hey, Cheese, where did you get all this stuff?"

Cheese slides his headphones down over his neck, "I went to an outlaw garage sale a few years ago. No, I'm kidding. Another buddy I served with ran a private investigation company. They went out of business and he asked me if I wanted any equipment. Hey, be quiet, I hear the Mayor. He just walked into his office."

TC bursts out laughing, "You bugged the Mayor's office?"

"I sure did, the DA's office too. Hey Joey, turn that recorder on. He's making a phone call."

Cheese reaches over handing TC and Joey each headphones and point to the jacks. "Plug in boys it's going to be a long day."

* * *

The Mayor's aide gently knocks on his office door. He waves her in as he's hanging up the phone. "Mayor, there are two detectives waiting to see you, a Mr. Komo and a Mr. Fletcher."

"Yes, I've been expecting them, please send them in."

The Mayor briefly makes two quick calls, one to the DA's office and the other to the Police Chief. As he holds the phone to his ear he waves at both detectives, pointing to the coffee pot. "Hey, Chief Lewis, I've got Phillips on his way over and our two detectives are already here… Okay, we'll have a cup of coffee waiting on you."

The Mayor leans back in his leather chair, "You fellows look like you've been up all night."

Komo turns around with a wild-eyed look, "We've been up for the last three nights."

DA Phillips walks through the door with Chief Lewis right behind him. The Mayor's aide peaks around the two men walking in front of her, "Will you gentlemen need anything else?"

The Mayor gives her a haughty look and says, "No, that will be all.

Just make sure we are not disturbed and close the door behind you. Gentlemen, grab a cup of coffee and let's step into the conference room."

The DA, being the first one to sit down, asks, "How in the world did we get tangled up with the Columbians? I thought we were dealing with just one man, the Russian."

Mayor Dalton asks, "What do you mean? We are dealing with one man, Nikolai."

"Well, I had an interesting phone call last night from South America and it scared the crap out of me. How they got my personal number is still a mystery."

Dalton shakes his head in disbelief, "What did they want?"

"They're wondering what happened to their money."

The Police Chief slaps the desk. "You weren't the only one. They called my house also, and were asking me, where we wanted to be buried. They're giving us three days, and if we don't deliver, it's over."

The Mayor, with a worried look, leans forward on the conference table. "How much were they asking for?"

Chief Lewis widens his eyes, "Twenty million, that's how much! They said we weren't doing enough to protect the Russian."

Phillips places both hands over his face. "The Russian —I hate that slob."

Phillips glares at the two detectives, "Have you guys turned anything up on Nikolai? Maybe he's still alive."

Detective Komo elbows Fletcher, "No sir, we haven't found him yet. Out of 16 bodies, he wasn't in the mix. The only one they've got ID on so far is the Mayor's stepson, by the way Mayor, sorry for your loss."

"Thanks, Fletcher, but no loss to me. He was a piece of garbage!"

Phillips slams his empty cup down. "That Russian slob might be the one that orchestrated this whole thing."

Komo stutters, "We don't think so, we believe it's five bikers who made the hit, and we have a pretty good lead on one. He lives in Lafayette."

Chief Lewis smiles, "I don't think we have anything to worry about. I have full confidence in my detectives."

Suddenly State Representative Jerry Brown bursts through the door with the Mayor's aide right behind him, "Sir, you can't go in there… The Mayor is in a closed meeting!"

Mayor Dalton waves at the aide, "It's okay, Mindy. Let Jerry in and close the door behind you. Jerry, I thought you were scheduled in Baton Rouge today."

"I was scheduled, but after getting a strange call from some crazy Columbian speaking broken English threatening my entire family, I thought I might better get down here and find out what the heck is going on!" Jerry exclaimed.

Chief Lewis walks around the conference table pouring everyone a fresh cup of coffee, "Like I was saying just before you came in, I have full confidence in these two detectives. They have a good lead on the men responsible for the Bayou Rose bombing. With the help of several handpicked deputies that are on my personal payroll, they should have this cleaned up shortly."

After taking a sip of his coffee, DA Phillips gives Chief Lewis a sarcastic look, "Speaking of cleaning up, why is that newly elected Belle River Sheriff still breathing?"

Chief Lewis almost stuttering, "Well… after discussing our situation with my detectives, we thought we might want to wait before we get rid of Sheriff Bradford. You fellows need to understand, one of our trusted policemen was killed at the Pawn & Party the other night, along with the owner. Shortly after that, this biker gang blew the Rose up, leaving 16 charred bodies behind. Not to mention that trash getting away with a butt load of our money. So, I don't think we should make a hit on Bradford, at least not right now. Killing him would probably be just enough to bring the Feds down on us. We don't want the federal boys snooping around."

Mayor Dalton, who has a long vendetta against Sheriff Bradford, shows anger. "He's the one snooping around, you idiot! I want that Bible-thumping do-gooder gone. I want to read in the Morgan City Times, *Sheriff Bradford found dead floating in the Gulf of Mexico.* Do you understand me, Chief Lewis?"

Lewis turns to his detectives, "Okay. Y'all heard the man, but first run these bikers down!"

Komo and Fletcher both quickly stand, "Yes sir, we'll get it done. You can count on us!"

As the detectives make their way for the door, Mayor Dalton stands up with a big smile pasted on his face. "Look, gentlemen, I think we all need to be out of town as this unfolds. From the worried looks on your faces, I believe we all need a short vacation. So this is what I propose: while those detectives take out the trash, we're going to have a little fun. Mr. Brown, would you like to join Phillips, Lewis, and me for the weekend? We are going down to my beach house. I've got six fine heifers lined up and plenty of whiskey."

Representative Brown walks over to a small sink and pours out his cold coffee and says, "That actually sounds appealing to me; I've been in need of letting my hair down for a long time. Count me in, gentlemen!"

Dalton jokes around, "Let your hair down, you can't let your hair down. You're almost as bald as I am."

They all laugh heading for the door as Dalton places his arms around the shoulders of Brown and Phillips, "So let's quit worrying about the Columbians and go have a little fun."

* * *

Cheese Hound removes his headphones, reaches over and turns the recorder off. "Boys, we've got those stinking maggots!"

Joey is grinning from ear to ear, "I thought we were going to be here all day. We snagged enough information within a few minutes to send those slime balls straight to Angola!"

Cheese holds his hand up, "Not so fast. We don't know who to trust with law enforcement. Hang on and let's think about this. With this much condemning information involving the Mayor, the Chief of Police, the DA, a State Representative, two detectives, and God only knows how many cops—this could be one of the largest take-downs in Louisiana history. So boys, we need to get this one right!"

Joey loses his smile and replaces it with a concerned look, "If we go to the cops, we're dead."

TC butts in, "What about Sheriff Bradford? They're planning to kill him. I'm sure he would love a copy of this recording!"

Cheese grabs a donut, "Yes indeed, we could give him a copy and share it with a few newspapers. Heck, we can run copies over to the TV and radio stations."

Joey joins in, "Hey, what about the internet? Let's load it up."

Cheese shakes his head, "No way, they could trace that right back to us. We need to stay in the shadows. Speaking of shadows… y'all remember when I hid at the end of my road the night we blew up the bar?"

"Yep, you were making sure we weren't being followed."

"That's right." Cheese points across the parking lot, "You see those two detectives getting in their sedan? Well, I've seen those same two guys rubbing elbows with the Russian several times in the past. The night we hit the bar, I saw that same car fly by my road. I'm positive that's Komo and Fletcher, hit-men for the Mayor and his gang."

With a worried look Joey says, "Oh crud, they're on their way to find Matt!"

Cheese points to a plastic crate, "TC, look in there and snag one of those magnetic trackers. We need to get one on their car. Joey, you take this tracker and I want you to head towards Lafayette. First call Matt and let him and Bones know the detectives are coming. We'll drop you at your bike, and however you see fit; attach the tracker to their car. We'll know every move they make. Joey, I hate to say it, but you guys might have to take both of those cops out. I guess it's a 'kill or be killed' thing. In the meantime, TC and I are heading back to the camp. We'll duplicate the disk, and then figure out how to get it into Sheriff Bradford's hand, without being noticed."

Just a couple blocks away the white surveillance van slows down as Joey jumps out near a laundromat parking lot. Joey rushes over cranking his custom bike. With almost perfect timing, he watches the two detectives drive past. Within seconds, Joey pulls up behind the detectives as they come to a complete stop at a red light. Due to heavy traffic, Joey easily places the magnetic tracker underneath the detectives' bumper without being noticed. To insure not being seen, he backs away allowing several vehicles to get between him and the detectives as cover. Now that they're on Highway 90, he follows the detectives north, to Lafayette.

* * *

Chado Cole and Uriel watch as the Cajun surveillance team drives away in the white van. "Uriel, I know it's time to go, right?"

"Yes, as your dad used to say, 'It's time we make a block, kiddo.'"

Still sitting on a curb near the parking lot of the Morgan City courthouse, Uriel looks around to ensure no one is watching as he reaches over taking hold of Buck and Chado. Within a flash, they're suddenly standing in Lafayette near the loading dock of the Burnt Skillet Steak House.

Chado says with expression, “Hey, I recognize this place. I used to sit in traffic and complain how they need to synchronize the red lights, especially here on the corner of Johnston and Ambassador Caffery.”

“Yes I know, I had to listen to you moan about traffic for years.”

Chado laughs, “Okay, Uriel, what are we doing here?”

“Well, my friend, you need to pull out the old Martin guitar and do a little pan-handling. We are going to set up on the opposite side of the street and just wait.”

“Wait for what?”

“Wait for your buddy Matt.”

31

Evil Deeds

Cheese Hound's cell phone rings… it's Bones, "Hey, Cheese, what's up?"

"Bones, we got trouble heading your way. Has Joey called you?"

"No, I just got out of the shower and I noticed I had a missed call from him. I tried calling back, but no answer."

"Yeah, he probably wouldn't hear you. He's on his bike heading for Lafayette to hook up with you and Matt. Is Matt there with you?"

"No, he loaded Lela on the back of his bike early this morning. They ran down to New Iberia to some restaurant. Matt said he was craving shrimp and grits and there was only one place that really knew how to cook it. Cheese, what do you mean, we got trouble heading our way?"

"Bones, there are two crooked detectives who are inbound for Lafayette. They have kill orders from the Chief of Police and the Mayor. We need to call Matt right now."

"Well, that's going to be a problem, Cheese Hound."

"Why's that?"

"His cell phone is sitting right here on the table."

"Oh crap, Bones, listen to me. We have a recording of everything they're up to. Their first order of business is to track our team down, and I believe they're heading straight for you. Bones, grab his phone, go find Matt and Joey, and y'all high tail it back down here. We'll meet you guys at the shack."

"Okay, Cheese."

"Wait… It would probably be wise to dump the bikes. They're looking for a biker gang, and they probably already have Matt's license pegged. So snag your car and get in the wind. Keep me informed, Bones."

"Will do, Cheese."

Bones rolls his bike over to a neighbor's garage, and within a couple of minutes, he's heading toward New Iberia in his Dodge Hellcat. Blasting from one red light to the next, he's having a minor panic attack as he makes several attempts to contact Joey.

Bones carefully watches the oncoming traffic hoping to spot Matt and Lela heading north. Just past the Lafayette Airport, Joey finally answers his cell.

"Joey, you lug head. I've been trying to call you. Matt's in trouble, two detectives have kill orders and are heading in this direction!"

"Calm down, Bones, I know what's going on. I was with Cheese and TC when we listened in on their plan. I'm about a quarter mile behind those detectives."

"What's their location right now?"

"Oh, I guess they're around six or seven miles south of New Iberia."

"You've got to be kidding!"

"No, what's wrong Bones?"

"Matt and Lela went to New Iberia this morning for breakfast, and they're probably due to get out on Highway 90 right about now."

"Oh, my goodness, they could run right into those cops!"

"Joey, I'm around two miles past the airport and I should see you here in a couple minutes. Oh man…"

"What's wrong?"

"I'm getting pulled over by a good ole State Trooper. I was running around 75 in a 60. Joey, just don't let those detectives out of your sight, and as soon as this state boy gives me my ticket, I'll try to find Matt."

"Okay, call me as soon as you can. Oh yeah, I forgot to tell you, we have a tracking device on their car."

"Cool deal, stay safe, Joey."

"Don't worry, Bones, we'll find Matt, and before you know it we'll be eating fried alligator and drinking cold beer back at the shack."

Bones steps out of his Dodge Hellcat with paperwork in his hand.

The state trooper walks up tapping his clipboard with his pen. "Son, do you realize you were doing 78 miles per hour in a 55?"

"I'm sorry, sir, I actually thought it was 60 through here, and with low traffic this morning, I admit I had a bit of a heavy foot."

"The 60 zones don't start for another half mile or so, but that wouldn't have actually helped much. Let's take a look at your license, registration, and proof of insurance."

"Yes sir, here ya go. It's all in order and up to date."

"If you don't mind, stand in front of my car while I run your information. It won't take but a few minutes."

Bones leans back against the trooper's car just as Matt and Lela zoom past heading north on Highway 90. Suddenly, Bones' heart skips a beat when he sees a black sedan within 50 yards behind the couple. For a second he hopes it's just another cop car, but with all the dumb luck in the world, he spots Joey tagging along a quarter mile behind, just as he said. He's positive it's the detectives.

Looking back at the state police, Bones has a strong desire to spill the beans on the whole situation, thinking this trooper would somehow save the day. Fear comes over Bones, sending chills over his whole body. He whispers to himself, "What if all these cops are tied in with the drug lords? It would be the end for the whole crew."

The state trooper walks back out handing Bones his paperwork, "You okay son? You look like you just saw a ghost."

"Oh, no sir, I'm fine. I'm just a few minutes late meeting up with some of my friends."

"Son, you caught me on a good day. Your record isn't the best in the world but owning a hot rod like this you're not doing too badly. So I'm letting you off with a warning. But, before I allow you to leave, tell me what kind of horsepower this thing has."

Bones smiles, "Well, I bought it brand new, and it was pushing around 700 horses. Me and some of my buddies tinkered with it and bumped it up a nudge over 800."

"Good grief, my cruiser is only pushing around 400 horses. I'm glad I didn't have to try and run you down."

The kind state trooper slaps Bones on the shoulder with his ticket book, smiling as he heads back to his car.

Without wasting any time, Bones makes a U-turn at the next light waving as he passes the trooper. Just as he starts to call, his audio system informs him of an incoming call. It's Joey.

"Hey, Bones, we've got trouble, man. I'm still behind the detectives and they're right behind Matt and Lela. What do I do?"

"Does Matt know they're behind him?"

"I don't think so. My goodness, Bones, how's that for bad luck? Matt must have pulled right out in front of these guys just as they drove up on Highway 90."

"I know. What are the odds of that?"

"Bones, we need a plan."

"What's your location, Joey?"

"They turned off 90 onto University and we just drove past the college."

"Okay, I think I know where they're headed. He'll probably turn onto Johnston. They're headed to one of Lela's friend's house, who lives off of Ambassador Caffery."

"What should I do, Bones?"

"Just follow them. I don't think they'll try anything out in public. If I don't get pulled over again I should be there in around five or six minutes. Joey, try to stay back a few cars. We don't want them to know we're here."

* * *

After enjoying a wonderful Cajun breakfast, Matt and Lela feel the warmth of the morning sun while moving along with traffic through the streets of Lafayette.

Lela presses her face against Matt's back feeling safe at last, after living through the horror she had experienced being enslaved by the Russians. She notices a vehicle in the other lane with two kids smiling as they point at Matt's beautiful custom bike. Smiling back at the kids, she throws kisses at both of the children. They burst out laughing as they wave returning the gesture. Lela begins having thoughts that suddenly turn into questions. "Matt, sweetie, have you ever thought about having kids?"

"Kids… What, are you pregnant?"

Lela hits him on his helmet, "No… I'm not pregnant. I just think it would be nice to someday have a couple kids. You know, settle down and raise a family like normal people."

Matt reaches around patting her on the leg, "Weren't those shrimp and grits delicious?"

She punches him in the side, "Don't change the subject. I'm serious. I would love to leave this life behind and settle down out in the country. I would like to own a chicken, cow, dog, cat, and maybe even a horse for the kids."

Matt leans over on the tank as he bursts out laughing, "Girl... you are as crazy as a bessie bug."

"Yeah, but don't you love me?"

"I guess I do a little, but I don't want any stinking chickens. Maybe a dog... yeah, I think I could probably stand a dog."

"What about a little Matt Jr. or a little girl to bounce on your knee?"

"I'll think about it, sweetie."

Lela presses her face against his back once more as they slowly roll down Johnston St.

* * *

Chado Cole, Buck, and his guardian angel stand on a busy street corner in Lafayette, Louisiana. They're panhandling, dressed as bums.

Smiling and waving at passing cars, Chado strums the old Martin guitar. They give kind nods at the occasional Good Samaritan tossing change over into the guitar case, totally blending in with their surroundings. "Uriel, you know, this isn't such a bad job. I should have been doing this, instead of deep-sea diving. I might have lived a little longer."

Uriel gives Chado a friendly tap on his shoulder, and then points back down the street at the oncoming traffic. It's Matt, one of Chado's best friends. A friend he had labeled when he was among the living as his adopted little brother.

Being only one block away, Chado notices a dreadful sight behind Matt and Lela. It's the two detectives in a black sedan, and unknowingly, they have with them several demons swirling around their car. Just a few yards above these spawns of Satan were three large fallen angels. All are on a mission to destroy Matt.

Just as Chado is overcome with fear for his friend, Uriel reaches over giving him a gentle nudge. "Stand firm, Little Soul."

Unexpectedly, out of nowhere, another angel of God appears. Invisible to the living, this warrior angel is decked out with armor and sword in hand. He now stands beside Chado and Uriel.

As the detectives approach the intersection, the fallen angels hovering above their sedan, spot the panhandlers. They stare with a deep hatred that could only be fueled by Satan himself. Even though Chado and Uriel are dressed as bums, they no longer fool the fallen angels. They are exposed for who they really are.

* * *

Matt has no idea Detectives Fletcher and Komo are only a few feet behind them, as they roll up to the intersection. Matt happens to look over and recognize the same two bums and mangy dog that were at the Bayou Rose. While sitting at the red light, Matt quickly reaches in his front pocket pulling out a $100 bill, and motions for Chado to come over. Just as Chado takes hold of the bill, Matt looks deep into his eyes. He suddenly recognizes his best friend that had died five years ago. That dreadful day flashes through his mind as Matt remembers Chado lying on a stretcher with the EMT shaking her head, as they covered him with a sheet.

Tears fill Matt's eyes as he holds onto the money in a way to make his long lost friend stand still, "Chado, it's you. How can this be possible? I watched your family grieve as we buried you."

"Old friend, '*This corruptible has put on incorruption, this mortal has put on immortality. Death is swallowed up in victory. O Death, where is your sting? O Hades, where is your victory?*'

"Matt, God has chosen you for something very special. You are about to take a journey into the darkness. But know this my friend, we will be with you."

Before Matt has time to respond, the detectives slam into the back of Matt's bike, launching him out into the crossing traffic. Within a split second, an oncoming beer delivery truck hits Matt and Lela broadside. Matt and his bike tumble across the four lanes ending up underneath the truck. Lela goes airborne, slamming into the windshield of an oncoming vehicle. Her limp body ends up in the front passenger seat of a car.

Chado stands at the edge of the street corner still holding half of the torn $100 bill in his hand. After watching his best friend and Lela tumble through the air, Chado glances at the demons and fallen angels as they laugh and snarl while hovering around the debris of the crash.

With blacked-out plates, dark tinted windows, and no markings on their vehicle, the two detectives drive away unnoticed by the public.

Chado advances, feeling anger toward the demonic forces and the two evil men. Uriel quickly grabs Chado's arm gently pulling him back from the street corner. "Slow down, Little Soul, we need to stand back and let this scene go as God planned."

Being overwhelmed by compassion for his friend, Chado pulls away from Uriel and runs out into the street crawling under the truck. "Matt, I'm here! I'm here with you, buddy."

Still on his stomach, he manages to crawl past the crushed bike farther underneath the truck, until he finally comes face-to-face with his unconscious friend. "Matt, it's me. Your ole buddy, Chado."

With no response, he takes Matt's bloody wrist and feels for a pulse. "Come on, Matt, you hang in there."

Lying on his side, Chado stares at the broken bloody body of his long-time friend. He continues talking to Matt, when he notices a small sign of life. Matt barely cracks his eyes open, whispering, "Chado, is Lela okay?"

Before Chado can answer, Matt passes out. He is silenced from his critical injuries.

Within seconds, first responders arrive on the scene. Chado feels two Lafayette cops grab him by the ankles sliding him from underneath the truck.

One of the policemen asks with a gruff voice, "Were you involved in this wreck?"

"No, sir, I was just trying to help."

"We appreciate your concern, but we'll handle it from here. You need to move along."

Chado humbly walks back over to Uriel, "I'm sorry for disobeying and not listening to you. But I couldn't just stand by and not do anything. That's my best friend on Earth underneath that truck."

"It is okay, Chado. No need for apologies. I knew you were going to do just what you did. Otherwise, I would have been saddened if you had chosen to just watch. This is another example of why God selected you for this mission. Your actions display evidence of a true heart."

Chado gives Uriel a sad smile as he turns his attention back to his friend. With a cloud of despair covering his heart, he realizes Matt has denied Christ all the years that he's known him. He patiently waits for the demons to tear out his soul and spirit. The demons are coiling around him like snakes, each one snarling with excitement as they wait for his last breath. Waiting on this dreadful moment, he notices the demons are backing away as the EMT's load Matt into the back of an ambulance.

"Uriel, what's going on? Is he going to be okay?"

Abruptly, one of the fallen angels along with two demons hover just a few feet away from Uriel, "You think you can save this one? He belongs to me! This mortal will soon taste the wrath of hell. As a mortal he has been a slave to sin and rejected the Christ. Now he will become a slave to hell. It is our right; we have authority and ownership of his soul. Angels of the Carpenter, you have no part in this. So I say, away with you."

The fallen angel slowly flies backward over the intersection until he hovers directly above Matt. This action resembles a dominate animal that just made a fresh kill, and now has claimed his bounty.

The mighty warrior angel standing behind Uriel replaces his sword in its sheath. Within minutes they closely watch the fallen angels and their demons follow the two ambulances as they transport Matt and Lela to Lafayette Hospital.

Chado squats down beside Buck, closes the guitar case, and looks up at Uriel. "What just happened? I just knew we would be on our way to Hell's Gate."

"Patience, Little Soul, it is always God's timing, not ours. Come along, we need to stay close to Matt, and when the chosen time comes, he will take his journey, and we will be there to protect him."

* * *

Bones pulls up behind Joey as they both watch the two ambulances carry Matt and Lela away. Traffic is still shut down as everyone waits for wreckers to clear the road. Joey gets off his bike and jumps into the car with Bones. "Joey, what the heck just happened?"

Joey with a frightened look responds, "Those two detectives just killed Matt and Lela, or at least they both looked dead when they were loaded on stretchers."

Without saying anything, Bones calls Cheese Hound on his cell. "Hey, Cheese, I've got you on speaker, and I've got Joey here in the car with me."

"Did y'all find Matt?"

Bones hits Joey on the leg. "Tell him, Joey."

Cheese butts back in, "Tell me what? Did you find him, or not?"

With hesitation, Joey says, "Cheese… we've got bad news. Those two detectives were sitting behind Matt and Lela at a red light, and right when a huge beer truck was crossing Johnston Street, they hit Matt's bike from behind. They pushed them right out in front of that beer truck. It's bad, Cheese. I got as close up as I could and they both looked dead when the ambulances carried them away."

Without answering Bones and Joey, the phone goes silent for a few seconds. Suddenly, they hear Cheese Hound on the other end, cursing and tearing a room to pieces.

Joey whispers to Bones, "I believe we are about to go to war with these turds!"

After a couple of minutes of anger management, they hear a calm cool voice coming from Cheese. "Joey, look at your tracking device and tell me where the detectives are at."

"Cheese, it looks like they're headed back towards Morgan City."

"Okay, this is what I want y'all to do. Joey, you dump your bike, cab up with Bones, and you guys get back down here as soon as you can."

"Okay, my dad's shop is only a couple of blocks from here. We'll drop my bike there, and we'll be in the wind."

"Wait, run by the hospital, and check on Matt. No… scratch that. I'm about to get y'all killed. For right now, we don't need to be seen anywhere around Matt. Forgive me boys, I'm not thinking straight. Just get back down here so we can get our heads together and figure out what to do."

"Okay, Cheese, we're on our way."

32

THREADS OF LIFE

Chado points to a row of thick hedges, "Buck, you go hide in there for a while. I'm sorry, ole buddy, but they don't allow dogs inside hospitals."

Chado slides the guitar case underneath the shrubs, takes the leather pouch holding the scroll and hangs it around the huge canine's neck. "Old friend, don't let anyone put their hands on this scroll."

Buck looks around as though he's checking to make sure no one sees him as he slips behind the thick hedges.

Chado and Uriel chuckle at Buck as they make their way inside to the ER waiting room, thinking how funny he gets when he's in undercover mode.

Being dressed as bums, their appearance causes suspicion in other people sitting in the waiting room. Uriel slaps Chado on his knee, "I will be right back."

He walks off down the hall and within a few minutes he returns with a small plastic bag. "Come with me, Chado."

Chado follows Uriel to the nearest restroom, and as they enter, Uriel hits Chado in the chest with a set of hospital scrubs. "Put those on and be quick about it."

After they are fully dressed in surgery room scrubs, even down to the cloth booties that cover your feet, they toss their smelly bum disguises over into a nearby trashcan.

With a very busy emergency room, no one notices Chado or Uriel as they stroll around, pretending to be helping. Chado notices the same demons that were at the wreck are swarming around Matt. They apparently are waiting for him to take his last breath. Two rooms away, more of the same type of demons, are hovering around Lela. The demons are unaware of Chado and Uriel's presence, as they are totally focused on their victims.

Chado, standing only a few feet away from Matt, hears some of the medical team's conversation. "This young man barely has a pulse and probably won't make it through the night. Too much internal bleeding, he needs to go straight to surgery, immediately!"

The lone ER doctor orders the nurse to put him on life support. Then he walks out of the room heading for Lela.

After inserting a breathing tube, nurses continue working on Matt's external injuries, as two scrub techs wheel him down the hall to emergency surgery.

Chado whispers while cleaning out a trash can, "Hey, Uriel, how long will we be here? It looks like Matt might go at any time."

"I do not know. We just have to wait and be ready when he does."

Suddenly a sheriff's deputy walks into the ER and speaks with the doctor. "Hey, Doc, I need to find out about the man and woman that were just brought in. We didn't get any ID on either of the two."

The doctor hands over Matt's Louisiana license, "Deputy, the lady didn't have any ID on her, and if you don't mind, get in touch with this guy's family. We're going to do everything we can, but considering his injuries, he probably won't make it through the night."

The cop smiles, "So what you're saying is, he needs a miracle."

"Yes, I guess so."

"Well, Doc, I'm a praying man, and I intend on sending out an e-mail to a slew of prayer warriors. So don't you folks give up on either of those two just yet! I don't know why, but I feel a strong urge to lift them up to the Lord. In the meantime, I'll chase down their next of kin."

"Thank you, deputy. I'm sure the families will appreciate your compassion. However, we are way understaffed today and I need to get back to it."

"Say no more, Doc. Have a blessed one."

* * *

After several hours of surgery, Matt continues hanging onto a small thread of life as they wheel him into ICU. The surgeons both have low confidence in his survival.

Coleen Ann Cole, a nurse who has worked the ICU floor for years, comes on duty at 11:00 pm. She looks at her patient's charts and talks with Glenda Johnson, the nurse she is relieving.

"Hey, Coleen, how was your day off?"

"Oh… girl my days off are actually a thing of the past. Raising my grandson keeps me pretty active."

"Hey… that's right, you lost a daughter a few years back. I'm so sorry."

"Yes, Nathan was almost one year old when Summer got killed. I'm his momma now, at least until we all get to Heaven."

"I hate to pry, but didn't you lose your husband in an offshore accident?"

"I did, it was five years ago when I lost Chado. He was a deep-sea diver out in the Gulf of Mexico. All I ever found out was that he drowned. A friend of his said he was working around 200 feet deep when it happened. The dive company never came clean on what really went on that night. I just remember that awful late night call."

"Coleen, it sounds like you've been through it."

"That's ok. I get comfort knowing Chado is probably up there in Heaven with Summer, and they are enjoying themselves."

"Coleen, you said your husband was a diver? This is kind of weird that we're on this subject. They just brought in a guy who was in a motorcycle crash, and he has some kind of dive tattoo on his right shoulder. Who knows, you might know him. He's in ICU 7."

"I'll be right back."

Glenda, being curious, follows Coleen to Room 7, carrying his chart with her. As Coleen enters the room, she realizes the patient is unrecognizable from the swelling to his face and dried blood over both eyes. Without saying anything, she runs some water into a wash pan and begins cleaning his face. After several wipes over his forehead and cheeks, tears begin to swell in Coleen's eyes. Glenda, feeling compassion, swiftly places her arm around her shoulder. "I'm so sorry, sweetie. Apparently you do know who he is."

Glenda takes the bloodstained rag away from Coleen, tossing it over into the pan as she wraps her arms around her. Both are silent for several seconds with only Coleen whimpering on Glenda's shoulder, as one of the surgery doctors walks through the door.

"What's going on in here?"

Coleen looks up at Dr. Welch with tears in her eyes, "Give me a second, Doctor."

Glenda walks her out to the nurses' station, sitting her down. "Would you like a cup of water, sweetie?"

"Yes, thank you."

After only a couple of minutes, Dr. Welch comes out of Matt's room walking straight up to Coleen. "Okay, Nurse, talk to me. What's the connection, and do we need to get you a replacement for tonight?"

"His name is Matt Stone, and he was friends with my deceased husband."

"I understand. If you don't mind me asking, how long ago did you lose your husband?"

"He died five years ago. Doctor, is Matt going to make it?"

"Truthfully, we don't know. He's barely hanging on. We've got a neurosurgeon who will give us a report on brain activity here shortly. If we get negative results, it will be up to the family to decide how long they will want to keep him alive. Well I guess there is always a chance of a miracle. My question is, can you perform your duty as a nurse?"

"Yes, sir, I believe I'll be okay."

Glenda butts in, "Dr. Welch, I'll pull a double if you want me to stay."

"Thank you, Nurse. I believe that's a good idea. If you find yourself dozing off, grab one of the vacant rooms and get a few winks. You ladies call me if things get crazy."

* * *

Back down south at the Cajun Bat Cave, Cheese Hound, Joey, TC, and Bones all sit around a small table discussing their next move. The crew mumbles between each other, "I wonder if Matt and Lela might pull through."

Joey with a bit of sorrow, "If you'd have seen the shape they were both in, well I guess what I'm trying to say is, don't get your hopes up too high."

Cheese shakes his head as he dials the number to the Lafayette Hospital. "Yes, I would like to check on two people that were in a motorcycle collision this morning. Can you please check… yes thank you, I'll hold."

Cheese Hound, activates the speakerphone allowing the crew

to listen in. Piano music softly plays over the phone while they all patiently wait. No one is saying a word as they all stare at the phone lying in the center of the table. There is a clicking sound as the music is silenced, "Sir, are you still there?"

"Yes… Ma'am, I'm here."

"Our records show a Mr. Matt Stone went through surgery and is now in ICU. At this point, the young lady is listed as an unknown and she is also in ICU. Would you like for me to transfer you to the intensive care unit?"

"Yes, please."

"ICU, this is Nurse Johnson, can I help you?"

"Yes Ma'am, can you give me a report on Matt Stone and Lela Gentry?"

"Are you a family member, sir?"

Cheese, realizing they probably won't give out information to just anyone, hastily decides to lie.

"Yes, ma'am, I'm Matt's brother, Steven Stone, and Lela is his girlfriend."

"Well, Mr. Stone, I hate to give this kind of news over the phone, but they are critical and barely clinging to life. We have both patients on life support at this time. The sheriff's department has been trying to find their next of kin. If you want to see your brother alive, you probably need to get here as quickly as possible. I'm so sorry for the bad news."

"I understand, Ms. Johnson, thank you."

"Yes sir, goodbye."

* * *

Coleen walks up to the nurse's station just as Glenda is about to call the sheriff's department. "Hey, Coleen, just got a piece of good news on our patient, Matt Stone. His brother just called. He said his name is Steven Stone."

Coleen, with a strange look on her face says, "Matt doesn't have a brother. He's got one sister that lives somewhere in Minnesota. It must be some kind of a mistake."

"Why in the world would anyone do that?"

Coleen replies, "I don't know, I hope he wasn't mixed up with the wrong crowd."

33

Cajun Justice and the Glass Bottom Boat

Back down in the swamp, Cheese Hound leans back in his chair rubbing both hands across his face, "Okay, fellows, here's my thoughts. I know we kicked a hornets' nest when we shut down that drug ring. We knew when we started, that the Russians were involved. On the other hand, we didn't know the Columbians and these crooked politicians were connected. Don't get me wrong, I didn't mind one bit killing those Russians or anyone else that's involved with their drug enterprise. Saying this, I want to ask you guys, do you want to take the money and run? In other words, get as far away from all this as possible."

Bones sets his coffee cup down, "What are you going to do, Cheese?"

"With or without you boys, I'm going to kill them all. I don't want to look over my shoulder for the rest of my life. Besides that, I'll be getting revenge for what they've done to Matt and Lela."

Bones looks into the eyes of each man at the table. "I was hoping that's what you would say, Cheese Hound."

TC slaps the table, "Heck yeah, let's kill 'em."

Cheese pulls out a hidden drawer underneath the table, "I originally had plans on getting these recordings to Sheriff Bradford. I just don't believe him or his two deputies have the experience or the firepower to go against this mob. On top of that, this bunch of crooked politicians will probably get smooth out of it."

Joey looks at his watch, "It's almost midnight. Are we doing anything tonight?"

Cheese smiles, "Yes, we are going to do the unexpected. Those fools probably think we're on our way to Canada by now. Joey, you got that tracker on you?"

"Sure do."

"Where are those two detectives?"

Joey does his famous grin, as he replies. "It looks like they are just off Pelican Cove about a mile or so. Hey, you reckon that's where the Mayor's beach house is located?"

Cheese nods, "That's exactly where it's at. We have the whole herd in one place. Remember when we recorded those crooks? They were bragging about drinking whiskey and having the young heifers waiting. This looks like a chance where we can totally catch them off guard."

Joey and Bones begin digging in the gun lockers as Cheese opens a small canister. "I've got a crazy idea that I want to throw in the mix."

Cheese pulls out several chemical darts and hands each man a high-end dart gun. "Fellows, we're going to capture those guys."

Joey with a bewildered look, said, "I thought we were in the killing business tonight?"

Cheese loads one of the dart guns. "I have big plans, Joey. If the Mayor, DA, Police Chief, and a State Representative are involved, I just wonder who else might be connected. I'm just saying that if we're going to make a dent in the fender, heck, let's wreck the whole car."

Joey asks, “How do you figure on squeezing information out of them?”

Cheese replies, “We’re doing a night raid on their beach house by way of sea. Tag’em and bag’em, then bring their whole crew out in the Gulf. Don’t sweat it fellows, I’ve already loaded what we need on board and know exactly what to do. By the time we finish, we’ll know all their dark secrets. So arm up, grab fresh batteries for your night vision, and let’s go.”

This gang of modern day outlaws cruise south in the narrow backwater bayous leading to the Gulf of Mexico. Traveling in total darkness using military grade night vision, they quietly idle up to the beach within an hour. Cheese switches to infrared scopes, easily spotting a small security detail roaming the property. He motions everyone into a huddle. “Okay, fellows, we’re going to make this look like the Columbians hit this place. So don’t say anything in front of those girls, unless you can speak Spanish. Joey, grab those two dead chickens out of the ice chest.”

Joey chuckles, “What do we need chickens for?”

Cheese smiles, “It’s a Columbian drug lord thing. Let’s go.”

Within a couple of minutes, the security detail is down, and the outside perimeter is secure. There is no movement inside. It seems that everyone is passed out drunk or asleep. The team quietly moves from one room to the next, popping each person with tranquilizers.

Four of the girls wake up facing these masked vigilantes and begin to scream. Cheese motions for his crew to turn off their night vision, as he reaches over turning on the lights. He holds his finger in front of his lips as to kindly tell the girls to be quiet. Without uttering a word, he points at the huge leather couch. With a little help from TC and Joey, they gently sit the girls down.

Only taking a couple of minutes, Bones, TC, and Joey use duct tape to secure and gag their captives. Cheese Hound takes the chickens and cuts their throats. With his internet education on Columbian voodoo, he paints the walls in Spanish with several different symbols, along with a note, written in chicken blood:

The venom runs through the blood of life, my fangs sink deep into the heart of America. All who betray the snake shall inherit the sorrow of my ancestors.

As a safety precaution, they tie up the teenage girls, collect all the cell phones, and cut the power. In the meantime, TC and Joey make a couple of trips using the Mayor's fancy golf cart delivering all six men to the beach. With help from Bones and Cheese Hound, they roll their unconscious bodies over in the hull of the huge powerboat. Within minutes, they head out to sea.

Running the powerboat in total darkness, with only the instrument panel glowing, Joey's curiosity overcomes him. "Cheese, you mind telling us where we're headed?"

"You divers will like this. You see, I have a favorite abandoned oilrig that sits pretty close to a trench that the locals call Dead Man's Trough. It's a shallow trench that extends up from the Sigsbee Deep."

Bones butts in, "Hey, we know that area. We've laid several pipelines near there. That Dead Man's Trough is around 2,800 feet deep. Not too much farther past that, it drops off to around 14,000 feet deep. Cheese, why would you want to go that far out?"

The Hound laughs, "More dramatic. I want the best for our elected officials."

With the calm Gulf waters, the huge craft makes good time as they glide along the unusually slick surface. Cheese points at the blinking light on the abandoned offshore rig. "Hey, TC, check on our guests and see if the drugs have worn off yet."

TC opens the small hatch shining a penlight down into the hull. "Yep, it looks like they are all bright-eyed and bushy-tailed."

Cheese pulls back on the dual throttles as they approach the rig.

Idling the last few hundred feet, Joey knows what he has to do. When you work in the Gulf for years, you know how to tie off to a rig, so that the current will push your boat away from the structure. For an added precaution, you always let out additional slack just in case the current changes. "Good job, Joey, we don't want to scratch our pretty boat."

Bones crawls down in the hull cutting the duct tape from each of the seven men's ankles, leaving their hands and mouths still bound. One by one, they are directed up onto the deck.

TC stands on the front of the powerboat looking down the barrel of an AR-15, as each of the condemned men exit the hull. As they step out, Cheese sits each one down on a long bench seat. Staring into their eyes, some display a look of anger—others a look of fear. Having no idea of what's going on, each one tries to talk, but with duct tape covering their mouths they sound like men without tongues, desperately trying to explain themselves.

Other than the small waves hitting the hull of the powerboat, a silence falls over this scene. The bound men stop trying to talk as they each look around at their captors, all wearing black ski masks covering their faces.

The dive crew are all wondering what Cheese Hound is about to do, and patiently wait with their weapons directed at the condemned. Without saying anything, Cheese pulls out the Mayor's cell phone and scrolls over to the recording app. "Gentlemen, what you say over the next few minutes may or may not save your lives. I would recommend the truth and nothing but the truth. I am going to give each one of you an opportunity and, like I said, you might want to come clean."

Cheese reaches over to peel away the tape from Detective Fletcher's mouth. "Okay, worm, what do you have to say in your defense?"

With a strange look on his face, Fletcher humbly asks, “Are y’all working for the Columbians?”

Cheese Hound lies, “Yes we are. Where’s our money and who killed the Russian?”

Joey can’t help himself as he chuckles. Cheese briefly looks up at Joey slightly shaking his head. Being a bit embarrassed, Joey quickly zips it, while he continues to admire Cheese as he displays his cunning tactics.

Now being very attentive, Fletcher explains. “We know who hit the Bayou Rose and we know where they’re at. We were planning on taking their whole crew out at daylight this morning.”

Cheese whispers through his mask with a scratchy voice like an old west gunfighter. “Who are they…? Where are they?”

“It’s a biker gang and they’re hid out in an old fishing camp down on the bayou.”

“How could you possibly know that?”

“We tortured a call girl that works for the Russian, and she told us where and who they are.”

“How do you know she gave you the facts?”

“She’s friends with a girl named Lela. This girl is sweet on one of the bikers, and a cousin to a guy named Cheese Hound.”

“Cheese Hound, now that’s an odd name.”

The crew burst out laughing along with the detective as he snickers. Cheese reaches up and pats Fletcher on the head, “I have to say, you might get out of this after all. So tell me how many men were you bringing in, to make the raid on this fellow you call Cheese Hound?”

“We’re hiring outside help, to make the hit, because we are a little shorthanded. The best deputy we had on the Russian’s payroll was killed in a Morgan City pawnshop, the night the bikers took down the Bayou Rose.”

Cheese reels Fletcher in like a fish, "How do I know we can trust outsiders?"

"Oh, don't worry, they're good men. They're ex-military and we've used them in the past. Trust me, they are very thorough."

Cheese turns and winks at Joey as he pries more information from Fletcher "Have you given your military guys the biker's camp location?"

"No way, I trust them, but not that much. Komo and I are the only ones who know where it's located. You've got to understand, there are several million dollars involved in this. I wouldn't trust my own mamma with that much cash."

"What about the prostitute, how much does she know?"

"The prostitute is out of the picture. After we beat all the information out of her, we dumped her corpse into the Mississippi River."

Cheese gives Fletcher a subtle smile as he asks, "Well, I guess the only other loose end would be the girl named Lela."

The detective laughs, "No loose end there. We took her and her boyfriend, Matt Stone, out this morning. Trust me, they are history."

Cheese Hound walks over to the console, "Gentlemen, do you guys ever watch any animal channels on television? Personally, I like the historical shows, but occasionally, I flip over to those animal shows. Sometimes they have the underwater videos. I guess what amazes me is the food chain down under the ocean. Those big and small fish swim around all day eating on anything that looks tasty."

Cheese flips a switch on the console and the floor underneath the feet of the condemned men starts to retract, unveiling a glass bottom in the luxury powerboat. With the pristine blue water and the bright lights of the offshore rig they can see around 50 feet deep. Multitudes of fish are visible, different species ranging from small chigger fish, barracuda, along with a few sharks.

Cheese tosses a dive harness over to Bones, "Slip that on our new friend." He reaches underneath the console pulling out what divers call a "spare air kit". This small bottle has a mouthpiece attached to the top of a mini tank. The tank only holds three cubic feet of air. It's only good for a few minutes in shallow water. Cheese walks over to a hidden compartment underneath one of the seats and drags out several weight belts along with a roll of climbing rope.

"Mr. Fletcher, I'll need those clothes you've got on."

The detective begins squirming and pleading for his life. "What are you doing? I'm not taking off my clothes. You people are crazy! I've told you everything. If you kill me, you'll never find your money, and you'll need me when we get another lab up and running."

Cheese smiles, "Calm down, Mr. Fletcher. Here, let me help you out of those clothes."

Cheese whips out a razor-sharp skinning knife, and starting at his belt loop, slices down both sides of the detective's trousers. With nothing remaining but his boxers, he begins swearing at Cheese. "So help me, I will make you pay if it's the last thing I do!"

"Well that wasn't very nice. I was going to leave your shirt and boxers on, but you being all hateful and stuff, I believe we better get them off too." Cheese reaches up with a couple quick slices, and now, other than a dive harness, the detective stands on the bow buck-naked.

Bones realizing what the Hound's intentions are, places the heavy weight belt around Fletcher's waist, then ties the rope to the harness. Bones forces Fletcher backward until he's standing just a few inches from the edge.

For one final surprise, Cheese attaches a six-foot string of shiny silver fishing spoons onto the harness, and smiles. "My advice to you would be to conserve your air and hold on, because this is gonna be a wild ride. Oh yeah… the mini tank is only good for a few minutes."

Before the detective can respond, Cheese jams the spare air kit into his mouth. He then takes his razor-sharp skinning knife and makes several small cuts on the detective's extremities. Just before a single drop of blood hits the boat, Cheese hits Fletcher square in the chest, sending the detective overboard.

Cheese points at the spool of rope. "Bones let out about 35 feet of slack. This should be a pretty good show."

Observing through the glass bottom, they all watch as the detective hangs helpless below the boat. At first the fish swam away, annoyed by the naked man squirming about. The first fish to show up are the sheepshead. They've always been a pain for divers due to having teeth resembling a human's. They tend to swarm around you, kind of like mosquitoes, darting in and out, constantly nipping and biting at your skin. You could say they're more of a hindrance than a danger. As long as you wear a good thick wet suit, you're okay. Now being completely naked, you have a totally different outcome.

The detective squirms and kicks at four small sheepshead. He's totally unaware of several barracuda lurking in the shadows of the rig. They are enticed by the shiny silver lures attached to his harness. Within seconds, and traveling at high speed, three barracuda rush in attacking the lures. Similar to a Saturday morning fishing show, the three barracudas are now attached to the fishing lures, with each trying to go in different directions. They jerk Fletcher around, and he looks like a rag doll being tossed about. Another six-foot barracuda cuts one of the sheepshead into two pieces. With scales and pieces of fresh fish floating, and the smell of human blood in the water, a twelve-foot tiger shark comes up out of the dark depths. He wants in on the feeding frenzy. With precision, the shark makes a pass taking the left leg of the naked detective.

The Mayor turns his head away. He can't stand watching as the beautiful blue water just turned red with Detective Fletcher's blood and floating pieces of fish. Cheese reaches over and tears the duct tape away from the Mayor's mouth. "Hey, Your Honor, I'm so sorry. I didn't realize the fish channel was going to be rated R tonight. Okay, who's up next for a swim?"

Bones and Joey point at Detective Komo as Cheese gives them an order. "Hey, you guys, pull in Fletcher, we need his harness and I bet you, he's ready for a towel."

The Mayor breaks his silence, "You people are crazy. You're not with the Columbians. Who the heck are you? Tell me what we've done to deserve something as horrible as this. Who ever heard of being tortured to death by fish?"

Cheese smiles, "Yes, I would have to say this is a bit diabolical."

The Mayor pleads, "I beg you! Is there anything, I can say or do that would cause you to spare us?"

Cheese reaches over and peels away the duct tape from the other gagged men. "Okay, let's see which one of you sleaze balls can talk me out of deep-sixing each stinking one of y'all, starting with you, Mr. State Representative."

"My name is Jerry Brown and I have a family…"

Cheese interrupts, "You see, you blew it right there. When you used your name and the old… 'I have a family' trick, you blew it. You need to understand, I read a lot. What you're trying to do, is jack with my conscience. Make me feel all sorry for you and crap. Let's try this again and here's a little hint, we need information."

Abruptly, Bones and Joey pull Detective Fletcher's corpse to the surface, "Wow, look at that. There's not much left to him. What do we do with the rest, Cheese?"

"Take the harness and put it on Komo. Leave the weight belt on Fletcher and send him to the bottom. I have plenty of belts. Now, you were saying, Mr. Brown?"

They hear the splash as they all watch through the viewing glass, as Fletcher's remains quickly sink out of sight.

Mr. Brown, now crying, begs, "Please, tell me how we have wronged you. I promise we can fix it. We've got money; we can set you guys up with a fortune."

Holding his hand up to his mouth, Cheese Hound, signals Brown with the zip-lip gesture. He then turns and notices the guys have Komo standing on the edge, stripped down to his birthday suit, with an air bottle hanging out of his mouth, ready to go. "Hey, fellows, I changed my mind. I think we can cut Mr. Komo a break."

Komo nods his head 'yes' in agreement with Cheese, thinking he might get to live.

Cheese steps up face-to-face with Komo, "Take his harness off and one of you guys explain to this gentleman about water pressure."

TC steps up and says, "Let me see, where to start… I guess I can give you a quick version. You see, your body can take the depth pretty good up to a few hundred feet deep. The problem for someone like you is, it's all about the ears. I know this sounds crazy. Nevertheless, just stay with me, and I'll try to explain. When a person dives off into an eight-foot pool, and heads for the bottom without popping their ears, they begin to hurt. If you don't pop them pretty quick, you have to come back up a few feet to relieve the pressure, pop them again, and then you can continue, going deeper, continually popping. You feel me, Detective?" Komo, nods his head yes.

"Okay, so here's the tricky part. Right where we're sitting the depth gauge says we're in about 300 feet of water. But the current is pushing to the south, and about ¼ mile in that direction is what we call Dead Man's Trough. It's two or three thousand feet deep. I would guess your ole bud Fletcher is slowly heading in that direction. Forgive me, I got a little off track. We were discussing pressure. Now, where was I? Oh, yeah, the ears. You see, out here in this extreme depth as you're going down, you pass through a different atmosphere every 33 feet. Do you realize what happens if you can't pop your ears after going through the first atmosphere? Your eardrums explode! Nevertheless, the pain will eventually be gone. You want to know why?"

Komo starts crying, shaking his head no as Cheese pulls TC back, "That's enough, you're scaring the poor guy."

Komo, overcome with fear, looks behind him at the water as Cheese gently pulls his chin around until they are face-to-face. "Now, now, there's no need to tear up in front of all these men. You're either about to be a hero or a zero, so be careful and answer me wisely. Which one of you two was driving when you and your bud killed that biker trash that stole our money?"

Cheese reaches up, taking the air bottle out of his mouth. Komo smiles thinking he is about to make some points with the Columbians. "I was driving. I waited for the perfect opportunity and I bumped them out in front of a beer truck. Let me go and I'll kill every stinking one of those guys."

Cheese Hound and the rest of his crew, all at the same time as though it had been well planned, pull off their ski masks to reveal their true identities.

Reaching up scratching his head, Cheese Hound tosses his mask on the console and looks deep into Komo's eyes. "Hello, Mr. Detective, let me introduce our little crew, or what y'all have been calling 'biker trash.'"

The detective and the rest of the condemned men's hearts sink as he continues. "I'm the one they call Cheese Hound. That's TC and Joey. The guy with the long hair holding that rifle to your head is Bones. I hate to say it, but we're missing two other buddies, that no longer are here with us. Matt's not here because you snakes killed him yesterday. The other fallen member of our crew, well… that was Chado Cole, a dear friend who died five years ago out here in this Gulf."

Cheese points down at the water. "You see, he died down there on the bottom, and it being his anniversary of leaving this world, I think it would be an honor if you fellows go pay him a visit."

The condemned men continue begging for mercy, promising they would do anything to make this right.

Cheese holds his hand in the air, "Hold on now, fellows. Y'all are going to have to be a bit more convincing than that. You see, Matt was a dear friend to all of us, and my sweet little cousin Lela you killed was just an innocent kid. Now the young girl you two beat to death and threw in the river, well… her dad is a close friend of mine. Nope, I don't think there's anything known in the human language that might save your souls."

Cheese jams the mini air bottle into his mouth, pulls out his Colt 45, and shoots the detective in the kneecap, as he shoves him overboard.

"Now, who else wants to die tonight? Bones bring me the police chief, if you don't mind. We need to hurry this along. It'll be getting daylight soon."

Joey laughs, "Hey, fellows, he's a fat boy. We probably need to put two weight belts on him."

Chief Lewis struggles against the muscle-bound divers as he pleads for his life. "Please have mercy; I'm not a bad man. I beg you, please have mercy!"

Cheese pushes him closer to the edge with Lewis still begging, "Wait, just wait! Don't I at least get a few last words?"

"Answer this riddle, why did the evil men decide to destroy Louisiana with drugs?"

The Chief stutters, "Wait, wait…"

Cheese doesn't give him an air bottle like the two before. "You want to be a man and jump, or do I have to throw you in?"

The Chief falls to his knees begging, "Please have mercy, please!"

Bones steps up and kicks the police chief under his chin sending him flying back into the water, "Where was your mercy when you ordered a hit on my friend, Matt? You sorry sucker, you're headed for a place called, Hell!"

Cheese turns around, "Who we got left, Joey?"

"We still have the mayor, DA and the state rep."

"We're pushing daylight boys; let's do two at a time. Heck, they can keep each other company on their way down. Bring me DA Phillips and Mayor Dalton. Not only can they keep each other company, they can hold hands when they cross over into the fiery furnace. Come to think of it TC, how old do you think those young girls were they had back at that fancy beach house? They didn't look a day over 16 if I had to guess. You two child molesters move on up here."

TC replies, "You don't have to guess, I looked at their IDs. Three were 17, and the fourth was barely 16 years old."

Cheese looks over at Dalton, Phillips, and Brown, "For the life of me, I don't understand you power grabbing, sick monsters. How can you stand to look in the mirror knowing how many innocent lives you've screwed up? If I was a betting man, I would bet there is a special place in hell for your kind. You could still have a life of luxury being an honest and God-fearing servant of the people. However, you swine decided to get mixed up with the Russians and Columbians. You sit back smoking big cigars and drinking fancy whiskey while they feed drugs to the community. Do you three even have a soul?"

State Representative Brown whispers to Mayor Dalton, "Tell them what's really going on. A federal prison would be better than dying out here."

Joey, standing close enough to hear their whispers, bumps Brown in the temple with the barrel of his AR-15. "Tell us what?" He reaches over further, taping Mayor Dalton on the head with his rifle, "You turds better come clean. This is your final countdown."

DA Phillips says with a loud voice, "Okay, okay… We'll come clean if you promise to let us go. I have to agree with Brown. A federal prison would be a step-up from dying out here. Can you guarantee our safety?"

34

Apollyon Mastema

Cheese Hound activates the cell phone video recorder. "Bones, for insurance, hit the recorder on that other phone. I would hate to miss out if this one was to crap out. Okay, you skunks, I want all three of you to state your names, and tell us what you do for a living. Then, I want DA Phillips to give us details about everything. Alright boys, let's hear it.

Each taking their turn, the bound men one by one look intently into the cameras.

"My name is Jerry Brown, and I am a Louisiana State Representative."

"My name is Marcus Dalton, and I am the Mayor of Morgan City."

"My name is Raymond Phillips, and I am the District Attorney for St. Mary Parish. I am here with a group of unknown men that have forced my three friends and me at gunpoint into confessing our crimes against the citizens of the United States. Before I begin, please understand that I have always felt ashamed of my decision to be a part of what I'm about to reveal. At first it seemed harmless and just a great scheme to make extra money, but I got pulled down a rabbit hole with no exit. At this point, I'm glad to finally reveal this madness. With my confession, it is my hope to be relieved of this heavy burden that has haunted me for the last several years. I am now asking you and my God to forgive me for what I've been a part of."

Cheese Hound gives a short handclap, "Mr. Phillips, I like what you're dishing out. Please continue."

"Well… what some might call petty crimes within our organization of drug trafficking, prostitution and murder, I have to say it can't be compared to a much larger crime against our great country. On the surface, all you see is a drug ring, but as you dig deeper, it's just a single tentacle connected to a worldwide organization. They have one goal, and that goal is to take down the United States from within. This didn't just start last week; this well-organized plan has been in play for several years. The leader of this socialist group has elected officials scattered throughout the entire country, including our past president. They all answer to one man and we call him the Master.

"Our secret society has funneled money by way of drugs, human trafficking, and prostitution toward our cause. However, this is just a small part of the funding. The majority of the monetary resources are from several billionaires. They proudly donate very large contributions, insuring top positions in the new world order.

"Everyone involved has taken an oath to unite with other socialist countries such as North Korea, China, Venezuela, Iran, and Russia. They have each promised asylum and great wealth if we help tear down our government from the inside.

"To further this madness, the politicians are pushing for open borders to create a financial drain on our country. Along with the thousands of illegal's entering the heartland on a daily basis, the Columbians won't be noticed, as they filter in with them. They have been hired to transport biochemicals and trained chemists across our borders. They're preparing, as we speak, to infect certain areas of the US with the Omega virus. If they fail, the Master has a back-up plan he initiated with the North Koreans.

"The North Koreans plan to release several POWs back to the US in good faith, as a step toward joining the world as a peaceful nation. This gesture of peace is a lie. These POWs unknowingly have biochemicals surgically implanted within their bodies. They each have a type of dissolving capsule that is totally undetectable. Within a few days upon their arrival, these capsules will dissolve spreading the Omega Virus like wildfire. They also have other targets such as Great Britan and Israel.

"Here in the United States the Iranians, along with the North Koreans, plan to take out targeted areas with electromagnetic pulse bombs. The EMTs, along with dirty bombs, are secretely being smuggled into the country on cargo ships entering through two different ship channels. Their first entry point is New Orleans up through the Mississippi River. The other is the Houston ship channel. If they're successful, they will disable our entire communication and electrical grids. They have also targeted several key pipelines and production facilities. All this will be a coordinated attack inside each Christian nation. When this happens the invasion will begin."

Joey jams the barrel of his rifle into his temple, "When is all this supposed to go down?"

The DA flinches as he continues, "If our presidential candidate, Hilda Clanton, would have won, the date was set for 2024 for the invasion. She was planning to have open borders, and disarm the citizens, which would guarantee our success; but she lost. This election loss angered the Master, now he has moved the date forward."

Cheese and Bones step forward, "Hang on, Bones, I got this. Mr. DA Man, who is this 'Master' that you mentioned? And please tell me who else is involved in destroying our good ole, USA?"

"His name is Apollyon Mastema. He is like a god to his servants.

He promises great fortune and status among the people that pledge to his cause."

Cheese reaches over digging his thumb into the DA's shoulder. "Yeah, he sounds like a super cool creep. You need to finish telling us who all is involved in Apollyon's invasion plan!"

"When the last Republican President was elected, Mastema sent word that it was our time to act. Our first mission was to overturn the presidency; either by sabotage or assassination. Through this secret society, that controls the media—which in turn controls the wicked hearts of the population—we thought we could get him impeached. That plan seems to be falling apart, so they are probably planning to take him and the Vice President out."

TC clicks the safety off on his rifle, "Let me put one right between his eyes."

Cheese holds his hand up, "Hold on, TC, I'm beginning to like this guy. Let him finish. Please, Mr. Phillips, continue."

"Well, like I was saying, controlling the population was the easy part. Now controlling the government, is taking a bit more time and planning. We've worked for several decades to strategically place politicians and government officials in key areas waiting for this very moment. The Master has people sitting at the highest levels of government, ready to do his bidding. Apollyon has several governors in key liberal states across the US and each governor has many elected officials, such as myself, down in the ranks, which are onboard. Further up the food chain are senators and congressmen sprinkled around the Capital. The most potent are at the highest levels, which include our past president; the heads of the FBI and CIA, are all involved too. Their goal is to restructure our government into a socialist nation actually creating a 'One World Government' under one leader, one currency, and one religion, all being led by the master, Apollyon Mastema."

DA Phillips goes on, "Gentlemen, I, Raymond Phillips, being of sound mind, stand guilty of these crimes and by my confession, this statement is true. Without purpose, I have left nothing out of my testimony and it is my hope that you would show mercy by sparing my two friends and me."

Cheese turns off the recorder, "Wow, Phillips! When you come clean, you really mean it. My question to you is… how do I know if we let you go that you won't run straight for your crooked buddies, and have me and my friends taken out?"

DA Phillips looks out across the calm Gulf water, "With the information I've given you, it's an automatic death sentence for me. There's no place on Earth I can go to be safe from the Master. He has eyes everywhere. As soon as you make this public, you've placed a bull's eye on our heads and your team. Trust me, no one on this boat will live very long after he finds out. You have to understand, this is way out of our hands. It's so vast, covering so many countries, and so many people in power, that it's just too late to stop it."

Cheese pulls his sleeve back, glancing at his watch. "Bring me Mayor Dalton and Brown and put a couple of those weight belts around their fat little tummies."

Both are crying and pleading as they kick at Joey and TC with the Mayor swearing, "You said if we came clean you would set us free. Please, you can't do this! Please let us go!"

Cheese steps up, jamming a mini tank respirator into the Mayor's mouth, with Joey doing the same to State Representative Brown. With both men still trying to talk, Cheese holds his finger in front of his lips, "Please, gentlemen, calm down. I feel like there's a special sharing moment about to come over me and if I don't gift everyone here with it, I truly believe I'll burst."

TC, Bones and Joey chuckle, "Now, fellows, don't laugh. This is truly dear to my heart."

Cheese turns and points to the east. "I want both of you guys to look at the morning sun that's getting ready to peak over these Gulf waters. You know, with me being a military man and serving this great country, when I see the dawn's early light, I immediately get all patriotic. Call me crazy, but I still love the good ole USA. As a matter of fact, some of my best friends have died standing as close as you are to me right now. One second they were alive, and the next, well… they were gone to see the Lord. Now you politicians seem to have never had any love for our country, or just lost your patriotism somewhere along the way. Given the information the District Attorney just laid out so eloquently, I believe we should have court right here in the boat."

Cheese Hound continues, "I, being the Captain of this vessel, appoint my trusted crew as jurymen. With my status as Captain, I hereby self-appoint myself as acting judge. With my military background and being of sound mind, I accuse you two fellows with treason. Now, I turn sentencing over to our nominated jury. You all have heard the testimonies of these elected officials. With this overwhelming evidence through testimony, what say the jury?"

TC, Joey and Bones, each one taking turns with a low subtle voice, say, "Guilty." "Guilty." "Guilty."

Cheese looks out over the Gulf as the morning sun sends its first rays across the calm, slick water. "You know fellows, from what we've found out here tonight, our nation is about to be attacked, and we can't just sit back and watch it happen. We've got to figure out who we can trust with this information."

He reaches down to pick up an empty shell casing from the deck and tosses it over the side. "Fellows, it looks like we have a lot of killing ahead of us. So we might as well finish up out here and get to it."

Cheese Hound turns from staring at the rising sun and slightly motions to his men, with a silent nod.

Without hesitation, Joey and TC shove State Representative Brown and Mayor Dalton overboard. With their hands bound behind their backs and wearing heavy weight-belts, they head to the bottom like torpedoes.

Cheese cranks the twin engines and idles toward the rig giving slack to the rope, as Joey easily unties the boat. Now heading north, Bones is curious as to why he's allowing DA Phillips to live. "Hey, Cheese, don't you think this is risky? You know he's going to turn us in for killing those animals."

Cheese responds, "Get him out of the hull, and cut him loose."

Within seconds, the DA is standing beside Cheese. "Mr. DA, I've got a proposition for you. Back there when you said you never wanted to be involved, but got pulled down a rabbit hole and couldn't figure a way out… If you're up for it, I believe I've found you a way out."

The DA smiles, with an unsure nervous look. "I'm all ears!"

Cheese tightens his grip on the steering wheel, "I don't know why, but a part of me must have believed you and that part of me is why you're still breathing. You get me, Mr. DA Man?"

"Yes, I get you, and I did mean it. I'll be a man of my word, and I'll do anything I can to help stop Apollyon Mastema. Maybe, God will forgive me someday."

"Well, that's what I was hoping you would say. Hang on a second."

Cheese throttles down the huge speedboat to an idle. He turns on an auto pilot system and carefully sets his GPS in the direction of the Mayor's beach house. He then motions for everyone to gather around, as he bumps the throttle back up to a cruising speed of around 60 mph. Now gliding along the silky smooth Gulf water, they all kick back on the bench seats as Cheese lays out a plan.

"Okay, fellows, here's what I propose we do. Oh, yeah, if you disagree or have a better idea, jump in at any time. I know y'all are concerned about why we're allowing DA Phillips to live. Well, boys, he has just become a very important ally. With his position, he can feed us information that will hopefully, stop some of this madness. Bones, back to your concern—in case you're worried about the DA turning on us, and he makes a decision to do so—we'll introduce him to Little George."

The DA butts in, "Who is Little George?"

Joey laughs, "That's Cheese Hound's pet alligator. Trust me, you don't want to meet him. FYI, I know he likes to eat Russian and would probably love the taste of a DA man."

Cheese bumps Joey in the chest, "Calm down Joey, I believe he gets the picture. Okay fellows, as I was saying. Everyone so far will think the Columbians took out the Mayor and his cronies. We're going to let District Attorney Phillips out a mile or so down the beach from the Mayor's camp. He can come up with a story about how he was taking a late night walk on the beach when the Columbians made their raid. On the other hand, if he wants, he can slip back in the camp, untie the girls, and claim hero status. It's entirely up to the DA.

The Hound continues, "He will then carry on as usual, feeding us information on this guy he calls the Master. In the meantime, we're not going public with this information. Instead I've got a couple of old friends of mine that work inside the Pentagon."

Bones looks at Cheese with doubting eyes "Don't worry Bones, if you cut either one of my friends at the Pentagon with a knife, they'll bleed red white and blue. Trust me. They are solid and love a good fight."

35

Soul Harvest

A few miles north of the Gulf of Mexico in the town of Lafayette, Louisiana, Chado Cole and Uriel pose as hospital orderlies. They slip in and out of the Intensive Care Unit undetected by the demons now swarming around the bedside of Matt Stone.

Two ICU nurses, Coleen Ann Cole and Glenda Johnson, are working the night shift and notice the two new orderlies. "Hey, Coleen, who are the new guys working the floor?"

"I'm not sure, but they're pretty good. The ones we've seen in the past just walk around acting busy. Those two are actually working."

Glenda laughs, "It's nice to see orderlies following hospital rules, both are wearing germ masks and safety glasses."

Coleen drops her pen on the desk and leans back in her chair as she glances over observing the orderlies. She has no idea one of the men is her deceased husband, and he's standing only a few feet away.

Chado Cole sprays disinfectant on the counter-top of one of the empty nurse's station. He can't help himself as he looks up and makes eye contact with Coleen. Underneath the dust mask he's grinning from ear to ear. He wants so badly to tear off the mask and reveal his true identity, run over to embrace his wife, telling her all the wonderful things he's witnessed in Heaven. Above all, how he spent time with their daughter, Summer, as they walked together on the beaches of Heaven with Jesus in the presence of angels.

Uriel realizes Chado is having a hard time with the strange circumstances of being in the same room with his wife. He swiftly comes to Chado's rescue and blocks his view.

Coleen, having no idea she is staring at her deceased husband's ghost in the flesh, finds herself caught in a daze. She quickly shakes her head, turns away, and reaches over to take a swallow of diet cola. "Wow… that was strange."

Glenda mumbles, "What's that, sweetie?"

"I don't know what just happened. I believe I just had some kind of déjà vu or something. It happened when I looked over at that orderly. Something strange… no, I should say something familiar, with his eyes. Forgive me, Glenda. This whole shift has been strange. I still can't get over the fact that my late husband's best friend, Matt, is lying in the next room hanging on by a thin thread."

"Say no more, Ms. Cole, our shift will be over soon and you can get home to that sweet little grandson, Nathan. One smile from him and you'll be right as rain."

"Oh… thank you so much for saying that, his smile always heals my heart."

Uriel motions for Chado to help him move a portable x-ray machine out into the hall. "Little Soul, it is time. Do you see how those demons have gotten still and are hovering just above Matt?"

"Yes, that looks so wicked!"

"Chado, they can smell death from a mile away and they know Matt is about to pass over."

Suddenly both nurses rush into Matt's room as they watch the heart monitor flat-line. Coleen quickly begins CPR as Glenda announces over the hospital intercom, "Code blue, code blue, ICU 7! I repeat, code blue, code blue, ICU 7!"

Chado Cole and Uriel, standing just outside Matt's room, watch as two demons of hell pull the soul and spirit from his body. Both are snarling and laughing as Matt's soul struggles against their claws.

Chado pulls his germ mask away from his face to allow Matt to see him. "Chado, what's happening to me? What are these things? Help me, Chado, help me!"

Chado wants to run in and take hold of Matt's extended hand. "Chado Cole, please help me!"

Uriel swiftly sticks his arm in front of Chado's chest, "Be still and hold firm, Little Soul. It is not our time."

The cardiopulmonary team rushes in just as the two demons drag Matt's soul and spirit through the wall.

Coleen, still administering CPR, backs away as she allows the code team to do their work. She happens to turn just in time to catch a glimpse of Chado pulling his germ mask back up over his face. She suddenly freezes in her tracks. "Chado… Is that you? This can't be real!"

Glenda immediately grabs Coleen around her shoulder as Chado and Uriel quickly exit the ICU facility. "Are you okay, sweetie?"

"Glenda, I believe I am totally losing my mind."

"Talk to me, girlfriend, what in the world is going on?"

"You have to promise me, that you won't utter a word of this."

"I promise, cross my heart."

"Glenda, I believe I just saw my deceased husband. The smaller of those two orderlies was standing right here. When I stepped away from Matt's bedside to allow the code team to take over CPR, I looked up and as plain as day, there he stood."

"Sweetie, they were both wearing masks."

"I know they were but he had lowered his and I saw his face. It was him. I know it with all my heart."

Glenda reaches up, kissing Coleen on the forehead, "I believe you, sweetie. I believe you."

* * *

Chado and Uriel rush out the front door of the hospital Emergency Room. They both step over behind the heavy shrubs where Buck, the large canine, is patiently waiting.

Uriel rubs Buck on the head as he takes the scroll, handing it over to Chado. "Do not forget the guitar. You are going to need it where we are going."

"I thought we were headed for Hell. Why in the world will we need a guitar in Hell?"

Uriel laughs as he kneels down, placing his arm around Buck while reaching out for Chado's hand, "Hold my hand, Chado; I will tell you when it is time."

Within a flash like that of an old-timey camera, they're standing in front of Hell's Portal on God's Mountain.

"I guess I don't have to ask where this portal leads."

"No, Little Soul, you do not. However, before we leave, the Almighty has something for you. I guess you could say… you have moved up in the rank of immortals."

Uriel points to a cobblestone bench and table underneath a row of spruce trees. In the center of the table is a large piece of sackcloth, covering something underneath. "Go ahead, Chado. See what lies beneath the cloth."

Chado, in his excitement, trots over and grabs a corner of the cloth. He then turns, smiling at Uriel, and with a swift pull, he unveils this gift from God.

Chado stands speechless as he lightly rubs his fingertips across his prize. "Thank You, Lord, thank You!"

Uriel places his hand on Chado's shoulder, "Little Soul, what scripture does this remind you of?"

Chado, with tears of joy, looks up at his mighty guardian angel, and recites the scripture. "Ephesians 6:10-18, *'Finally my brethren, be strong in the Lord and in the power of His might. Put on the whole armor of God that you may be able to stand against the wiles of the devil. For we do not wrestle against flesh and blood, but against principalities, against powers, against the rulers of the darkness of this age, against spiritual host of wickedness in the heavenly places. Therefore, take up the whole armor of God that you may be able to withstand in the evil day, and having done all, to stand. Stand therefore, having girded your waist with truth, having put on the breastplate of righteousness, and having shod your feet with the preparation of the gospel of peace; Above all, taking the shield of faith with which you will be able to quench all the fiery darts of the wicked one; and take the helmet of salvation, and the sword of the Spirit, which is the word of God; Praying always with all prayer and supplication in the Spirit, being watchful to this end with all perseverance and supplication...*'"

Chado dresses himself with this heavenly gift as he quotes the scripture. Now filled with happiness and standing adorned with the whole armor of God, Chado watches Uriel raise both hands toward Heaven and with a shout says, "We praise you, Father God!" Uriel instantly transforms from his earthly disguise into his true identity. Behold, the mighty warrior angel, Uriel.

He looks down giving Chado a subtle smile. "Little Soul, I have to say this is a step-up from those hospital scrubs you were wearing."

"Wow, Uriel, I've never worn armor before."

"Well, Little Soul, we are about to travel into dark territory and your gift from God is appropriate.

"Hey, I've been meaning to ask you something. You know the first time I laid eyes on you, I noticed markings on your shield and sword. I asked Allayer and Nipper what it meant and they said to ask you. Now that I've received these gifts from God and my shield has the same inscriptions as yours; can you tell me what it all means?"

"Maybe later, we have got an appointment with hell right now."

Suddenly, out of one of the other portals, ten huge warrior angels appear. Chado stands in amazement as he watches the warriors walk across the plateau. The sounds of their armor and footsteps remind Chado of when he would ride his horses back home, with the squeaks of the saddle leather and the hooves hitting the ground.

With no one uttering a word, they follow behind Uriel, Chado, and Buck as they all step across the golden threshold.

They are now positioned directly in front of Hell's Portal and Uriel whispers to Chado, "Draw your sword, Little Soul, cast your blade into the earth, and kneel."

All in one accord, they fall to their knees. Each one drapes their hands over the handles of their swords, while bowing their heads in reverent prayer.

Chado, being filled with spiritual adrenaline, and the lack of patience, takes a slight peek before the angels stop praying. He slowly opens his eyes and stares through the portal. He can still see the spruce and evergreen trees on the other side of this strange rock doorway. Suddenly, the beautiful background of the trees and mountain peaks begin to disappear. The background becomes a blur. It's now being replaced with a watery sheen. An eerie darkness begins to swallow up the beautiful background as Chado closes his eyes and whispers a prayer. "Heavenly Father, help me to be strong within this dark hour. Protect Uriel, Buck, and the other angels as we begin this journey into the depths of hell. I pray we save Matt from the clutches of Satan and complete this mission. As we stand before you, Lord, it is my prayer that we will be pleasing in your sight. I love you, Father God."

Just as the angels finish praying, a blinding flash of light fills the heavens. Within a twinkling of an eye it crashes against the plateau like a bolt of lightning. The booming sound echoes through the mountain range for several seconds. This breathtaking event surprises everyone. Chado and the angels, still on their knees, turn as they witness something beyond wonderful. They each fall on their faces when the Almighty God of Heaven and Earth, stands only a few feet away. With no one being able to look upon God with the naked eye, he stands before them in the form of a mighty lion.

Without saying anything, he walks past the angels allowing his crown of fur to lightly brush against each one.

Chado, still having his face pressed against the ground, feels the Lion nudge the back of his head with His nose. "Look at me, Little Soul."

Chado slowly raises his head while rolling his eyes upward, "I'm here, Lord."

Chado is now so close he feels the breath of God on his face. "Little Soul, do you have the courage to deliver the second scroll?"

"Yes, Lord, but not by on my own strength, but only through the courage and strength that comes from you. If I am able to complete this mission, I pray, Father God, that we do not fail you."

"Little Soul, remember when I asked you where did your confidence go? Did it fly away in an eagle, or swim away in a fish? I believe you have truly found it within. You have done well, but to enter the dark realm is another matter. I will tell you a mystery; when I created Hell, I designed several measures. Within the measures is a place of light. This place of light cannot be conquered by the darkness, nor can the darkness enter therein. As the keys of Hades were used to set the captives free, the footprints of the Savior marked this place of light. In its circle of light grows a single tree. This single tree represents the beginning of life, and the fall of man. If you are overcome and need refuge, run to the circle of light. There, I will restore your strength.

"Little Soul, Lucifer knows you are coming, but he will not be expecting this."

Suddenly, within a flash of lightning, the Lion vanishes, leaving Chado confused. "Uriel, what did he mean? Lucifer won't be expecting what?"

Before Uriel answers, Chado begins laughing as he realizes what God meant. He had just changed the appearance of the angels and Buck. Their silvery white wings and armor were now transformed into a dark grey color, resembling that of the fallen angels. Looking down, he notices his appearance has also changed. "God is so cool! Now they won't see us coming!"

Uriel bumps Chado with the tip of his wing, "This disguise will help with the demons and some of the fallen angels, but Lucifer might be a little harder to deceive."

"Uriel, I've got a question."

"Go ahead Chado, we are listening."

"I remember when I was first brought to this mountain. Allayer and Nipper told me that this place is secret and not even Lucifer himself knows it exists. Saying that, is this portal only used by God's angels?"

"Yes, Little Soul, only His angels."

"So… they won't know we're coming?"

"That is correct. This portal will allow us to access hell without being detected."

Chado reaches down, petting Buck, "Wow, I still can't wrap my head around what we're about to do. I'm standing here with eleven warrior angels and one of my favorite dogs about to embark on a journey into the bowels of hell. This is totally unbelievable!"

Chado, filled with excitement, and a huge smile painted across his face, turns to realize the eleven angels aren't smiling. It is the total opposite. They each have a stern and very serious look in their eyes. Now almost to the point of embarrassment, Chado swiftly apologizes. "Hey, fellows, I'm sorry for being so childish with my thoughts. It's just so wild. I actually feel like this is just some crazy dream and I need to wake up."

Uriel replies in a serious tone, "Little Soul, it is time you wake up. What lies beyond that portal is an eternity of pain and suffering filled with fallen angels and demons. They also use strange beasts to assist with the multitudes of lost souls entering hell's gates. Trust me friend; this journey into the realm of hell will be the most dangerous period of your existence. Remember, Chado, don't look the fallen angels directly in their eyes."

"I'll do my best."

Joel, one of the eleven angels, tosses Chado a large piece of sackcloth. "Little Soul, use this to cover yourself, that guitar and the sacred scroll."

Chado, still confused, says, "For the life of me, I don't understand why I need to bring this old guitar along with me to Hell. Uriel, can't I leave it here on God's Mountain and pick it up later? I could probably defend myself better if I didn't have a guitar hanging off of my back!"

Uriel smiles with the other angels, "Little Soul, the Lord wants you to bring it, and I would probably do as He says."

"Well yes, I guess I better!"

Now submitting to a request made by the God of all Creation, Chado squats down face-to-face with Buck, "Old friend, looks like we're carrying a guitar into Hell. You want to lead the way?"

Buck shakes his head no, and then barks at Chado as if tell him to go across first. Uriel and the other angels chuckle, as they watch Chado boldly step through the portal.

In a sudden blink after breaching the portal, Chado feels the same sensation that he experienced on other portal rides. The tremendous force pulls him through space beyond light speed. Enjoying this view of the heavens, he looks back over his shoulder at the angels and smiles. Suddenly he feels an abrupt change in direction as they merge with another tunnel. This galactic wormhole through space and time quickly changes. The panoramic view of the stars and heavens disappear, as the walls of this tunnel grow dark and narrow. You can no longer see the beauty of the galaxy.

Chado begins to sense an overwhelming feeling of deep sorrow as the tunnel grows darker. Thoughts fill his mind how millions of lost souls must have traveled down this same tunnel. He wonders if this dreadful wormhole could have been designed like this to take away any joy of a final view of the heavens.

Uriel hears Chado's thoughts. *Chado, you are beginning to understand. That is exactly why. When the lost souls are taken through the portals to hell, they are stripped of all joy, and that includes the beauty of the heavens.*

Chado answers Uriel with thought. *That has got to be a miserable ride. Can you imagine having to travel down this dark tunnel with a couple of demons at your side?*

36

The River of Sorrows

Within a short span of time, eleven angels, one immortal and his dog, Buck, step out onto the parched dead planet of Hell.

At the exact second of Chado's first breath, all five senses seem to explode. The pungent smell of rotting flesh and sulfur is so strong that he can almost taste it in his mouth. He feels the parched, dry wind against his face as it carries dying cinders across the wasteland. Chado curiously kneels down alongside Buck, dragging his fingers through what looks like dirty snow. He rubs his fingers and thumb together discovering that this dirty snow is simply dark gray ash, covering the surface of the dead planet.

Chado stares off into the distance as he witnesses thousands of lost souls being forced out of a giant portal, down through what looks like a trench. This long fissure is the same depth as a tall man and the width of six people standing shoulder to shoulder. This narrow trench looks to be several miles in length from the portal to the edge of the crater.

With only their heads visible, the condemned walk inside this shallow trench, their movement resembling a slow moving stream.

Uriel, hearing his thoughts, gently places his hand on Chado's back and says, "Little Soul, we call it 'The River of Sorrows'. Upon their first death, they enter this stream of lost souls leading out of the portal, down to the Sixth Gate of Hell. It flows into this crevice leading to what you are calling a crater. From the basin, you see in the distance they are herded like cattle over into the pit, never to be seen again.

"This planet has five other locations exactly like this one. Each one continually receiving thousands upon thousands of lost souls."

"My goodness, Uriel, if only the living could see this, they would turn from their wicked ways and seek the Lord with all their hearts."

"Yes, Chado, witnessing this causes your heart to be saddened, but I say woe to the ones who have turned away from Christ. Each of these you see before you have chosen to reject the Savior. Now they serve in hell for eternity."

"It breaks my heart, Uriel, so, so, sad."

"Little Soul, it breaks the heart of God also."

"Uriel, so if there are six gates in hell, and twelve gates in Heaven, do the numbers have significance in some way?"

"Yes, Chado, I will give you a mystery to think about. In the word of God, He has chosen numbers of completion and incompletion. He uses these numbers in many ways throughout the Bible, such as the twelve tribes, twelve disciples, twelve gates of Heaven, and so on. The number six is the opposite. It is a number of imperfections that He uses in other forms, such as the number representing the antichrist, 666, or, in this case, the six gates of hell."

Chado shakes his head and, with a look of grief, continues to observe their surroundings. Through the smoky haze, he can see several hundred of hell's angels circling over the giant crater. Some fall out of formation like giant birds as they dive down disappearing into the aperture to hell.

Still at a considerable distance, he notices a multitude of demons that have fulfilled their task of transporting the lost, vanishing back through a much smaller portal. Apparently, they're heading back to Earth in order to complete more of Satan's bidding.

To Chado's surprise, as he's staring through the smoky haze, he catches a glimpse of something that seems to be out of place or just doesn't belong. Unsure of what he's observing, he waits for the smoky haze to clear. Yes, he's now certain; much further away on the opposite side of the giant crater stands a magnificent cross. It must be at least 10,000 feet in height to be seen at this distance. This cross is burning with a brilliant white fire. The outside edges of this blaze seem to have a bluish tent that glitters against the dark hazy background.

"Uriel, why is there a cross standing on the planet of hell?"

"My friend, this is a message to everyone who enters the pit. Another reminder of what Jesus Christ sacrificed for all mankind. As the condemned walk down the River of Sorrow on their way to the pit, they have to face this empty cross. Each one knowing they rejected the life, death and resurrection of Jesus Christ, and now this truth is the last thing they see before going down into the pit of hell."

"My goodness, Uriel, I can't imagine the sorrow they must feel."

"Yes, devastating, but there is more."

"What do you mean?"

"Chado, do you see the trench they're walking in?"

"I'm with you, I see it."

"The floor of the trench they walk upon, is covered with crowns of thorns embedded in the ground."

"Wow, you mean they're literally walking on crowns of thorns?"

"Yes, Little Soul. As the thorns are broken off into the bare feet of the condemned, they immediately grow back, ready for the next footstep. It is a never-ending cycle."

Uriel points towards the line. "Chado, the whips they are using are exactly like the ones the Roman soldiers used as they tormented Jesus. With each lash, they are reminded of the pain our Savior endured."

"So hell is filled with suffering and gnashing of teeth just like it is written in the Holy Bible!"

"Yes it is, my friend. I see the haze is clearing and I now ask you to look upon the heavens. Do you see that blue planet across the gulf of stars?"

"Yes, it's beautiful. It almost looks close enough to reach out and touch. What's it called, Uriel?"

"Little Soul, you surprise me. Do you not recognize the white ring around it, and how it hovers above the sea?"

"Good grief, that's the Planet of Heaven! How could I be so shallow?"

"Chado, think back on scripture; does anything come to mind?"

Continuing to stare up at the planet of Heaven, Chado breaks out into a smile. "Wow, Uriel, I do remember a story in the Bible that relates to this. It's about a beggar named Lazarus and a rich man. The beggar was a believer and when he died, the angels carried him away to Heaven, but when the rich man also died, he was buried with his soul entering hell. The rich man lifted his eyes and saw Heaven afar. He then cried out to Abraham for mercy asking to send Lazarus that he may dip his finger in water to cool his tongue, for he was tormented from the flames. But Abraham said, '*Son, remember that in your lifetime you received your good things, and likewise Lazarus evil things; but now he is comforted and you are tormented. And besides all this, between us and you there is a great gulf fixed, so that those who want to pass from here to you cannot, nor can those from there pass to us.*'

"So, Uriel, in God's word the great gulf he mentioned simply represents a gulf across space?"

Uriel kindly smiles, "I believe so, Chado."

"Do you think all those lost souls look up and know that's the planet of Heaven?"

"I am sure of it. You see, every time those demons strike their backs with the whip, they each tend to look up crying out with pain. Each time as they raise their eyes, they face that giant cross and the planet of Heaven. Chado, the demons being as cruel as possible continually point out anything that might give the lost more sorrow."

"Uriel, I'm still curious about the cross. Why is it burning with the white, bluish flame?"

"Chado, do you remember when God filled you with the Holy Spirit at the little Friday Night Bible Study?"

"Yes, I was praying and had the vision of the cross burning from the ground up. Later when we prayed for the lady who had the demon, it felt like my feet caught on fire and then flowed up through my whole body. How could I forget that?"

"What about the other times?"

"Well, if memory serves me, it only happened once when I was alive on Earth. The other time, I was praying and worshiping after I got to Heaven."

"Little Soul, the burning fire that consumes this cross is like the fire that touched you each time. It represents the Holy Spirit. It is another message to the lost along with Lucifer and his fallen, that the Holy Trinity holds all power, even here in Hell."

Chado stands while brushing the ash from his hands. "Uriel, I know it's there to remind the lost, but just seeing that beautiful, fiery cross, sure is a comfort. Hey, shouldn't we be moving on? I would hate to somehow not reach Matt before they take him through the gate."

"Little Soul, before we go, you need to take a look behind you. I believe you will enjoy gazing upon this miracle."

Chado slowly turns, expecting to see other horrible scenes of hell, but, to his surprise, he experiences a breathtaking view of a giant tree. Suddenly he remembers what God had said.

"Hey, fellows, is this the mystery God talked about?"

Joel, one of the eleven angels, steps forward, "Tell us this mystery, Little Soul. If God said it, I am sure it is worth repeating."

Chado steps forward as he quotes what God told him. "He said, I tell you a mystery; when I created Hell, I designed several measures. Within the measures is a Place of Light. This place of light can't be conquered by the darkness, nor can the darkness enter therein. As the keys of Hades were used to set the captives free, the footprints of the Savior marked this place of light. In its circle of light grows a single tree. This single tree represents the beginning of life and also the fall of man."

Chado stares through the burning cinders and smoky haze at this spectacular sight. He's completely overwhelmed with its size and beauty. "Can someone explain what it all means?"

Uriel wipes away ash from his shoulder as he speaks, "Chado, what God is calling, 'The Place of Light', is a location positioned at another gate that no longer exists. This place was called The Gate of Hades. At the time of Jesus' death, burial, and resurrection, he took the keys to Hades and set the captives free. These are the ones who lived by the Mosaic Law before God sent his Son.

"After they were released, upon this location, God closed the gate forever. He then turned the parched, dead ground into a fertile place. At that time, he planted the tree you see before you. This place of light is located directly in the center, being the same distance between all six gates of hell. From each gate, it is visible to all creatures that walk out of any of the six portals. As with the cross, it is another reminder to all who gaze upon it, God is in control."

"That's pretty deep, Uriel, but I don't remember reading anywhere in God's word about anything like this."

The angels chuckle while Joel places his hand on Chado's shoulder again, "Little Soul, do you not remember reading in the Bible about the hidden mysteries of God?"

"Oh yeah, I get your point."

Uriel motions to everyone, "Let us move along. Chado cover your head with that sackcloth. We do not want to be spotted. I would like to slip through without having to fight our way in!"

As they head toward the River of Sorrow, Chado is still thinking about the giant tree. "Hey guys, I was trying to figure out just how big that tree really is. How far would you say it is from here?"

Uriel smiles, "Do you want that in earth miles, heaven miles, or hell miles?"

Chado laughs, "Earth distance would be fine."

"Little Soul, it is approximately 300 miles from where we stand."

"Three hundred miles; what the heck, Uriel, back on Earth you can't see the mighty red woods over 10 or 20 miles away!"

"I have to agree, the redwood trees are spectacular, but this tree is around 2,000 years old and, not to mention, God breathed life into it. I will give you an example, if you sat a 500-year-old redwood beside this tree, the redwood would favor a tall weed. Chado, the small limbs on this tree are as large as the trunk of a full-grown sequoia. You haven't seen them yet, but if we make it out of this, I will show you trees in Heaven that will actually dwarf the one you see before you. Just keep in mind, God wanted everyone who sets foot outside any of these portals to be able to see it."

* * *

Still trying to overcome the distinct smell of sulfur, Chado looks down as they walk along. He notices that the ground has wide cracks in the parched surface. The cracks remind Chado of how a lakebed looks during a severe drought as the fissures run in all different directions. Through these cracks, you can see what looks like crude oil or tar. It seems to be smoldering just below the temperature of combustion.

Looking over at the angels, he notices the tips of their wings brush the surface causing the ash to form a small dust cloud behind each one. With their darkened clothing and armor, Chado determines they should easily pass as fallen angels. Especially with some of them carrying, visible scars enhancing their dark look.

As they approach the backside of the giant portal, several demons on their way back to Earth, using the smaller portal, glance over, not being alarmed at all. They are actually so unaware of Chado, Buck and the angels; they pay no attention as they go about their task of fetching souls from hell.

Just past the smaller portal, Chado spots an odd sight. It's a different type of demon than the ones being used to transport. These are a bit larger and carry themselves with the impression they have more authority. They must be higher in rank because they were riding on the backs of animals. Very strange animals, a species that Chado or no one else from Earth had ever seen before. They resembled the very description given in the book of Revelation, Chapter 9.

'And he opened the bottomless pit, and smoke arose out of the pit like the smoke of a great furnace. So the sun and the air were darkened because of the pit. Then out of the smoke locust came upon the Earth. And to them was given power, as the scorpions of the Earth have power. The shape of the locust was like horses prepared for battle. On their heads were crowns of something like gold, and their faces are like the faces of men. They have hair like women's hair and their teeth are like lions teeth. And they have breastplates like breastplates of iron, the sound of their wings are like the sound of chariots with

many horses running into battle. They have tails like scorpions meant for torture.'

Chado is curious to know if John the Revelator's visions written in the Bible were describing these odd-looking animals, or something else. He knows it would be too much of a risk to ask questions while walking in the midst of demons and fallen angels.

Uriel hears Chado's thoughts. *Little Soul, protect your mind. If I can hear you, so can those fallen angels sitting on top of the portals. I will tell you all about the creatures later. For right now, we need to split up. Chado, you and I will head for the upper left side. Joel, you and the warriors take the right side. We should be able to spot Matt from above. Just do not make eye contact with the fallen.*

Being totally focused on the horrible creatures that the demons were riding, Chado hadn't noticed they were walking directly underneath several fallen angels, all who are perched on top of the portals. They sit in a line with their dark wings draped over the stone ledge resembling vultures waiting on someone to die. They hardly even notice the heavenly group, as their attention is directed on the condemned exiting the portal. It's as if they're waiting on someone in particular to egress from the portal. Chado slowly reaches up to pull the sackcloth even further over his head, casting a shadow across his face. With similarity of what the larger demons are clothed with, Chado passes underneath the fallen angels undetected.

Still following close behind Uriel, they slowly make their way down the left side, above the trench, and away from the fallen angels. Now with a clear view they can easily see down inside the narrow channel that leads to Hell's Gate.

Overwhelming sorrow falls over Chado as he walks within a few feet of the lost. Being able to see the sad countenance on their faces pierces his heart. Unbearable to witness and wanting to turn away, he knows he can't because his best friend is somewhere among these condemned souls.

As Chado and the angels continue searching for what seems like hours with no sign of Matt, they realize they have to enter the crater.

Abruptly, out of nowhere, a demon pushes his way past Chado and Uriel as he rides on the back of a monster. He's popping his jaws and swinging a whip, proudly tormenting the lost. Showing off his talent, he wheels the beast around near the edge with perfect accuracy as this monster curls his long scorpion tail, easily delivering targeted hits. The demon laughs and pops his jaws even louder as he hears the screams from the defenseless souls. Wasting no time, he goes out of sight down the steep slope of the crater continuing his torture.

* * *

Chado stands beside Uriel and Buck overlooking this giant chasm that shadows the Sixth Gate of Hell. This deep crater resembles an ancient mining operation that may have lasted for thousands of years. On the other hand, God might have used a large meteor to blast away a huge chunk of hell. The hole itself is several miles wide and at least a mile in depth. The entire floor of the crater is covered with a dark red glow, as if to be on fire. The unending lines filled with people of all races circle down and around the cavern walls. A multitude of demons are scattered throughout the lines, as they herd people like lambs to a slaughter.

Uriel motions to the angels standing on the opposite side of the trench to begin their decent down inside the cavern. With no demons or angels nearby Chado feels, it would be safe to have a conversation. His concern for Matt's safety gets the best of him, "Uriel, I'm really getting worried. What if we don't reach him before he goes through the gate?"

"Do not worry, we will find Matt."

"Yeah, but what if we don't. Can we go inside the gate? I mean… will we survive if we have to go inside?"

"Okay, Chado, calm down. If it will make you feel any better, I have got a trick up my sleeve, as you humans say."

"I'm in. What's your trick?"

Uriel points to an area where a large piece of cliff wall had fallen off and formed a small maze of boulders on the floor of the crater. "Do you see that pile of rocks?"

"I see it. Can you get us there without being seen?"

"Yes, but first, I have a task for Buck."

Uriel pulls out a small piece of Matt's clothes that he snagged back at the Lafayette Hospital. "Here you go, Buck."

The large canine runs up to sniff the cloth. "Okay, boy, go find Matt then meet us at that pile of boulders down there. Watch out for hellhounds. They usually dwell closer to the gate."

Buck does his grinning trick and wheels around vanishing over the edge of the crater.

"Uriel, you think he'll be okay?"

"Chado, you worry too much. Take hold of my hand."

Just before they supernaturally transport to the bottom, Joel looks back at Uriel, as to be connected with his thoughts. He then slowly nods his head, agreeing with the plan.

* * *

Within a split second, Uriel and Chado appear within the confinement of the boulders. Although hidden from the demons and fallen angels, to Chado's surprise, he suddenly begins to feel pain on the bottom of his feet. Looking down, he realizes he's standing in a shallow lake of fire. "Uriel, what do I do?"

"Be still, Chado. You can take it for the short time we will be here."

"That's easy for you to say. You're an angel!"

"Stop whining. It cannot consume you. Look at your feet. They haven't changed. Trust me, Little Soul, you will survive the flame."

"Uriel, if it's this bad outside the gate, what's it like inside?"

"Do you remember what God said about the different measures of hell?"

"Sure I do."

"Well, Little Soul, this is nothing compared to the many levels beyond that gate."

Being concerned with the annoying pain caused from the shallow lake of fire, Chado hadn't noticed the sounds coming from within the pit. This odd noise resembles that of millions and millions of hummingbird wings. This constant low tone is causing a vibration to pass over the entire floor of the crater.

Chado, still concerned with the flames, finds a small ledge hidden in the boulders where he can pull his feet up just above the blaze. "Now that's a little better. I just don't see how anyone can stand it down here." Almost mid-sentence, Chado stops talking and starts moving his hand around on the rocks. "Hey, Uriel, you feel that vibration? What the heck is that humming? It sounds like a giant swarm of bees or something!"

"Keep it down, Chado! We need to stay undercover as long as possible."

Chado cups his hand and whispers, "I'm sorry, bud. This whole walking around in hell, and feet on fire thing, has got me a little flustered. So what's making the sound?"

"Chado Cole, the sound you hear is the groaning of millions of lost souls coming from beyond the gate."

"Oh my goodness, I thought it might be swarms of locust or some kind of a beast out of the pit of hell. That's horrible. I just want to get Matt and get the heck out of here!"

Chado shakes his head as he steps back down into the fire, edging his way to a small crack between the boulders. He has a clear view of the entrance. "Hey, Uriel, come here and look at this. We can see everything from here. Wow, I thought the gate would be built out of something special. It looks like plain old wood."

Uriel leans over, "It is made out of something special. It's made out of gopher wood."

Chado smiles, "Wasn't that the same kind of wood Noah used to build the ark with?"

"Little Soul, you are going to love this. Why do you think no one ever found the ark?"

"I haven't a clue."

"God used pieces of the ark to build all six gates to hell."

"You're pulling my leg! Hell is definitely no place to be joking around. If the gates to the pit were built with wood, wouldn't it just burn up?"

"Hardly my friend; do you not remember the burning bush or the story of the fiery furnace with Shadrach, Meshach, and Abednego? If you really think hard about the stories in the Bible, there are a lot of examples." Uriel starts laughing and points at Chado's feet. "Little Soul, you have been standing in this shallow lake of fire for a while now and your sandals and feet look just fine. So if God does not want the gates of hell to burn, trust me, they will not."

"So tell me, of all material in creation, why did God choose wood from the ark?"

"Think about it Chado. Everything you have seen so far here in hell have been reminders. When those lost souls walk through any of the six gates to hell, the last thing they see until the Great White Throne Judgment is a wooden gate built from gopher wood. A piece of material he used in a vessel to give humanity another chance. It was just a simple old wooden ship designed and blessed by God as a refuge for man and the animals."

Uriel reaches over bumping Chado on his arm, "There is your dog. It looks like he is attempting to work his way around that rock ledge."

"Yes, I see him, but I don't see Matt. Uriel you think he's already gone through the gate?"

"I do not think so. We will know very soon."

Within seconds, Buck darts past Uriel and Chado as he jumps up on a small boulder that allows his feet to be just above the flame. Chado quickly hops up beside his canine on the rock. "I don't blame you old friend, I can't stand it either."

With Buck staring intently back at the line of souls, he begins to communicate with Uriel.

Uriel smiles as he pats Buck on his head, "Thank you, Buck. I see him."

"There he is, Chado. Matt is just this side of those two demons near the base of the cavern."

"I see him, I see him, Uriel! What do we do now? Can we snag him and get the heck out of here?"

"Not yet. God wants him to actually see down inside the pit of hell. We are going to intercept Matt just in front of the gate. It is going to be a little tricky, but that is what the God of all creation desires."

"Hey, Uriel, I see Joel and the other ten angels. They're just a few yards behind Matt."

"Perfect, if our cover is not blown, we might not have to fight our way out."

No sooner than Uriel stops talking, fallen angels begin pouring out of the sky, filling the giant courtyard.

"What's going on Uriel? Have we been spotted?"

"I am not sure. It could be something else happening."

37

Horns of Hell and Dragon of the Pit

Within a few seconds of the fallen angels arriving in the courtyard, several demons appear in front of the open gate. They are each leaning back with all their strength, holding chains attached around the necks of dogs. These hounds of hell resemble Rottweilers, a breed found back on Earth. Each one has the appearance of a dog with rabies, as drool mixed with blood drips from their mouths. These massive canines continually lunge against their chains, snapping at the nearby souls walking through the gate. Their hellish masters laugh as they allow the hellhounds within inches of the condemned.

After displaying their hatred toward the lost, these demons and their dogs of darkness walk out mid-way of the courtyard and form a line across the center. This action stops the continuous flow of lost souls coming from the portal in their tracks. The remainder of souls continued through the gate, leaving the courtyard in front of the gate clear.

"What are they up to, Uriel?"

"Little Soul, this mission just got complicated."

"What do you mean?"

"I believe Lucifer himself is about to show up."

Chado and Uriel, peek through the cleft of the boulders, and watch as six fallen angels walk out of the pit of hell. They split with three standing on each side of the entrance, armed with large horns made from some kind of an animal.

All in one accord, they begin blowing through these instruments of darkness. The awful sound created from these crude horns resembles the cries of a thousand mothers at childbirth. This awful piercing sound echoes across the burning wasteland, creating a vibration. The shallow lake of fire surrounding the courtyard suddenly gets brighter. Even the ripples upon the fiery water appear to be rejoicing as it dances and flickers. With this vibration, more small boulders fall from the unstable cliff walls landing only feet away from Uriel and Chado's hidden location.

Uriel swiftly places his wings over Chado and Buck as the small rocks from overhead continue peppering the trio.

Under the protection of his guardian angel, Chado continues to peek through the small crack in the rocks as he witnesses something beyond belief. Slowly being unveiled from within the Sixth Gate of Hell, is the head of a giant dragon. With only his nostrils and eyes exposed from the fiery furnace, Chado quickly reaches up grabbing a leather strap on Uriel's armor as he prays, "Oh, God of Heaven, please protect us! Uriel, I can't believe what I'm seeing! This has got to be a bad dream."

Uriel edges closer to Chado as he peeks through the crack, "Fear not, Little Soul."

"Uriel, is that Lucifer? The last time we saw him he was in the form of a man. If that's him, he looks a little more intimidating than before."

"Yes, that is he. Do not let his appearance frighten you. He is no different from the archangels. Lucifer takes this cursed form to pass fear over the lost souls and his fallen angels. I ask you, Little Soul, what scripture does his appearance remind you of?"

"Revelation 12:3 says, '*And another sign appeared in Heaven: behold, a great, fiery red dragon having seven heads and ten horns, and seven diadems on his heads.*'

"Is that the one Uriel; or, is it in verse seven? ' *And war broke out in Heaven; Michael and his angels fought with the dragon; and the dragon and his angels fought, but they did not prevail, nor was a place found for them in Heaven any longer.*'"

"That is close enough, Chado. That is close enough."

Suddenly a heated wind filled with smoke and cinders belch out of the pit as the dragon emerges. This wind begins to form two small fiery tornados over the courtyard. The swirling fire seems to grow and move along beside the dragon as he walks across the opening. This reptile of hell walks out, stopping just behind the demons holding back the line of souls.

"Hey, Uriel, what do the fiery tornados represent, or do they have any meaning at all?"

"Yes, the whirlwinds of flame have meaning. Satan has always been an impersonator of the Creator. He tries to mimic everything God does, but he does it in a sinful and wicked way."

"How so, Uriel? I mean how does he try to imitate God?"

"Well, you understand the Holy Trinity, right?"

"Sure I do. It's the Father, the Son, and the Holy Spirit."

"Okay, Chado, what you see before you, is the unholy trinity. The flaming tornados located on each side of the dragon, represent the antichrist and the false prophet. Something else Chado; every demon and fallen angel, including Lucifer himself, believe they will one day rule over all creation."

"Hey, Uriel, something's happening with the dragon."

They quickly move to another peephole in the boulders to have a better view of the courtyard.

Sadness comes over Chado. "Oh… Uriel, I can see Matt again. He's standing at the edge of the lake of fire. Uriel, look at their faces. Their eyes are darkened and empty without any hope."

"Chado, we are here for just one. The rest have made their choice."

Overwhelmed with a heaviness of sorrow from witnessing this awful scene, Chado slowly shakes his head as they continue to watch. The smoke thickens around the dragon as the consuming darkness is now blocking their view.

Without warning, bolts of lightning begin to hit the surface of the burning lake creating deafening claps of thunder. This tremendous amount of energy is displaced as it bounces off the walls of the cavern echoing across the planet of Hell. Without a command, the well-trained servants of hell begin forcing the thousands of lost souls to their knees. Looking back as far as the eye could see everyone including the demons and fallen angels are now bowing before the Prince of Darkness.

Hidden within the fire and brimstone, the dragon transforms into human form. With the dark cloud of burning cinders dissipating, a tall woman having the appearance of a man stands alone in the center of the courtyard.

"Uriel, is Lucifer male or female?"

"I am not sure Chado. This is strange, even for Lucifer."

"What's he up to?"

Uriel holds his finger in front of his mouth signaling to be quiet. He then turns pointing as the fallen angels rise to their feet, with each one being focused on their master. Lucifer, without uttering a word peers into the eyes of his captivated audience as though to be searching for someone. The lost souls standing only a few feet away from the Prince of Darkness have a look of terror mixed with hopelessness pasted over their faces. For the first time of their existence, they are standing face-to-face with Satan himself.

To everyone's surprise, Lucifer holds his hands and arms out in a friendly, but sarcastic gesture, as if to welcome everyone to his kingdom. Breaking from his prideful stance, he squats down touching both hands to the surface of the burning lake, and with almost a sonic boom, he launches. From the power of his liftoff and the force created, it sends a huge wave over the lake of fire. Within almost a split second, the fallen angels surrounding the courtyard follow behind him.

With a handful of demons, and very few hellhounds left to guard the gate, Chado, Uriel and Buck begin to make their way around the edge of the burning courtyard.

"Hey, Uriel, where do you think Lucifer and those angels are headed off too?"

"They have suspicion we are coming, they just are not sure which gate. I would imagine they are checking the other five."

"Well, I hope they don't come back before we finish up here."

"Chado, I was really concerned about the fallen angel we saw back in Lafayette at the scene of Matt's incident. I just knew he would be watching Matt here at the sixth gate anticipating our interception. Either he thought after they took Matt's soul, it was final and over with, or he has forgotten. Well, I guess we cannot leave out the possibility of a trap."

"A trap! Let's just pray that doesn't happen."

Remaining undetected, they inch their way around a lone demon that's mounted on the back of his scorpion beast. The demon seems to be curious of the trio. He wheels his beast around and tries to intimidate Chado, as the monster he is riding waves his scorpion tail overhead. Uriel rapidly steps in front of Chado, staring deep into the eyes of the demon. This spawn of the pit humbly backs down, and turns his hellish steed around, heading across the courtyard through the oncoming lines of lost souls.

With almost perfect timing, they reach the gate intersecting and blending in with the multitudes of lost souls. Joel, one of the eleven warriors, has worked his way up alongside Matt. He gently cups his left wing around Matt while slowly leading him to the right side of the entrance.

With all hope lost, Matt is totally unaware of what's happening. Wrapped inside a cocoon of metallic feathers, he is encapsulated almost to the point of total darkness, other than the flames that surround their feet. Now overwhelmed with deep sorrow, he looks down at the fiery liquid having memories of his best friend. A best friend that loved him enough to share the many stories about God, and how he pleaded with him to give Jesus a chance. The voice of Chado echoes through his heart. 'Run from sin, Matt, run!'

Standing at the edge of the Sixth Gate of Hell, Joel gently removes his wing from around Matt, exposing a clear view down inside the fiery furnace. Matt immediately falls to his knees crying out with a loud voice, "It's real! Oh… my God, it's real!"

Two demons standing nearby are alarmed as they see Matt on his knees crying out to God. They hastily run up popping their jaws, snarling profanities, and allowing their hellhounds to attack. With the sound of chains clattering from the hellish dogs, mixed with the horrible smell and moaning from the pit, Matt closes his eyes hoping these horrible dogs will end his existence. Now they are only inches away from Matt's face. Unexpectedly from out of the shadows, a huge buckskin canine, glides through the air and with precision, rips the hound nearest to Matt almost in half. With unbelief, Matt looks up as Buck disappears into a puff of smoke that belches out of the pit. Within a split second, Buck reappears and from out of the black smoke, he does it again. Another precise hit; Buck breaks the spine of the second hellhound. The two demons, being totally caught off guard, advance toward Buck. This mighty dog of heaven is still violently shaking their hellhound in his mouth. He's positioned with his back to the demons, totally vulnerable. The two advancing demons focused on destroying Buck, turn just in time to see a glimpse of Joel and Uriel's blades as they are destroyed.

Matt, still on his knees after witnessing this odd scene, continues to stare down inside the pit of Hell. He watches as the steady flow of souls are forced deeper and deeper. The smell of burning rotting flesh mixed with the pungent odor of sulfur burns his eyes and nose. Unbearable waves of heat constantly rise from the fire below escaping up through the shaft. Pale green, yellowish colors of sulfur cover the entire ceiling and walls of this giant cavern. The walls and ceiling seem to be alive as the fiery pit cast shadows from the movement of thousands as they make their way down. Deep out of the pit giant swarms of locust fly through the air like flocks of birds. They swarm around the lost tormenting each one as they bite and sting. Other types of insects are flying and crawling over anything moving, including the demons. This pestilence of hell, along with the fiery brimstone is so agonizing the lines of people seem to have slowed down to a crawl. A constant roaring sound of wailing and gnashing of their teeth can't be compared with anything Matt has ever witnessed.

Shrouded in defeat, Matt feels someone's hand on his shoulder, and hears a familiar voice, "Matt… they tell me what you're looking at is only the first level of the horror that lies beneath. The other levels are much worse."

Being totally confused and at a loss, Matt slowly turns to see someone standing with a shadowy face, covered with sackcloth.

"Who are you?"

"You know who I am, old friend. Do you remember when you were lying almost dead in the middle of Johnston Street, and I told you we're going on a journey?"

"Chado… Is that you?"

"Yes, friend, it's me."

"Chado, why are you in Hell? I thought you believed in God, but you're here in Hell with me. What happened? How could this be? I know I deserve hell, but you love God and you should be in Heaven!"

"Please slow down, Matt! Truth be known, we all deserve hell, but only by the saving grace of Jesus Christ are we delivered from this destruction. Matt, you do remember what I preached to you over and over back when we worked together?"

"I confess, Chado. I heard you back then and I just didn't listen. However, I do remember the part about if you want to truly be saved, you have to surrender your heart over to Jesus. After getting a close look at this place, I wish I could get another shot. Just look at us. We're literally standing in fire, and you just said the worst is yet to come."

"Matt, I have to tell you, God, for whatever reason, has chosen you to be a part of something really special."

Uriel cuts in on their conversation, "We need to go, now! Those demons over there are on to us, and they have a way to communicate with Satan."

Uriel turns to Joel and the other angels, "Take Matt and meet us at the tree."

Uriel takes hold of Buck and Chado, kneels down in the fiery liquid and just before vanishing, they see Lucifer and his angels arrive at the entrance of the Sixth Gate. Lucifer deviously makes eye contact with Chado and just as he points his finger toward the trio, they all vanish.

38

Bound for Darkness, Saved by the Light

A little over 300 miles away from the Sixth Gate of Hell, they all step off the scorched dead surface onto plush fertile ground.

Matt, just being plucked out of the pit of Hell, and supernaturally transported to what looks like the largest tree in the universe, stands totally confused and speechless.

Like an overgrown child, he embraces his adopted big brother, Chado, with tears streaming down both cheeks. Without warning, a sudden weakness comes over Matt as he drops to his knees. He begins shaking his head with disbelief. "This can't be real. It's has to be just a really bad dream." Matt suddenly begins slapping himself on the cheeks. "I have to wake up."

Chado reaches down, grabbing both hands. "Hey, Matt, look at me friend."

Matt slowly lifts his head with muddy tears dripping from his chin as he whispers. "Chado, please wake me from this awful nightmare."

"Matt, I assure you this is not a dream. We are here with you and these events are unfolding. Let me ask you this. Do you feel the thorns broke off in your feet, or where the lashes of the demons whip struck you? Do you smell the odor of death and burning sulfur? Matt you are suspended between life and death. Your soul and spirit dwells here on this planet of Hell, while your body awaits all three to be rejoined back on Earth."

Matt attempts to gain his composure and clear away the tears. He reaches up with soot-covered hands and unknowingly smears ash across his face. Chado and the angels chuckle at Matt.

"What's so funny, Chado?"

"Sorry, Matt, it's just the ash smeared around on your face looks like you've been working in a coal mine. How about you get off your knees and accept what's going on."

Chado pulls off the sackcloth he's wearing, tosses it over to Matt. "Here ya go, bud. Use this old cloth robe to clean your face."

"Wow, Chado, I really like your armor."

"Yeah, it's pretty cool. God gave it to me before we had to make this trip to Hell."

Uriel holds his hand in the air, "Enough small talk. We need to finish up here and get Matt out. Lucifer will soon know our location."

Matt, continuing to wipe away the ash and soot from his face, leans over whispering, "Hey, Chado, who are all these big angels?"

Uriel steps forward holding his hand out in a gesture of friendship. "Matt, I am Uriel, Chado's guardian. The others you see before you are warriors. We were sent here on a mission from God to rescue you from the pit of Hell. I apologize, but we do not have time for introductions, so I will get to the point.

Uriel continues, "Matt Stone, God has chosen two vessels. One who was bound for destruction and the other, a child of light. Both are to be part of a mission that could save millions of lost souls back on Earth. You are one of the chosen vessels. You, Matt Stone, were the one bound for destruction."

Just before Matt begins to reply, Chado quickly places a hand on his shoulder, "Shush, Matt. Let Uriel continue. Just listen to him."

Uriel looks intently into Matt's eyes, "You will remember everything you have witnessed here in Hell, and when it is time, you will give testimony. Matt, you will fall under great persecution and be called a liar. However, in these times, you shall seek the Lord God Almighty in prayer. He will give you strength to stand strong in these times of trouble.

"Matt, God's word says in Matthew 10:18-22, '*You will be brought before governors and kings for My sake, as a testimony to them and the Gentiles. But when they deliver you up, do not worry about how or what you should speak. For it will be given to you in that hour what you should speak; for it is not you who speak, but the Spirit of your Father who speaks in you. Now brother will deliver up brother to death, and a father his child; and children will rise up against parents and cause them to be put to death. And you will be hated by all for My name's sake. But he who endures to the end will be saved.*'"

Matt looks around at the angels as if he's confused. "Chado, I don't understand all this. Why in the world would God choose me? I've never believed in God, and he chose me? This must be some kind of a mix up. Trust me. I wish I would have listened to you back when we were diving in the Gulf. How could I have been so stupid? Now seeing all this, I truly believe it's real. I know there is a Hell and if that thing we saw back at the gate was the devil, there must be another place called Heaven, and there has to be a God that runs it all. Chado, why can't I understand? I want to believe. I just don't know how."

Chado steps in front of Matt and stares deep into his eyes. "Matt, you look at these things as a mortal man, only believing what you see. Understand this friend, until you believe, and have faith as of a child, your eyes won't be opened. Jesus said, '*The kingdom of Heaven is like a drag net that was cast into the sea and gathered some of every kind, which when it was full, they drew it to shore; and they sat down and gathered the good into vessels, but threw the bad away. So it will be at the end of the age. The angels will come forth, separate the wicked from among the just, and cast them into the furnace of fire. There will be wailing and gnashing of teeth.'*

"You see, Matt, until you're saved, and only then, will your mind, heart, and soul be opened."

"Well, I want to be saved. Chado, can you or the angels save me?"

Chado smiles, "No, little brother. Only through Jesus Christ can you become reborn as a child of God."

Matt's eyes filling with tears again, "Tell me how Chado, please tell me!"

The eleven angels all in one accord kneel down with their blades stuck in the ground, bowing in prayer.

"Matt, this is one of the simplest actions, but without a doubt, the most important, a person could ever do in a lifetime. Let's kneel down with the angels and go to the Lord in prayer. Matt, first you must consider your life and then turn away from everything in it that is contrary to what God wants. This turning away from selfishness and toward God is called repentance. Ask God to forgive you of your sins. Second, you must acknowledge that Jesus Christ died on the cross to forgive you of sin. You take Him as your Savior to cleanse you from sin—as the substitute who paid the price due for your sin. Then you must ask Him to be Lord of your life, acknowledging openly and verbally that Jesus is not only your Savior, but your Lord."

Matt lifts his eyes staring across the mighty gulf of stars at the beautiful planet of Heaven and begins to pray. "God of Heaven and Earth, I ask you to please forgive me of my sinful life. Help me, dear Lord. I want to turn away from my sinful ways. I repent of my sins. I believe in you, God, I believe you sent your Son to die on the cross and paid the price for my sin. I want to be yours, dear Lord. I want to serve you, and not my will, but your will be done in my life. I love you, God. Amen"

Chado and the angels gather around Matt with each one reaching out patting him in gestures of love and happiness. Uriel reaches over bumping Chado with the tip of his wing, "Chado, it is time to give Matt the scroll."

Chado reaches for his leather pouch quickly pulling out the scroll. "Matt, this is something of great importance and it will be used along with testimonies from you and a pilot named Christy Moody, when the time comes. This action will eventually start a mighty revival among the saved and the unsaved."

Chado slowly reaches over handing Matt the ancient scroll, as Matt asks, "Chado, what's written in it?"

"Matt, God brought me to a special place where he had me document everything I experienced during this mission. He also added a message along with what I wrote inside the scroll for the people of our planet Earth. Whatever you do Matt, don't break the seal!"

"Who gets to break the seal? And who do I give it to?"

Chado replies, "Listen closely, Matt. The only one who can break the seal, or is able to read the ancient text is a child of my bloodline."

"So this child of your bloodline, who is it?"

"It's my grandson, Nathan Cole. He doesn't know it yet, but God has given him the ability to read the oldest known language on Earth."

"Isn't Nathan the son of your daughter who got killed back in 2008?"

"Yes, he was only nine months old when Summer got killed."

"I'm so sorry, Chado."

Chado chuckles as he explains. "Don't be sorry, Matt. I just saw Summer not long ago. She works in a place Heaven calls, 'The

Valley of The Children'. Oh by the way, the best way to get this scroll to Nathan will be through Coleen. She adopted Nathan after Summer was killed. Just tell her not to let anyone talk her out of this scroll. It's especially for Nathan, and no one else. Matt, be sure to tell Coleen that Summer and I are doing fine. Oh… one other thing. If she doesn't believe any of this, remind her that she actually caught a glimpse of me in ICU. Uriel and I were disguised as orderlies. Right when the demons were carrying you away, I briefly lowered my mask and Coleen spotted me. Don't worry, she'll remember. I saw the funny look on her face."

Chado chuckles again… "Well, Matt, you think you can handle what's ahead of you?"

"Yes, I think so. I've walked several miles through crowns of thorns, been scourged with Cat-of-Nine-Tails, been stung by some kind of scorpion beast, and just a few moments ago we were standing ankle deep in a lake of fire. Yes, I can handle just about anything from this point on."

Chado grins as he looks over at Uriel and the other angels. "So… are we ready to go?"

Matt butts in, "Hey before we go, could you guys explain what this beautiful piece of ground is all about. It just seems really odd something so plush and full of life way out here in the middle of this dead planet; and what's the deal with that huge tree over there?"

Uriel places a hand on Matt's shoulder. "My friend, that will be a good conversation piece during our travels, but we really need to get you back. Our time is limited; the doctors are desperately trying to save your life right now as we speak. We wouldn't want them to give up on you and have to dig you out of the morgue."

Matt and Chado burst out laughing as they all line up, ready to transport, when Joel quickly turns his head. "Listen, can you hear that?"

With an alarmed look Chado asked, “Hear what?”

Uriel swiftly steps in front of Chado and Matt as they witness several thousand dark winged angels diving from out of the smoky atmosphere of Hell. Within seconds, this legion of fallen angels begins to land and the constant rumble of their feet hitting the ground sound like bass drums. The dust and ash they disturb creates a huge cloud around the entire army of Hell. This cloud of ash and cinder is so thick they disappear like ghosts. Within moments after the last one lands, something like a bolt of lightning strikes the surface within a few yards in front of Uriel. With the ash hanging in the air like a heavy Louisiana fog, you can hear their armor clattering as they begin to advance. Still hidden inside the haze of smoke and ash the sound of their footsteps comes closer and closer. Suddenly, lines of fallen angels in military formation appear out of the cloud of burning cinders, with Lucifer himself leading the way.

With each footstep, he exhibits power and talent by changing his appearance. At first, he looks like a tall man, having the face of a beautiful woman. Another step, he takes on the appearance of a priest, another step the face of a demon. Another, a gorgeous woman with long shiny red hair; then just before reaching the edge of God’s fertile plush ground, he stops and has the same appearance he had when he visited Chado on two different occasions. It is the gothic 1940’s preacher outfit. His dark flat brimmed hat is pulled down over his forehead, matching his charcoal lifeless eyes. Along with the black bowtie and long black jacket, he favored what a preacher or undertaker may have worn in those days.

Uriel and the ten warriors create a line of defense near the edge of the fertile ground. Chado, Matt, and Buck are tucked away behind Uriel and Joel. Just before drawing their swords, Lucifer raises a hand with his wrist remaining limp as some ancient Roman king would do to his servants. With this action, the fallen angels immediately halt their advance. The hot dry wind quickly clears away the dust cloud created from the fallen angels march.

Lucifer displays arrogance like no other as he leans to the side, and peers deep into Uriel's eyes. "Are we breaking your God's law this day? Upon what authority have you trespassed into my kingdom? You come boldly against my will and have taken a lost soul that only I have right to. What say you, leader of angels?"

Uriel steps closer to the line, "We come with authority of The Great I Am. It is His will."

Lucifer smirks, "Angel, it is my right. I now own the unbeliever. Hand him over and we will allow you to pass freely back across the gulf."

Uriel takes another step forward, "Son of perdition, I command you under the authority of the Almighty God to allow passage!"

"Silence, angel, you command no one here. You forget you stand inside the circle of the tree. You cannot transport unless you step across and when you do, my servants will destroy you all."

Chado whispers to Joel, "Is that true? We can't transport behind the line?"

Lucifer chuckles as he leans to the side again, "Little Soul, is that you back there? My, oh my, haven't we been busy. I knew the Maker was using you, but I had no idea it would be to visit me here in my kingdom. This lost soul that you protect, holds a parchment in his hand. It looks as if it displays a seal of your God. Hmm… it must be of great importance."

Satan directs his attention back to Uriel, "I know the Creator has set a plan in motion, but this is where it ends. Angel, return to your God and tell Him you have failed. His power has no place here. Tell Him his feeble attempt to save the fallen away will also fail. They have turned from his teachings and embraced my ways. I am the Prince of the Earth, and I alone rule over the multitudes whom

He hopelessly loves in vain. Behold, do you not witness this legion standing before you? I say woe unto thee. If I raise my hand you will be destroyed, and I grow weary of this pitiful display of courage. Make your decision, angel."

Uriel turns to Chado and whispers, "Little Soul, pull out that Martin guitar and play like you've never played before!"

"What are you saying, Uriel? I don't think it's time to serenade Satan and his angels."

Uriel places both of his huge hands on Chado's shoulders as he smiles, "Listen to me. Do you not remember the power that comes from praising God? Now you take out that old Martin, and you play with all your heart to the Lord. I say this to you, Chado Cole, dig down into the depths of your soul and give God the praise and love He deserves!"

"I will, Uriel, I'll do it!"

While kneeling down and opening the worn out guitar case, Chado looks up at the planet of Heaven off in the distance, and prays to God. "Heavenly Father, we are trapped here in Hell and held captive. You and You alone are our refuge. Please, Father; deliver us from this dark place. Give us strength and fill our hearts with the power of your Holy Spirit."

Chado boldly steps between Uriel and Joel with the old Martin guitar hanging from his neck facing the enemy. Lucifer and his legion of Hell's angels are caught off guard at this sight of an immortal displaying a six-string weapon. After a short moment of silence, they begin pointing and laughing with the surety of an easy victory over God's chosen vessels.

Looking down and closing his eyes, not as a sign of defeat, but of reverence to the Lord. At this very moment, Chado feels a spiritual fire begin at his feet. This anointing of the Holy Spirit rises up through his legs continuing to saturate his entire body as he begins to play to the Lord. The sounds coming from the old guitar are magically amplified as it penetrates throughout the masses of angels. Their laughter is silenced as the eleven warriors begin singing Psalm 18, blending the words along with the sweet melody Chado plays.

'I will love You, O Lord, my strength. The Lord is my rock and my fortress and my deliverer; My God, my strength, in whom I will trust; My shield and the horn of my salvation, my stronghold. I will call upon the Lord, who is worthy to be praised; so shall I be saved from my enemies. The pangs of death surround me, and the floods of ungodliness made me afraid. The sorrows of Sheol surround me; the snares of death confronted me; in my distress I called upon the Lord, and cried out to my God.'

As the twelve continue to praise and worship with song and scripture, a small ray of light the size of a needle breaks through the smoky atmosphere. Striking the surface in the midst of Chado, Matt, Buck and the eleven angels, the ray of light begins to grow. Within a short span of time, they are bathing in this bright light from God.

Lucifer goes into a mad rage as he realizes God is about to take away his bounty. He quickly gives orders to attack, and without hesitation several of his fallen angels standing at his side rush in with their swords swinging violently at Chado. Without ceasing, Chado continues playing his spirit filled melody with unmovable faith as he watches the razor sharp swords of Hell bearing down. Right before their weapons make contact, Chado smiles as he closes his eyes. This evidence of strong faith angers Lucifer even more as he watches his angels attempt to penetrate the light. To Lucifer's surprise, as the blades touch this brilliant light of God, their swords and the angels wielding them, instantly disintegrate. Witnessing this destruction, immense fear sweeps over the multitude of fallen.

The advancing legion suddenly stop in their tracks as they watch the ashes of their fallen comrades float with the wind back into the face of Satan himself.

Lucifer, with great anger, slowly reaches up dusting off each shoulder from the floating ash of his fallen servants. "You may think you have escaped my wrath, but this is only the beginning of sorrow. We will hunt you down and destroy any hope you have of saving the souls of Earth. This feeble plan of the Maker will fail."

While Satan continues uttering his threats toward God and humanity, the beam of light grows brighter and brighter until suddenly, within a twinkling of an eye, they vanish.

39

Soul Habitat

Chado, Matt, Buck and eleven angels walk out of the Portal of Hell. Now standing on top of God's Mountain in Alaska, the fresh clean air replaces the stench inside their nostrils of burning sulfur. As soon as they arrive, Joel and the other warriors head straight for the Portal to Heaven. They all turn just before stepping through giving subtle waves to Chado, Uriel and Matt.

As always, human curiosity takes over. "Chado, where are they off too?"

"Matt, my friend, they're probably headed back to Heaven. Old buddy, there are seven different locations inside the walls that God calls, The Angel Strongholds. That's pretty much where the warriors hang out. Or they might be off to another mission. Who knows?"

"Oh wow, so that hole in that rock leads to Heaven?"

Uriel and Chado chuckle, "It does old friend, the holes in these rocks as you call them are portals"

"Well can you guys give me a quick tour of Heaven?"

Uriel tucks his huge wings behind him as he smiles, "Not yet, my friend. We have a mission to complete and, Matt, it is time to get you back to the hospital."

From out of the Portal of Heaven, two childlike angels appear.

Chado, surprised to see his old friends is suddenly filled with overwhelming joy. He dashes over and embraces Allayer and Nipper. Uriel, Buck, and Matt walk up behind the trio with smiles as they witness the happy reunion.

"Hey, Matt, I want you to meet two very special angel friends of mine, Allayer and Nipper. Guys this is Matt. He's one of my best buds from when I was alive and kicking back on Earth. We just helped rescue him out of the pit of hell. I have to tell you, that's a trip I hope to never endure again."

Allayer and Nipper walk straight up to Matt, not shaking his hand, but giving warm hugs. Nipper, with his childish humor says, "Matt, you don't know it, but you seem to be known throughout Heaven as someone special."

"What do you mean? I'm not special!"

"Allayer, you want to tell him?"

"Sure, Nipper, I would be honored. Matt, from the time when Jesus Christ went down into Hades and set the captives free, no one has been saved out of the clutches of Satan. The talk around Heaven is that you accepted Christ standing on the planet of Hell. That has to be a first, and before you start asking a thousand questions, we need to be on our way, we are running out of time."

"So you guys are taking me back?"

Nipper reaches up patting Matt's shoulder, "Have no fear, we do this all the time. We serve God in this capacity. You know, comforting and transporting."

"What about you, Chado? Will you, Buck, and Uriel be going with us?"

Chado smiles, "Don't worry, Matt, you're in safe hands with Allayer and Nipper. If they can rescue me off the bottom of the Gulf of Mexico, they won't have any trouble returning your soul and spirit back to your body. Let's just say we'll be in the shadows watching over you. Matt, just don't forget what to do with that scroll, and when it's time for your testimony, tell it like you saw it."

Chado reaches out giving Matt a manly man's bear hug. "Goodbye my friend."

Allayer and Nipper reach out taking Matt by his hands, and with a flash, they vanish.

* * *

Within only a second passing, Allayer, Nipper, and Matt are suspended above a lifeless body lying in ICU 7 of the Lafayette Hospital. A team of doctors and nurses work feverishly as they're losing hope in saving the life of Matt Stone. He is a victim in an attempted murder, when two crooked detectives used their car to push Matt and Lela out into oncoming traffic as they sat on his motorcycle waiting at a red light.

Nipper squeezes Matt's hand, "Before we join your soul and spirit back to your body, let us show you something."

They slowly float across the nurses' station and with clear view to Lela's room, Allayer points, "Matt, do you recognize the nurse taking care of your girlfriend Lela?"

"Yes, that's Coleen, Chado's widow! I have to get this scroll to her and she has to get it to their grandson, Nathan. How is this going to work? I'm just a spirit and they can't see me!"

Nipper smiles, "Calm down, Matt, you'll see."

"How's Lela? I mean is she going to make it?"

"Yes, she will survive. She just needs a little time to heal."

"Oh thank God. I really care a lot about her. Now that I'm saved, our lives are going to change from here on out."

Allayer tugs at Matt's hand, "Come with us. We want to show you one other thing."

They glide through the walls of the ICU into a small waiting room down the hall. "Mr. Stone, do you recognize any of these guys?"

Matt burst out laughing when he sees his whole dive team, along with Cheese Hound. They all are sitting around a table drinking coffee. "Wow, all my friends are here. This is so cool. Yep, they love me! You know those rascals have always played jokes on me because I'm from Minnesota. They call me Yank. They mean no harm; it's always been their rough way of kidding around. Although I wish I could spook them a little bit, you know just a little payback."

Nipper looks over at Allayer grinning from ear to ear wanting to kid around with Matt's friends. Allayer shakes his head and says, "Nipper, we don't have time for this."

"Come on, Allayer, let's have a little fun!"

Matt gets excited, "What can we do, Nipper?"

"Watch this." Nipper begins moving from one to the next lightly pinching each of their ear lobes. Matt bursts out laughing as he watches their reactions. They each quickly grab their ears, as they look around totally confused. Nipper makes another pass as he pulls at their nose hairs causing each one's eyes to start watering. TC and Bones react to the point of sneezing. They all jump up with Cheese Hound rubbing his ear lobe with one hand and his nose with the other. "What the heck is going on?"

Joey starts laughing, "Man, they must have a hospital ghost up in here, or someone spiked this coffee."

Bones, still having a sneezing fit, heads for the door, and says, "I'm going to see if I can check on Matt. Y'all take care of the haunted waiting room."

Matt, Allayer, and Nipper glide back into ICU 7. "Okay, Matt, are you ready to rejoin the living?"

"I reckon so, Nipper. Hey, thanks for kidding around with my friends. I'll ask them about getting their ears pinched and their nose hair pulled later. Maybe that will help convince them, to believe my story."

Allayer and Nipper with their childlike appearance, give Matt a kind loving smile as they gently lower his soul and spirit down until he disappears into his lifeless body.

Just outside ICU 7, Nurse Coleen is having a conversation with Matt's friend, Bones. "I'm sorry sir, but you can't be in here. The code team is doing everything they can to save your friend's life."

"What's a code team? Is he dying?"

"Sir, they've lost him several times, but something keeps him holding on."

Suddenly a carbon monoxide alarm trips inside ICU 7, "Is that Matt's room? What's going on?"

"Sir, please leave, I don't have time to explain."

Nurse Coleen trots over to Room 7 with Glenda Johnson right behind her. To their surprise, the room is filled with a pungent odor of sulfur. The emergency team backs away from Matt's bed in total disarray. The monitors begin to show signs of life as his pulse rate and blood pressure rise. One of the nurses runs out of the room overwhelmed from the foul odor.

Bones, looking over the shoulder of Coleen and Glenda takes out his cell phone and begins to video this strange event.

Dr. Welch reaches up disarming the alarm, and as he turns, Matt begins to move around on the bed. First his left arm, and within seconds his legs begin moving violently with the sound of cloth being shredded. At first, Dr. Welch is happy with saving his patient life and makes light of the odd commotion with a funny remark. "Someone hold this guy's legs down, apparently he hasn't cut his toenails in some time and their shredding the sheet."

An aide and one of the code team nurses attempt to hold both of Matt's legs down as he continues to regain consciousness. With his left hand, he pulls at the breathing tube taped to his mouth, finally ripping out the entire tube. The doctor notices he's breathing on his own. "Welcome back from the dead, young man."

Matt barely cracks open his eyes, as he's faced with the bright overhead lights. With a dry, parched voice he manages to utter, "Water, give me water."

Groaning with severe pain, he passes back out.

"Nurse, if you would, grab a sponge and let's dampen the inside of his mouth. This poor boy is thirsty. Would someone please go get a cup of ice chips?"

The nurse holding his legs, notices something strange about his feet, "Dr. Welch, would you mind taking a look at this?"

"Nurse, x-rays didn't show any broken bones. What are you talking about?"

"You just need to see for yourself. I don't really know how to explain."

The doctor throws the sponge down and turns his attention to Matt's feet.

"What in the world is that? Was he riding that motorcycle barefoot? Where's the ICU staff nurse?"

Coleen and Glenda, standing just outside the room speak up, "We're the ICU nurses, Dr. Welch."

"Did ER send up this patient's belongings?"

Coleen steps closer, "Yes sir, in the cabinet to your right."

Dr. Welch turns as he opens the cabinet door. "That is just what I thought. He's got a pair of leather riding boots, leather chaps and a thick leather jacket. That's probably why his lacerations are minimal. Nurse, hand me a set of tweezers, I want to know what the heck this is in his feet."

The nurse's aide folds the sheet further back, completely exposing his ankles and feet. The foul odor of sulfur becomes stronger as the aide points, "Would you look at that? What in the world is that black, scorched residue?"

Dr. Welch leans over with his nose within inches of Matt's feet. "Woe, I believe we've found the source of that foul odor. Does anyone know if this man received burns during his incident?"

Nurse Johnson with a kind voice answers, "There wasn't any mention of it in the report we received, and from the looks of his clothing, I would have to say, there is no evidence of burns."

The curious doctor begins plucking several foreign objects from the souls of his feet. He holds one of the larger pieces up to the bright lights, "Being from Louisiana, I would have to say this looks exactly like locust thorns."

He hands the tweezers over to one of the nurses, "If you would, pull these thorns out of this poor guy's feet, and let's get them down to the lab. I would really like to know where they came from. I guess you could say my curiosity is getting the best of me; this is just too odd."

The nurse's aide widens her eyes in unbelief. "Doc, if you think that's odd, you need to take a look at this weird scroll thing in his right hand. It looks really old."

Dr. Welch makes his way around the left side of Matt's bed as he looks down at this object clinched in his right hand. "Okay, young fellow, what in the name of science do you have here?"

The doctor slides a short metal stool over near the bed. He sits down, takes Matt by the wrist as he holds it up to examine. "Well that looks like a scroll of some sort. Hmm… this is very strange. It even has some kind of seal stamped on it."

The doctor gently tries to take it out of his hand, but with Matt's strong death grip, he fails to do so. Dr. Welch stands as he slides the stool out of the way, "Okay, someone find a video camera. We need to record this."

Glenda runs to her desk fetching her cell phone, "Here ya go, doc."

"Nurse Glenda, is it?"

"Yes, sir."

"Would you mind documenting? I know this might be a bit strange, but better safe than sorry."

"I don't mind at all, sir."

"By the way, who is the guy standing in the hall filming?"

"That's a friend of the patients, and we've told him to leave."

"Well, I have no secrets, and he's not in the way, so I guess as long as he stays in the hall he'll be fine. Okay, nurse, start the video."

"Yes, sir."

"My name is Dr. Welch and we are here at Lafayette Hospital with patient Matt Stone. Mr. Stone was involved in a motorcycle accident and was close to DOA when he arrived in ER. He was placed on life support and remained stable until 1:28 am this morning. Code Blue was activated with my emergency team responding. We lost patient Stone several times during this process, which was over the last several hours. At this stage, he is in and out of consciousness and seems to be stable at this time. The reason for this video recording is due to several different and very odd discoveries. At the time of showing signs of life, this entire ICU Room 7 was overtaken with the strong smell of sulfur. Yes sulfur. It was so strong it set off safety alarms in the room and made some of our staff nauseous to the point of almost vomiting. In our second discovery, patient Stone appeared to have what looks like locust thorns in both feet. He also has a black residue on his lower extremities, resembling a tar-based chemical with a very strong odor of sulfur. The mystery behind this is we have confirmed the patient was in fact wearing leather-riding gear, including boots, which have almost no damage. Note: There were no reports of chemical or fire involved in the incident. Upon further discovery, we found an object in Mr. Stone's right hand that cannot be explained. Nurse, if you would pan your camera over to his right side. Thank you nurse; as you can see in Patient Stone's right hand, it seems to be some kind of a scroll."

Dr. Welch showing signs of aggravation, suddenly stops talking and begins shaking his head, then looks back at the camera, "I am totally at a loss with this mystery. We have worked on this patient for several hours and there were no thorns, no tar, and absolutely no scroll in this man's hand. We performed surgery on him and he was absolutely clean. It's almost as if someone invisible came in the room and did this. I am just saying these things appeared at the very moment patient Stone began showing signs of life. How could this be possible?"

"Dr. Welch, I'm sorry sir for interrupting, but I may have found something else that doesn't seem to fit either."

"Yes, indeed. What is it, Nurse?"

"Doctor, if you can help me roll him on his side."

"My Goodness, what do you make of that?"

"He looks like he's been whipped with no mercy!"

"Nurse Glenda, take a photo of this poor guy's back and someone get his leather jacket out."

Nurse Coleen drags the heavy biker jacket from the closet, holds it up and it has almost no damage at all.

"Okay, nurse, you can stop filming. That should be sufficient."

Dr. Welch sits back down on the metal stool, slumps his shoulders as if totally exhausted. "I'm no Dick Tracy, but I believe there has to be foul play. I just don't get it."

He looks into the eyes of his bewildered code team. "What do you all think? Should we call the police? Maybe they can figure all this out."

They all turn hearing Matt groaning with pain. Dr. Welch quickly kicks the stool to the side as he leans over Matt shining his penlight into each pupil. “Hey there, Mr. Stone, welcome back.”

With a scratchy weak voice, “Water, please give me water.”

“Sorry, bud, we can dampen your mouth with this sponge, but you can’t drink anything just yet.”

The nurse’s aide reaches around with a water soaked swab dampening the inside of his mouth, as the doctor turns to Nurse Coleen. “If you don’t mind, would you please go call the Lafayette Police department and ask them to send someone over? In the meantime, maybe Mr. Stone can shine some light on this mystery.

The kind doctor takes small pieces of ice and begins to lightly rub them across his chapped lips allowing small drops of water to disappear into his mouth. After several minutes of Matt coming in and out of consciousness, he rolls his eyes to look at each one in the room with more focus. The anxious doctor standing at his bedside leans in, “Mr. Stone, can you understand me? Can you hear me, son?”

Matt, faintly nods his head yes.

“Can you tell us what happened to you?”

With a dry voice, he struggles with his words, “Lela, where’s Lela? Is she okay?”

“Yes, Matt, she’s in the next room and she is going to be fine. She’s got a few broken bones and lacerations. She just needs a little time to heal.”

Matt slowly lifts his right hand to assure himself he still has possession of the scroll. The anxious doctor reaches out in an attempt to take it from Matt, causing him to tighten his grip and coil his arm closer to his chest. “Hey… Mr. Stone, I mean no harm.”

Matt slightly shakes his head no, holding the parchment even tighter. “It’s okay... No one is going to take it away. I just wanted to take a closer look at it. You see, we don’t understand what’s going on, and would like to ask you a few questions… if you feel up to it."

Matt whispers, "Please, give me water."

Dr. Welch reaches over placing a couple small chips of ice in his mouth. "I'm sorry, but we have to stay with the ice for now. Mr. Stone can you tell us where you got the scroll, and how you received those thorns in your feet? The injuries to your back appear to be from a whip. Can you tell us what may have happened to you?"

With a scratchy voice, "I was in Hell."

"I understand you've been through a lot. That was a pretty nasty motorcycle wreck, from what I was told."

Matt reaches out with his left hand grabbing the doctor's wrist, "You don't understand. I've been to Hell!"

The doctor kindly pats Matt on his arm, "I know you're hurting. We're going to give you something to help you sleep. Before you know it, you'll be right as rain."

Now filled with frustration he squeezes Dr. Welch's wrist. "Listen to me, Doc. I just came back from the Sixth Gate of Hell! Do you understand what I'm trying to tell you? Hell is real! I was there, I swear, I was there!"

"Okay, son, I believe you. Just calm down and try to rest."

Dr. Welch walks out of the room stopping just outside the door. He turns and stares at Matt's feet, with a lost look on his face. The entire ICU staff gathers around Dr. Welch for some kind of an explanation. He slowly turns placing his attention back to his ICU team. "Did you guys just hear that? Mr. Stone just claimed that he had been in Hell!"

Without anyone answering, the entire staff stands mystified as they all stare at Matt Stone lying in ICU 7.

Suddenly the silence is broken, with Bones mumbling behind their circle. "Doc, if my buddy Matt said he's been to Hell, well I reckon you need to take him at his word. Just saying, Matt might be a lot of things, but a liar, isn't one of them."

Dr. Welch ignores Bones, "Nurse Coleen, have you gotten in touch with Lafayette PD?"

"Yes sir, they're sending someone over as soon as possible."

"Well, from what we just found out, I don't think we need the cops. I believe we might need a preacher or maybe a priest."

Glenda holds her hand up as if she was back in grammar school. "Dr. Welch, we can call the hospital chaplain if you like?"

"Sure, why not. Give him a call. I welcome anyone who can help. Speaking of help, mister, what's your name?"

"My friends call me, Bones."

"Matt Stone is a friend of yours?"

"Yes, sir."

"Bring your camera, and let's all go talk to Mr. Stone and see if he can tell us more about his trip to Hell."

Nurse Coleen politely interrupts, "Dr. Welch, would you like me to talk with Matt. Remember he was my deceased husband's best friend."

Dr. Welch widens his eyes, "When was the last time you saw Stone?"

"It was five years ago at Chado's funeral."

"Chado, I take it, was your husband?"

"Yes, sir. He and Matt went through dive school and worked together in the Gulf of Mexico as deep-sea divers. They became pretty close friends before Chado got killed out there on one of their projects."

"So… he should recognize you?"

"Yes, sir, no doubt."

"Okay, let's see what we can find out."

As Coleen leads the way, the rest of the code team, along with Bones, squeeze into ICU 7. They find Matt with his eyes closed, resting. Coleen reaches over taking hold of his left hand, "Matt… Matt… it's Coleen. Can you hear me?"

Matt barely cracks his eyes, feeling the heavy sedation of pain meds. After blinking several times his eyes come into focus, "Coleen, is that you?"

"Yes, my friend. It's me, Coleen."

"I saw Chado!"

"I miss him too, Matt."

"No! Listen to me! I saw Chado! He travels with his dog Buck and a big angel named Uriel."

Coleen starts laughing, "Matt, you were always cutting jokes. I want you to be serious. We almost lost you! You crazy rascal! You've always had a good sense of humor, but we need you to be straight with us."

"No, please believe me. Chado, Buck, Uriel, and ten other angels, rescued me from a place they were calling the Sixth Gate of Hell. I'm telling you, Coleen, I was really in Hell."

Coleen, holding back her tears, looks up at the doctor and whispers, "Is this real?"

Dr. Welch motions for her to continue. Coleen nods, "Where's Chado now?"

"I don't know. He gave me instructions and said he would be watching from the shadows. He was here when the demons drug me away to Hell."

"What do you mean he was here?"

"Chado and that big angel of his were working as orderlies. He said he thinks you saw him. He lowered his lab mask for just a second and he thinks you may have caught a glimpse of him."

Coleen with tears continuing to swell looks over at Glenda discovering she has her mouth wide open and is speechless. "Glenda, I told you I saw Chado!"

Dr. Welch whispers, "Your deceased husband, and his angel were here disguised as orderlies?"

All but Coleen and Glenda begin smiling with unbelief as the doctor whispers, "This is better than any sci-fi I've ever watched. Coleen, please continue before he passes back out. Ask him about his injuries."

Coleen squeezes his left hand, "Matt, can you tell us where you got the lacerations on your back and the thorns in your feet?"

Small tears begin to drip from his eyes, "It was horrible, Coleen. Two demons took me from this room and brought me through some kind of a tunnel. Inside this tunnel were hundreds of other people, and they each had demons holding them captive just like the ones that held me. It seemed like we were traveling through space, but I'm not sure."

Coleen gives Matt more ice chips and says, "Matt, what happened next?"

"At the end of the tunnel was a strange gate. It was as if we stepped through a watery membrane held up by a weird rock formation. I guess it was some sort of a gate. As soon as we stepped through we were met by more demons, but they were much larger and more vicious. They were all riding some kind of strange beast like I had never seen before. The demons on the backs of these monsters beat everyone in the long lines of people with the same kind of whips they used on Jesus. The beasts had scorpion tails stinging people at random. It was awful Coleen! Their stings felt like coals of fire! These demons herded us down a narrow path toward the pit of hell and the floor of the path was covered in crowns of thorns. As we walked along, the thorns would puncture and break off in our feet. Between this and the beating from the demons, it was unbearable. When we walked out of the long trench, we entered a huge courtyard and it was covered with what they called a shallow lake of fire.

"We could hear the moaning of millions of people coming from down inside the pit as we walked ankle deep in this burning water. This is where the Sixth Gate of Hell was located. Just before I was forced down inside the pit… Chado and the angels rescued me and took me away. They magically transported me to another place on this same dead planet. I heard the devil call it the Circle of The Tree. While we were there, Satan ordered his angels to attack us, but from out of nowhere, a bright light from God came down and it took us up out of Hell. Coleen this really happened. You have to believe me!"

"I believe you, Matt. I believe you."

Coleen looks around the ICU room as she witnesses some with frightened looks, others with their eyes filled with tears.

Dr. Welch leans over whispering, "Nurse, he mentioned instructions. Try to find out what that's about."

Coleen dampens his face with a washcloth then slips a couple small chips of ice into his mouth. "Matt, are you still with me?"

Matt squints' his eyes, "Coleen, can you dim those bright lights? My head is killing me."

"Sure we can… Now, Matt, you mentioned Chado giving you instructions. What were they?"

He slowly lifts the scroll with his hand quivering, "Take this. It's from Chado."

"What's it for? I mean what would my deceased husband have me do with it?"

"Coleen, with testimonies from myself and one other, along with two separate scrolls, the world is about to have a wakeup call."

"Two testimonies and two scrolls, what do you mean? You lost me, Matt."

"I was told there is woman somewhere on the other side of the world that was given a scroll like this one. She will also have a testimony to share with the world."

"But what in God's name does it have to do with me?"

"Both scrolls are for your grandson, Nathan. He alone is the only one that can reveal the message inside. Chado called it The Bloodline of the Scrolls. You see, God chose Chado's bloodline to be the only one that could read the ancient text. I believe it's written in the oldest known language on Earth. Nathan is Chado's true bloodline, and God has gifted your grandson to be the one who can reveal it to the world. Coleen, Chado wanted me to tell you, don't let this scroll be taken away from Nathan. Protect them both. Satan knows God has a plan and he's going to do everything he can to stop it. Have no fear, Coleen. I believe when Chado told me they would be in the shadows, he really meant him, his dog Buck and that big angel he calls Uriel, would be watching over you and Nathan."

40

ADVERSARIES OF GOD

Nestled in the midst of giant skyscrapers in downtown New York, the president of the 'New York Extreme Times' receives an unexpected phone call. It's from the owner of the mother company, recognized as the 'Apollyon World Network'.

"Mr. Gavin, you have a call on line one."

With a haughty loud voice, "I told you, I did not want to be disturbed!"

"I understand sir. It's Mr. Apollyon Mastema. I'll send him to your voicemail. Sorry for interrupting."

Gavin makes a mad dash toward the phone, as he yells, "Wait... Trish, I'll take the call! Next time when he calls, you need to lead with its Mr. Mastema on line one!"

Gavin takes a deep breath before hitting the speaker button, "Oliver Gavin, can I help you?"

"Hello, Gavin, this is Apollo."

"Mr. Mastema, I didn't know it was you. How delightful it is to hear your voice."

"Gavin, I believe that will be quite enough with the pleasantries. Stop lying to me. Your secretary just informed you I was calling."

"I humbly ask for forgiveness, sir, I don't know what I was

thinking. I won't let it happen again, Mr. Mastema."

"For your sake, I should hope not. Now, let us deal with the business at hand. Are you aware of any videos or narratives surrounding a woman pilot coming out of London, England?"

"Yes, I believe a group of med-students were filming during the pilot's surgery. They are claiming she is some kind of diehard, hero pilot, who was shot down while saving almost an entire battalion. The medical students who were videoing caught an ancient scroll appearing in her hand during surgery. There seems to be a very interesting story developing out of this. The public is already claiming that aliens or a god are involved. I think its trick photography."

"That is exactly what I was afraid of, Gavin! I recommend you send two of your finest over to London. My desire is to prove this story to be simply a case of deception, a hoax, or whatever… The label you provide is entirely up to you. Just make sure it is excluded from social media. Whomever you decide to manage this project, make sure you do not send any Christians. I desire two people that absolutely have no faith or belief in a god or aliens!"

Gavin nervously laughs, "Apollyon, we have never employed any Christians here at NYET, and by no means, ever will."

Apollyon answers with prideful tone. "Well I am truly thankful for that, Gavin. I am also disturbed by another matter."

Gavin, with fear in his voice, replies, "Master, I am here to serve you. What else do you desire?"

"There is another similar event unfolding in your homeland as we speak. It is occurring in a place near your nation's gulf waters, in a place called Louisiana. I am unclear of the details at this time. As soon as your people tidy up the false reports in London, we will need their full attention on Louisiana."

A few seconds of silence fall over their conversation as Apollyon decides to continue, "Gavin, I do not care what extreme measures you have to take in destroying these stories. If this means sending in someone other than investigative journalists, so be it. Do you clearly read between these lines, Gavin? If you do not possess the skills, or shall I say the stomach, I can easily find another source for this line of work."

"I will not let you down, Master. We will do whatever is required."

"This pleases me. You will go far within our new kingdom. Gavin, remember… I will be watching."

The End

Acknowledgements

I would like to first thank God for giving me such a unique story to share through "The Portal Series". Unaware of the impact the first book, "Scars of My Guardian Angel", was having on readers, it was soon evident through their testimonies, that this series is no longer just an enjoyable story. It has turned into an extraordinary ministry. I am truly humbled at how God is touching lives with healing and hope through this little book.

To the many people, past and future, that read my "The Portal Series", I give special thanks to you! It is my hope you will continue the journey with us throughout the series. I ask you to become a part of this ministry by simply sharing your reading experience with others. I pray the love and blessings of our Savior will shine upon you all.

I would like to also thank everyone who has joined us, as they have dedicated their time, efforts, and unique skills to make this self-publishing experience possible. We couldn't have accomplished it without you! The talents of these friends cover a wide range of tasks, including Book Events, Cover Design, Editing, Formatting, Grassroots Marketing, Proof Reading and Social Media Marketing. To acknowledge and honor everyone involved, their names are listed here in alphabetical order: Deidre Fuqua, Wanda Harlan, Rebecca 'Beckie' Hicks, Melissa James, Debbie Kilgo, Jackie Lewis, Laura Martin, Gale Despino McGlothlin, Aaron Michiels, Jennifer Michiels, Cristina Morgan, Roselyn Nicewarner, Diana Rhodes, DeliveryMaxx & GospelMax

Russell L. Martin Biography

Russell L. Martin, known to his family and friends as Rusty, was born and raised in Grant Parish, located in central Louisiana. His family lived near the poverty level throughout his childhood. With a limited education and a strong desire for a better life, he hired out with a traveling construction company that installed oil and gas pipelines all across the U.S.A. Starting out at the bottom of the food chain, he worked as a laborer, for little to no money. He would camp out near creeks and rivers, to save money and survive the high cost of living away from home. When his strong work ethics became noticed by his supervisors, he was allowed to advance and work in all phases of the oil and gas industry.

After several years of working on land, Rusty decided that it was time to get a taste of installing pipelines in the Gulf of Mexico. To further his education in this part of the industry, he received commercial diving degrees at The Ocean Corporation in Houston, TX. After only a couple years working in the Gulf as a diver, he went back to land-lay operations. He continued working freelance for multiple pipeline companies, until finally retiring after 34 years in the oil and gas industry.

It was not until he decided to settle back down where his roots of life started in central Louisiana, that he surrendered to becoming an author. His love for God, paired with many strange events throughout his life, left him with a gift of telling amazing stories.

He has stated, and truly believes, God led him to the keyboard of his old work laptop. Surprising his family and friends, he unveiled a hidden talent that no one realized he possessed, including himself.

After writing the Christian novel, "Scars of My Guardian Angel", incredible reader reviews, stories, and testimonies played a very big role in knowing God was guiding these writings. Russell has been very inspired to continue his new writing career, completing the second novel in "The Portal Series", "Bloodline of the Scrolls". His work will continue, with yet another sequel in the series, "Revelation of the Scrolls", to be released in 2019.

Rusty has also written thirteen wonderful Christian songs, that he and his wife share in local churches around their community. Playing his Taylor guitar and singing Christian music is truly a deep passion of his heart. He and his wife, Laura, live a humble and quiet life on a few acres nestled in the middle of Kisatchie National Forest. They enjoy life with their two horses, Ellie Mae and Hollywood. This couple also loves two stray dogs they rescued out of the deep woods. The one they call Daisy May looks much like a redbone hound, and the other one, Nibbles, well he's just a dog.

Your Review Means the World to Us!

Please share your thoughts and feelings with friends and loved ones after reading: **Bloodline of the Scrolls**

Let us know what you think on our website:
www.russellmartinauthor.com
Here you also can read blogs and updates, and stay up on the release of Book Three.

We welcome any communication with the author via Facebook and Twitter @RussMartinAuth

Your honest review on Amazon, or the platform where you purchased the book, is greatly helpful to our ministry.

Join us and continue your experience throughout "The Portal Series"

Coming in 2019, Book Three:
Revelation of the Scrolls

Made in the USA
Middletown, DE
03 December 2020

26009563R00234